Fodor's 90

Arizona

FODOR'S TRAVEL PUBLICATIONS, INC.
New York & London

Fodor's Arizona

Editor: Denise Nolty, Alice Thompson
Contributors: Sarah Ellison Caldwell, Elin Jeffords, Marael Johnson, Kitty Loeb, Mariana Popp, Don and Barb Rosner
Maps and Plans: Burmar
Drawings: Michael Kaplan
Cover Photograph: Mark Tomalty/Masterfile

Cover Design: Vignelli Associates

Special Sales

Fodor's Travel Guides are available at special discounts for bulk purchases (100 copies or more) for sales promotions or premiums. Special editions, including personalized covers, excerpts of existing guides and corporate imprints, can be created in large quantities for special needs. For more information, Write to Special Marketing, Fodor's Travel Publications, 201 East 50th Street, New York, N.Y. 10022. Inquiries from the United Kingdom should be sent to Fodor's Travel Publications, 30–32 Bedford Square, London WC1B 3SG.

MANUFACTURED IN THE UNITED STATES OF AMERICA
10 9 8 7 6 5 4 3 2 1

CONTENTS

Foreword   vii
  Map of Arizona, viii

An Introduction to Arizona   1

Facts at Your Fingertips
  Tourist Information, 14; Tips for British Visitors, 15; When to Go,
  16; Climate, 16; What to Take, 17; What It Will Cost, 17; Hints to
  the Motorist, 18; Hotels and Motels, 19; Bed & Breakfasts, 21; Guest
  Ranches, 21; Hostels, 21; Dining Out, 22; Tipping, 22; Drinking
  Laws, 23; Time Zone, 23; Telephones, 23; Business Hours, 23; Senior
  Citizens' Programs and Discounts, 24; Photography and Camera
  Care, 25; Camping, 25; Indian Reservations, 25; Arizona's Fragile
  Desert, 26; Protected Plants, 26; Participant Sports, 26; Hunting and
  Fishing, 28; Rockhounding, 28; Hints for the Disabled Traveler, 28;
  Health and Safety Hints, 29

Phoenix   31
  Map of Phoenix, 33
  Practical Information for Phoenix, 36
  Exploring Outside Phoenix, 60
    Map of the Phoenix Area, 61
  Practical Information for Outside Phoenix, 64

Tucson   74
  Map of Tucson, 76
  Practical Information for Tucson, 78

Southern and Southeastern Arizona—Excursions Out of Tucson   99
  Map of Southeastern Arizona, 102
  Practical Information for Southern and Southeastern Arizona, 106

Western Arizona—Casa Grande to Yuma   113
  Map of Western Arizona, 115
  Practical Information for Casa Grande and Interstate 8, 116
  Yuma, 118
  Practical Information for Yuma, 121

North-Central Arizona—Prescott and Red Rock Country   125
  Map of North-Central Arizona, 127
  Practical Information for North-Central Arizona, 132

Northern Arizona—New Mexico to the Colorado River   138
    Map of Northern Arizona, 142–143
Practical Information for Northern Arizona, 150

The Grand Canyon   170
The Grand Canyon Through the Ages, 171
    Map of the Grand Canyon National Park, 172
Exploring the South Rim, 178
Exploring the North Rim, 184
Practical Information for the Grand Canyon, 187

Index   211

FOREWORD

Deserts, forests, plains, rivers, lakes, and canyons: the natural beauty of Arizona is inescapable. And if that isn't enough, the thriving cities of Phoenix, Scottsdale, Tucson, and Flagstaff; luxurious modern resorts; Indian ruins and monuments; and dozens of other attractions combine to make Arizona an exceptional vacation spot. *Fodor's Arizona* will guide you through all of it, helping you to tailor your Arizona holiday according to your personal desires.

The first chapter of this book is a brief sketch of the history and geography of Arizona. The following section, Facts at Your Fingertips, provides general information about the state and an overview of the attractions and activities of interest to tourists.

The succeeding chapters are organized geographically and provide detailed descriptions of various segments of the state. Each chapter begins with a descriptive introduction and then lists practical information regarding accommodations, restaurants, what to do, and what to see. Since the best way to see Arizona is by car, several of these sections are presented as driving tours. However, information on other means of transportation is always provided.

While every care has been taken to assure the accuracy of the information in this guide, the passage of time will always bring change, and consequently the publisher cannot accept responsibility for errors that may occur.

All prices and opening times quoted here are based on information available to us at press time. Hours and admission fees may change, however, and the prudent traveler will avoid inconvenience by calling ahead.

Fodor's wants to hear about your travel experiences, both pleasant and unpleasant. When a hotel or restaurant fails to live up to its billing, let us know and we will investigate the complaint and revise our entries where the facts warrant it.

Send your letters to the editors of Fodor's Travel Publications, 201 E. 50th Street, New York, NY 10022.

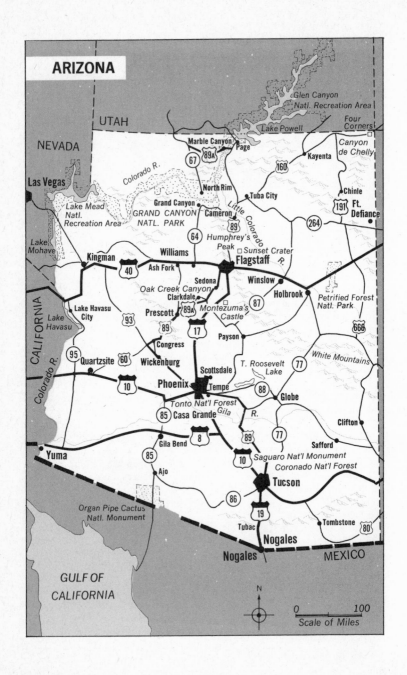

AN INTRODUCTION TO
ARIZONA

Contrary to popular belief, Arizona is more than a vast and sandy desert where nothing but a few rattlesnakes and cactuses lives. Within this state of 113,500 square miles there are at least a half dozen distinct climatic zones, ranging from hot scrub desert to temperate plateau to snowy alpine forest. On many days in the autumn and spring, both the high and low temperatures in the nation are registered here.

Arizona is a place where the ancient mingles with the modern, boasting both the capital city of Phoenix—the ninth largest city in the United States and one of the fastest growing—and the tiny Hopi village of Oraibi—the oldest continuously inhabited community in the country. Arizona was one of the first places in North America to be explored and settled by Europeans, yet it is the youngest of the continental United States.

Travelers to Arizona face a bewildering variety of sightseeing possibilities. Many come to visit the Grand Canyon alone, but a host of other natural and man-made phenomena can be enjoyed on the same trip. Arizona abounds with canyons, from the cool, cozy Oak Creek Canyon near Sedona to the dramatic purple-cliffed Echo Canyon in northeast Phoenix. The state is full of odd historical attractions, like the original London Bridge, which now spans Lake Havasu; and fascinating Indian towns and trading posts. In the northeast of the state lie the high desert wonders, like the Painted Desert where millennia of erosion have exposed mesas and ravines of blue, purple, red, and gold; Canyon de Celly, site of ancient

1

Indian cliff dwellings; and the Petrified Forest. In the cosmopolitan cities of Phoenix, Scottsdale, and Tucson, you can take a desert holiday without giving up any of the amenities of civilization. The five-star resorts are never far from natural beauty: Phoenix and Scottsdale are surrounded by desert mountain preserves, and Tucson claims part of more than one national park. An ambitious traveler could hit the major sights in a month, but even the remotest corners of this varied state are worthy of a few days' look around.

THE DESERT

The southwestern quarter of Arizona is the driest, warmest, and lowest section of the state, ranging from 70 feet of elevation in the Colorado River basin to 1,000 feet in the Phoenix area. Annual rainfall in the low desert averages three inches in the most arid parts and seven inches in the comparatively fertile river valleys. Typical of desert climates, daily temperatures fluctuate about thirty degrees between the cool dawn hours and the hot afternoons. The summer is just plain hot, with temperatures seldom dipping below the mid 70s at night and regularly exceeding 110° in the daytime. But mild winter weather makes up for any discomfort suffered from June through mid-September. Daily winter highs average in the low 70's and at night the mercury rarely drops below freezing. The arid, elevated regions to the southeast and north, including Tucson, Prescott, and the Navajo Indian Reservation, are called "high desert," and are usually five to 10 degrees cooler.

Plant and Animal Life

The Arizona desert abounds with flora, but to appreciate it one must dispense with traditional notions of verdure. Indeed, newcomers could be forgiven for mistaking certain healthy desert plants for queer geological formations or dead animals. The tall, spiny saguaro (pronounced sah-WAH-roe), that greyish-green cactus with fat arm-like branches beloved of cartoonists, is the official state tree of Arizona. Slow-growing, it stands only six inches high after its first 10 years. However, mature saguaros—they can live 200 years—reach a height of 50 feet and weigh 15–20 tons, 95 percent of it in water. Often taken for a young saguaro, the stocky barrel cactus has a purple or yellow tint and long curved spines. Its magenta fruit is the main ingredient in the cactus candy sold in souvenir shops. The palo verde is a thorny tree, green from trunk to tip, and covered with brilliant yellow blossoms in the spring.

Sit quietly in the desert for a few minutes and you will discover you are surrounded by animal life, too. Hummingbirds, cactus wrens, lizards, and cottontail rabbits are as common here as pigeons in city parks.

The national-park visitor centers throughout the state offer pamphlets, books, and exhibits about local flora and fauna, but without question the best places to get an introduction to the desert are the Sonora Desert Museum near Tucson and the Desert Botanical Garden in Phoenix. Morning is the best time to go. The desert is prettiest from late February through April, when wave after wave of trees, cactuses, and wildflowers bloom.

According to local humor, if a native looks up into the sky and sees a cloud he will shout "Monsoon!" and, with only two rainy seasons each year, one in early August and one in February, rainfall provokes a good deal of excitement. When it does fall, rain comes in torrents, washing away the layers of dust that have built up over the preceding months; replenished cactuses swell with moisture; and the fresh, planty fragrance of the creosote bush fills the air.

Desert Dangers

Arizonans are more concerned with protecting the desert from visitors than visitors from the desert. Removal or destruction of native plants is unlawful, and could land you with a heavy fine or a few days in jail. The state is so serious about protecting native plants that residents have to apply for licenses to transplant certain species into their yards. It is against the law to kill or remove animals without a permit, so leave the lizards and snakes alone. And, unless signs are posted to the contrary, it is illegal to drive off of established roads, which means no four-wheeling or all-terrain joy-riding.

You are unlikely to come across a rattlesnake and, even if you do, unlikely to be bitten unless you choose to harass it. A defensive, nocturnal animal by nature, it will be the first to flee in an encounter with a human if given the chance. In the presence of a rattler, stand very still or, if you're more than 20 feet away, retreat slowly. If somehow you do manage to get bitten, don't panic: the rattlesnake envenomates only 30 to 60 percent of the time and its bite is rarely fatal. If possible, immerse the bitten area in ice, and find a doctor.

Scorpions, black widow spiders, and poisonous insects dwell under rocks, in dark crevasses, and in holes. Keep your fingers and toes—and children's fingers and toes—out of these places and you probably won't be bitten. Scorpion and spider bites result in more deaths in Arizona than do rattlesnake bites—about 40 in the last decade—but most cause only temporary discomfort. If bitten, seek medical advice immediately.

The monsoon/drought cycle creates a few driving hazards particular to the area. Run-off from sudden desert rains can cause flash flooding. Watch for warning signs. And do not try to navigate across full washes: the powerful flow can sweep away a car. Dust storms—thick enough at times to make driving impossible—occur without warning in the summer. If you're on the road when a dust storm hits, keep your lights on. If you must pull over, however, be sure to turn your lights off, or you may be mistaken for moving traffic and rear-ended. Dust storms rarely last longer than 10 minutes.

Finally, tumbleweed grows in some parts of the desert. This almost weightless shrub dries up in summer and breaks off from its roots, depositing seeds as it rolls across the desert floor. Unfortunately, tumbleweeds don't stop for traffic and many collisions occur when startled drivers slam on their brakes to avoid hitting the poor, defenseless ball of twigs. If a tumbleweed should blow your way, keep going, and let the air currents around the car sweep it out of your path.

The biggest threat to your well-being in the desert is the sun. Year-round, the ultraviolet rays are intense and can burn fair skin in a matter of minutes. A more serious form of overexposure is heat stroke, an ever-present hazard when the temperature exceeds 100. Never set off for a hike or a drive in the desert—no matter how short—without water. If you are driving, bring along a 10-gallon jug of water for your radiator. If you get lost or if your car breaks down on a remote road, remember that it is easier for a rescue squad to find you than for you to reach help. Set up a distress marker that can be spotted by air-search teams and stay in the shade.

The Highlands and Mountain Ranges

Running north and south of the mountain ranges that dominate the center of the state are the semi-arid plateaus. Here the vegetation is transitional: You will find prickly pear cactuses interspersed among juniper bushes on grass-covered mesas, and stands of deciduous trees bleeding into pine forests at the foothills of the mountains. Temperatures in the lower highlands fluctuate broadly each day, ranging from a few degrees below freezing to the mid-50s in winter and from the low 60s to the low 90s in the summer.

Twenty percent of Arizona—an area larger than the state of Maine—is covered by pine forest. The pine forest is concentrated in the central and eastern mountain ranges: the San Francisco Peaks, the Mogollon Rim, and the White Mountains. It gets much cooler at these elevations (6,500–12,000 feet), and the average precipitation is over 30 inches per year, much of it delivered in the form of snow, affording a long downhill ski season.

The Grand Canyon is northern Arizona's biggest tourist attraction, but the area is rife with other record-breaking natural phenomena. The largest stand of Ponderosa Pine in North America grows near the Grand Canyon. These stately trees, valued for their lumber, can grow four feet thick and 180 feet high. Looming over Flagstaff is Humphrey's Peak, at 12,611 feet the highest mountain in Arizona. A perennially snow-capped peak in the San Francisco range, its lower slopes are covered with golden meadows and whispering aspen groves. Another rare species of pine, the bristlecone, grows in the neighboring mountains. Distinctive for its short and sprawling stature, this is one of the longest-lived species in the plant kingdom. Bristlecone can live some 4,600 years, though the bristlecone pines in the area are only 1,000 or so, due to a volcanic eruption that occurred in the year 1064 at Sunset Crater, the most recently active Southwestern volcano.

Meteor Crater, 20 miles west of Winslow, is a 570-foot-deep hole three miles in circumference, created by a 60,000-ton meteor that collided with the earth and disintegrated 50,000 years ago. The crater lies in the southwestern corner of the Painted Desert, where layers of sediment and clay have been exposed by thousands of years of erosion. In the middle of this eerie polychromatic sea of sandstone and shale is the Petrified Forest, where mineral deposits left by floods during the Triassic Period have seemingly turned trees into stone.

Water

Rafting through the Grand Canyon on the Colorado River is by no means the only water sport popular in Arizona. In fact, for several years Arizonans have led the nation in per-capita boat ownership. The huge man-made lakes that comprise the state's reservoir system provide opportunities for boating, swimming, and water-skiing. Fishing enthusiasts can avail themselves of highland lakes and streams where trout and bass are plentiful.

HISTORY

Prehistoric Peoples

It is up to archeologists to write the first chapter of Arizona's history, for Indians were living in the area thousands of years before the record-keeping Europeans arrived. The chronicle is by no means complete, but new discoveries that help to fill the record occur continually. A scant collection of fossils found in the northeastern section of the state shows that no less than 30,000 years ago, Paleo-Indians were living there. And archeological evidence from a cave near Bisbee reveals that 12,000 years ago, the prehistoric inhabitants were fashioning weapons and tools. However, other than the fact of their existence, almost nothing is known about these early humans.

The real story begins about 25 centuries ago. By this time, the prehistoric peoples of Arizona were divided into three distinct cultural groups: the *Hohokam,* who occupied the river valleys and deserts in the south-central part of the state; the *Anasazi,* who lived on the plateaus; and the *Mogollon,* who dwelt in the mountains of east-central Arizona.

The Indians of Arizona weren't just roaming around the plains shooting game before the Europeans came along to civilize them. On the contrary, three centuries before the birth of Christ, the agricultural Hohokams of the Salt River Valley—in which Phoenix lies—had completed miles and miles of an irrigation canal system through which they were to bring water to their farmlands for the next 17 centuries. At Casa Grande, midway between Phoenix and Tucson, they erected the first American apartment complex—a four-story building, thought to have housed several families, with an observatory on top. Amidst of the clamor and bustle of southeast Phoenix lie the quiet ruins of Pueblo Grande, a Hohokam village occupied from 200 B.C. to A.D. 1400. Excavations have uncovered meeting rooms, residences, and even a ball court.

Hohokam isn't what these people called themselves. The word is from the Pima Indian language and means "those who have gone." Perhaps drought was the cause of their demise, perhaps war, perhaps simply the decline of a civilization—the reason is unknown, but in the fifteenth century the Hohokams disappeared. Their canals dried up and their buildings crumbled into dusty ruins. Yet their legacy continues: The ancient canals are part of the water system that currently serves the two million people of Phoenix and the surrounding agricultural lands. In fact, if not for the Hohokams' having proven that the desert could be successfully farmed, Phoenix might never have been founded. Today, as valley residents dig up their backyards for swimming pools, patios, and gardens, they frequently uncover centuries-old tools, grinding stones, and pottery fragments of these ancient desert dwellers.

The story of the Anasazi Indians mirrors that of the Hohokam. They, too, had formed pueblo societies by the time of the birth of Christ and

subsisted on hunting and farming. They also accomplished some marvelous architectural feats and must be commended for their choices of location; nearly all of the Anasazi ruins are situated in awesome settings,
which make charming sites for educational picnics. On the shady side of
a small, sycamore-lined canyon in the center of Arizona, an Anasazi sub-
group, called the *Sinagua,* built a 20-room, five-story cliff dwelling—
dubbed "Montezuma's Castle" by later explorers. Its inhabitants probably
hunted and cultivated crops in the fertile valley below. Twenty-five miles
due northeast is Tuzigoot, another Sinagua pueblo ruin. Site selection was
undoubtedly based on defensive considerations, for this 100-room pueblo
perched on the crest of a tall hill affords a panoramic view of the surrounding Verde Valley. Like the Hohokams, the Anasazis seem to have disappeared; anthropologists date their demise around the year 1500.

Prodigious potters, the Mogollon Indians left behind an anthropological
treasure trove of shards and tools in the northeastern rim country. They,
too, subsisted by hunting and farming, and seem to have lived according
to a fairly organized social structure. At Kinishiba, near Fort Apache, and
at Bear Ruin, eight miles south of Show Low, archeologists have excavated
the 1,200-year-old ruins of Mogollon communities.

Spanish Exploration

By the early sixteenth century, ruins were virtually all that was left of
the prehistoric tribes. An altogether different set of Indians was on hand
to greet the Spanish explorers when they arrived. And though the Spaniards noted evidence of a recent upheaval in their travel journals, neither
they nor the oral histories of the extant tribes shed any light on what happened to the Anasazi, Hohokam, and Mogollon cultures. Evidence suggests that the Zuni, Hopi, and Pueblo Indians descend from these prehistoric peoples, but for the most part, the Indians the Spanish came across
had migrated to Arizona relatively recently. Some came north from Mexico; others, like the Navajo and Apache, were forced westward from the
Great Plains by more powerful rival tribes.

In the 1530s, rumors of a city of gold and riches in northeastern Arizona
reached the ears of the Viceroy of New Spain in Mexico. In response, he
sent a friar named Marcos de Niza to explore the region. Soon after setting
out, the cleric began to have trouble with his assistant, Esteban, a Moorish
slave who had traveled across the Sonora Desert as an Indian captive a
few years before. Esteban, it seemed, was more interested in the Indian
maidens he encountered than in claiming territory for his sovereign and
his exploits angered several Indian groups, endangering the mission. De
Niza and Esteban reached a compact: They would travel separately, the
Moor a few days in advance. As they got nearer to "Cibola," the mythical
city of gold, Esteban was to send messengers back to de Niza bearing crosses—the closer they got to the city, the larger the crosses should be.

Esteban sent back progressively larger crosses until he reached a good-
sized Indian pueblo called Hawikuh, near Gallup, New Mexico, and from
there he sent de Niza a man-sized cross. De Niza hurried to catch up, but
was forestalled en route by a message from the residents of Hawikuh: a
message delivered in the form of Esteban's mangled corpse. The mild-
mannered friar decided to go home.

Somehow, the farther de Niza got from Hawikuh, the more elaborate his travelogue became. By the time of his next audience with the Viceroy of New Spain, Hawikuh had turned into an Indian capital of 300,000 residents where the streets were paved with gold. The Viceroy wasted no time: He sent the renowned explorer and soldier Francisco Vasquez de Coronado to conquer the city. It was late June, the hottest, driest time of year, and Coronado and his small army were beset with hardship as they retraced the route de Niza and Esteban had blazed. Coronado, garbed in a golden suit of armor, was undoubtedly the most uncomfortable of the bunch. But visions of the magnificent plunder to be had at the end of their journey bolstered their spirits and they pressed on. U.S. Route 666, often referred to as the Coronado Trail, follows the path of the conquistador and his army, wending through some of the most spectacular scenery in Arizona.

In early July 1540, they reached Hawikuh and found not Cibola, the bustling city of gold and riches, but a dusty Indian village of 150 inhabitants. Perhaps out of sheer frustration, Coronado and his men skirmished with the warriors of the village in the first battle between whites and Indians in what is now the United States.

Having heard from the Indians of a Great River to the north, Coronado sent a detachment under Pedro de Tovar in search of it. Tovar and his men returned with barely believable stories of a *Gran Barranca:* a deep, red Grand Canyon through which flowed a great and raging river—an awesome work of God, impassable and wondrous.

Interest in the region waned over the next half century until, in 1598, the Spanish explorer Juan de Onate embarked on a series of expeditions through the southwest in which he claimed a huge portion of North America, from Arizona to Oklahoma, including everything south of Kansas, for the crown. He returned with ore samples that suggested potential mineral wealth.

Spanish Colonization

Throughout the New World, the Spanish crown practiced a two-pronged policy of colonization. Exploitation of mineral wealth and resources was half the plan, but recruiting converts to the Roman Catholic Church was of equal importance, for in those times—at the height of the religious turmoil that kept Europe at war for a century—the more subjects the Spanish monarch could muster into the Church rolls, the greater his power base against Protestant rivals. Moreover, the Spanish Roman Catholic mission system was a convenient way of maintaining local control over the natives and indoctrinating them into the white man's ways. Throughout much of Spanish America, it was the missionaries who first brought the Indians under Spanish dominion and Arizona was no exception.

In 1629, Franciscan friars established themselves among the Hopis in the northeastern corner of Arizona, but for reasons unknown they disappeared a few years later. The missionary effort did not actually take off until 1687 when a remarkable Jesuit priest named Eusebio Francisco Kino set out on a proselytizing tour of Arizona which would last the remaining 24 years of his life, cover 75,000 miles, and result in the foundation of 73 *visitas* (small local churches) and 29 missions. At each of these outposts, the missionaries set up not only houses of worship, but also lodgings for themselves and for the Indians, farm buildings and corrals, and workshops, in hopes of converting the native Americans not only to a new religion, but to a new way of living.

In an era when Spanish missionaries in the New World had gained a reputation for martinetism and lack of compassion, Kino was loved by almost all, and the example he set as a devout Christian led thousands to follow him into the Church. He built his first mission in 1692 at Guevavi; four years later he had founded another at Tumacacori, 25 miles north of Nogales; his third and most famous mission, San Xavier del Bac, 10 miles south of Tucson, was established in 1700. Mass is still celebrated at San Xavier del Bac.

When Kino died in 1711, his circumspect policies regarding treatment of the Indians fell into disuse, especially as the role of the Spanish military in colonizing the Indians grew. Antagonisms erupted between the Indians and the Spaniards, and in 1751 the natives rose up in revolt. In response, the Spanish erected a *presidio* (a walled, garrisoned city) at Tubac, near Tumacacori. Increasingly fearful that the Jesuits were amassing too much power in America, King Carlos III of Spain ordered their expulsion in 1767. Before a new contingent of missionaries—Franciscans this time—could move in to take the Jesuits' place one year later, Apaches had destroyed San Xavier del Bac.

Just when the missionary effort appeared to be on the brink of downfall, Francisco Tomas Garces, a Franciscan brother, arrived on the scene. Like Kino, he combined intelligence and compassion and he commanded tremendous respect and affection from the people he dealt with. After overseeing the rebuilding of San Xavier del Bac, Garces set out on a series of missionary expeditions. His travels took him far west, and he discovered openings in the Sierra Nevada to California and explored the northwestern section of the Colorado River in the process.

From Mission to Presidio

While Kino, Garces, and the other missionaries were busy bringing Indians into the fold, the military government in New Spain was looking into the possibility of exploiting Arizona's mineral wealth and position as a defensive salient. In 1736, a Yaki Indian led an inquisitive Spanish explorer to a watering hole 25 miles southwest of Nogales called *Aleh-Zhon,* a Papago phrase meaning "small spring." The small spring also happened to be the site of a lode of silver, which, when mined, netted 10,000 pounds for the royal coffers. Aleh-Zhon gained instant fame and eventually the Hispanized term "Arizona" was applied to the entire region.

As a result of Garces's discoveries, and the further explorations of de Anza, who ventured overland all the way up to Monterey, California, travel between Mexico and California increased. Not surprisingly, so did Indian attacks against the Spanish. In 1776, the Spanish constructed another *presidio* at Tucson on the site of an old Papago ranch. Today a small section of the wall is preserved in the Pima County courthouse in downtown Tucson.

From Mexican to American

Mexico won independence from Spain in 1821 and retained the Arizona territory in the process. The young nation had little use for the area, except as a buffer against the looming threat of the expansionist United States. For the next two decades, Americans became an increasing presence in the area. First the trappers and mountain men arrived; before long there were an estimated 2,000 of them working the Gila River region for beaver pelts and countless more hunting game in the northern mountains.

Tough, unscrupulous adventurers, these men presided over the most colorful period of Arizona's history. Bill Williams, a hard-drinking, horse-thieving fellow, first came west as a Methodist circuit-rider. Later he was made a chief in the Ute tribe and took a Ute wife. He used to disappear into the mountains for months at a time, emerging with a pile of wolf pelts that he would trade away for liquor and supplies. Leading a group of trappers over the Santa Fe trail in 1822, Ewing Young stumbled upon the Grand Canyon. Among the members of his party was 16-year-old Kit Carson, who had run away from an apprenticeship in the East to seek his fortune in the Southwest. Paulino Weaver, the son of an Indian mother, guided the Mormon Batallion in Arizona during the war with Mexico and helped gold prospectors uncover fabulous fortunes along the Hassayampa River. These are a few of the men who opened the southwest up for American expansion and their memories live on in the place names of the territory they covered—Williams, Mount Williams, Weaver's Needle.

In the 1830s and 1840s, while Antonio Lopez de Santa Anna exercised dictatorial control over Mexico, the "All Mexico" territorial expansion debate was heating up in Washington. Texas gained sovereignty in 1836 and the uneasiness between Mexico and the U.S. intensified. More and more, Arizona and New Mexico were following the pattern of the Lone Star State: American trappers and ranchers were moving in, carving out roads, settling down, and eroding the Mexican government's control. War finally broke out in 1847. It lasted only a few weeks, and the United States came out victorious. Under the Treaty of Guadalupe Hidalgo, signed on February 2, 1848, General Santa Anna ceded half his country, everything from the Gila River north to Wyoming. In exchange, America paid Mexico $15 million for the land and $3 million in indemnities for thefts and vandalism committed by the Indians. Santa Anna reserved most of the money for his personal estate.

Indian Wars

The Gold Rush began in 1848. People crossed Arizona in droves on their way to California, and the Apache Indians, who from the beginning had been hostile toward white men, increased their ruthless incursions. To protect the American travelers, the federal government erected a string of forts in the southwest, including Fort Defiance in the Four Corners area and Fort Mohave on the Colorado. The situation only got worse, however, for several prospectors had struck out on their own and had hit paydirt in the silver deposits of central and southern Arizona. Mines opened, and towns sprang up all over the state. Cattlemen discovered Arizona's wide, grassy ranges and before long the plains were covered with little dogies.

Naturally, the Apaches resented the encroaching white men and expressed their hostility in raids, cattle theft, and incursions against the more vulnerable settlers. To make matters worse, they could no longer seek refuge over the border with Mexico.

Meanwhile, the United States was growing increasingly interested in the territory south of the Gila River to the present boundary between Mexico and the U.S. For one thing, it was the perfect place to run a railroad across to California. Moreover, the U.S. hankered after the tremendous copper, silver, and gold deposits in the region. With these thoughts in mind, the United States sent James Gadsden to Mexico with an offer of $10 million for the 30,000 square miles of land. Apparently, Santa Anna felt he needed the money, for he readily agreed to the Gadsden Purchase, retaining a quarter of the money for his personal use.

Incidentally, schoolchildren in Arizona are taught that the Yankee surveyors of the Gadsden Purchase resorted to liquor to bring relief from the oppressive heat of the desert as they marked out the new boundary between Mexico and the U.S. And in their drunkeness, they swerved north, missing the Gulf of California—Arizona's lost ocean—by just 40 miles.

Over a period of 25 years, two great Apache chiefs, Cochise and Geronimo, succeeded in making life miserable for the white men in Arizona, which President Lincoln made a U.S. territory in 1863. Cochise and his Indian army actively assaulted the Americans for a decade beginning in 1861 during which over 5,000 people—white and Indian—were killed.

Finally, in 1871, U.S. General Oliver Otis Howard got the Apaches to agree to move to a reservation in the southeastern section of the state, though Cochise probably consented because of the potential for raids into Mexico. At any rate, the government deceived the Indians, sending them north to San Carlos instead. In November the Apaches rebelled. It took nine columns to quash the revolt, and even then the army's troubles with the Apaches weren't over. Geronimo and his marauding army of 40 warriors did not agree to surrender until 1886, largely because of an opportunistic group of merchant traders called the Indian Ring, who were making themselves rich selling supplies and ammunition to both the military and the Apaches. U.S. General George Crook had struggled for years to reach a peaceful solution to the conflict, but the night after he had at last got Geronimo to agree to move to a reservation, a delegate from the Indian Ring secretly visited the Apache headquarters. Plying the chief with liquor, the delegate informed him that what Crook really intended was to kill them. Violence erupted once again. In August 1886, 5,000 troops under General Nelson Miles marched in to conquer Geronimo and his scrappy little band of braves, bringing and end to the Apache wars.

Not everyone in the U.S. was excited about acquiring Arizona. Kit Carson declared that the territory couldn't keep a wolf alive. General William Tecumseh Sherman concurred: "We went to war with Mexico to get Arizona, and now we should go to war with her and make her take it back." When someone contradicted him, stating that all Arizona needed for success was less heat and a better breed of people, Sherman replied, "That's all *Hell* needs."

The Civil War

On February 14, 1862, Jefferson Davis declared Arizona a Confederate territory. No one bothered to object; the war was too remote, and, besides,

Arizonans had troubles of their own—Indians, for instance—to contend with. But somehow Union and Confederate troops managed to meet twice in Arizona. The only real battle occurred in 1862 at Picacho Pass, between Phoenix and Tucson. An officer, two enlisted men, and a mule were killed, but the Union forces prevailed, forcing the rebels to retreat, permanently, from the territory.

The Road to Statehood

The three Cs—cattle, copper, and cotton—were the sources of Arizona's development and prosperity. As pioneers staked out farms along the roads beaten by prospectors and trappers, towns took shape. It was due to the efforts of a few ambitious individuals, however, that the agricultural economy was able to take root. In 1858, Jacob Hamblin guided a group of Mormons across Arizona to the Colorado River, and over the following years hundreds of Mormons, seeking refuge from the religious persecution they suffered in the northeast, settled along Hamblin's route, gradually spreading down into the Gila and Salt River valleys. The Mormons were the first Americans to exploit Arizona's agricultural potential.

Perhaps one of the reasons for the early Arizonans' success was their willingness to experiment. In 1856, Congress agreed to appropriate funds for the army to import a herd of camels, accompanied by Arab drivers, to the territory. Camels were better suited to the desert climate, it was argued, than the standard army-issue mule. For several years camels carried supplies across the harshest terrain in the state, but, in the end, the St. Louis mule lobby and the Civil War terminated to the experiment. At Quartzsite, a pyramidal monument to one of the more popular camel drivers, "Hi Jolly"—his name was Haji Ali until the locals got hold of it—commemorates his last bivouac, and a few working camels can still be seen around the state.

Farming the central and southern parts of the territory seemed out of the question owing to the age-old water problem. But in 1867 an enterprising young post sutler at Fort McDowell won a contract to provide the fort with hay. His hay camp, located near what is now Sky Harbor Airport in Phoenix, was the first farm in the Salt River Valley. That same year Jack Swilling, an ingenious ex-Confederate soldier, undertook to irrigate the valley by clearing out the ancient Hohokam canals. The Swilling Irrigation Canal Company transformed large portions of the desert into fertile farmlands.

More farmers moved in and a little town grew up around Smith's Station, as the hay camp was called. The townfolk debated what to name the booming little community at an incorporation meeting convened in 1881. Swilling suggested "Stonewall." Others opted for the more descriptive "Salina." Then a man by the name of Darrell Duppa, a soi-disant English aristocrat, stood up to deliver a long speech on how the once-again fertile oasis that had sprung up out of an ancient Indian city harkened back to the myth of the Egyptian Phoenix bird, which rises from the ashes of its predecessor. His fellow citizens were so cowed by his comparative erudition that they accepted his suggestion, and even let him name a neighboring community, Tempe, which, he claimed, had often reminded him of the Vale of Tempe in Greece.

Charles Hayden erected a flour mill on the Tempe side of the Salt River in 1871. The mill was a boon to the area, for the nearest railroad was 40 miles away. Now local farmers could grow wheat, one of their most profitable crops, and have it processed locally. The Hayden Mill is still in operation, and the main thoroughfare through the pretty college city is appropriately called Mill Avenue. Hayden performed another great service to the state by siring his son Carl, who served in the U.S. House of Representatives, including a stint as Speaker, from the time of statehood, in 1912, until 1969.

The family of Michael Goldwasser, a Polish Jew who emigrated to America in 1848, came to the southwest in the 1860s and soon had a prosperous mercantile trade going. His sons opened a store in Phoenix, giving it the anglicized version of their name, and his grandson, Barry Goldwater, became another favorite son of Arizona, serving in the United States Senate from 1952 until his retirement in 1986, with one break in the 1960s to become the Republican nominee for president. The family sold their interest in the 1950s, but Goldwater's Department Stores are still prominent throughout the state.

The advent of railroads to Arizona led to a mining boom. Although now just a tourist-frequented ghost town in the mountains northeast of Prescott, Jerome was once a bustling copper center. Bisbee and Douglas are part of a network of mining towns that sprang up in the southeastern corner of the territory, and the mines are still open there—the Bisbee pit features guided tours.

The railroads also helped the cattle industry along. Cattle yards opened near the large railway centers—the Stockyards Restaurant in east Phoenix used to be a favorite stopping place of the cowboys bringing their herds in for slaughter and packing. These were the shoot-'em-up days of the Wild West. Even the relatively staid town of Phoenix was considered unsafe during drinking hours. The shoot-out at OK-Corral, made famous by the movie, occurred in the tough southeastern town of Tombstone. The Crystal Palace Saloon, where Wyatt Earp and Doc Holiday habitually slung a few back, is still open for business.

Statehood and Growth

Valentine's Day, 1912 marked the closing of the frontier that had for so long drawn Americans westward. Arizona became a state, with Phoenix as its capital, and George W.P. Hunt was elected governor. Typical of Arizona politicians, Hunt went on to serve seven terms. The state grew slowly until World War II, when the good times began to roll. Arizona's vast, remote expanses provided excellent ground for air-force bases, training centers, and defense plants. With the military came the seeds of high-technology industries that would flourish over the succeeding decades.

But Arizona wasn't just the home of dozens of army and air-force operations. Hundreds of Japanese-Americans from California were bused in to spend the duration of the war in three internment camps in Arizona and a German POW camp was set up a just outside of Phoenix. A group of soldiers incarcerated there obtained a map of the state and, noting that the nearby Salt River flowed into the Gila River and the Gila into the Colorado, plotted to build a raft and float to Mexico. It must have come as an awful disappointment when, after managing to break out of the camp and trekking several miles across the desert to the banks of the Salt, they found a dry river bed. Had they been aware that water runs in the rivers only a few weeks of every year they might have been spared the trouble.

One group whose aid to the nation during World War II is worthy of particular mention is the Arizona Indians. The military's search for an indecipherable code to use in secret communications came to an end with the recruitment of Navajos who, conversing in their own language over the radio, utterly confounded the Germans. In addition, hundreds of Arizona Indians served in the military overseas. In fact, the hero of the historic flag raising at Iwo Jima was a Pima Indian named Ira Hayes.

Many defense workers stayed on in Arizona after the war and manufacturing concerns moved in quickly to take advantage of the abundance of labor and land. The population grew steadily thereafter, more than doubling between 1960 and 1980. State and local governments have tried to encourage growth, for the most part eschewing laws and regulations that impede industrial development. In the last decade, particular emphasis has been placed on the introduction and development of high-technology industries. Tourism has increased significantly in recent years and is now a primary source of revenue for the state.

But unchecked growth has also introduced new problems to Arizona. Once a haven for sufferers of asthma, tuberculosis, and other lung diseases, Phoenix now has a serious smog problem that has proved as difficult to check as urban sprawl. The small-city charms of Phoenix, Tucson, and Flagstaff—shopping centers among cotton fields, horses grazing in front yards, pickup baseball games in city pastures—are being replaced by more cosmopolitan characteristics. Virgin lands in the deserts and forests up and down the state are being ripped up for the construction of condominiums, resorts, and vacation homes.

Arizona has the largest Indian population of any state, with 15 tribes, most of which occupy reservations under their own tribal government. But conflicts within and without have created problems for them, too. Living according to ancient customs amid the amenities and temptations of modern society is an increasingly unattractive proposition. Young Indians in particular feel the pressure to assimilate into mainstream American culture, and tribal leaders bewail the generational conflicts that have erupted over the last few years. Moreover, disputes—generally over land or jurisdiction—between various tribes and with the state government continue to erupt.

Clearly, Arizonans must find a way to overcome these new challenges, but the prognosis is optimistic. Arizonans have a history of surmounting obstacles—from turning a desert into an oasis to civilizing the cattlemen. In the meantime, Arizona offers the traveler a landscape it would take a lifetime to explore and a welcome it would take two lifetimes to wear out.

FACTS AT YOUR FINGERTIPS

TOURIST INFORMATION. Even if you have visited Arizona before, there is always something new to see. For instance, Arizona has more than 20 national parks and monuments—more than any other state.

Arizona also boasts the largest Indian population of any state—15 tribes occupy 20 reservations that cover more than 19 million acres. And the nation's oldest continuously inhabited community at Old Oraibi is located on the Hopi Indian Reservation.

Many who are not familiar with Arizona envision the state as a vast desert. In fact, Arizona has nearly every type of terrain thinkable—deserts, mountains, canyons, lakes, forests, rivers, rock formations, and more. Surprisingly, the greatest stand of ponderosa pine in the nation is found in Arizona along the Mogollon Rim.

Where else but in Arizona could you find trees that have turned to stone over a 200-million-year period? Or view the original London Bridge that once spanned England's River Thames?

And, of course, Arizona is the Grand Canyon State, named after the 10-mile-wide, 250-mile-long canyon carved by a single river over more than 6 million years.

Information on scenic tours, attractions, hotels, inns and resorts, restaurants, golf courses, and much more is available through the *Phoenix and Valley of the Sun Convention and Visitors Bureau,* 505 N. 2nd St., Phoenix 85004; (602) 254–6500.

Visitor Information Centers are located in terminals 2 and 3 at Sky Harbor Airport, and on the northwest corner of Adams and Second streets in downtown Phoenix. In addition, the bureau provides a Visitor Hotline that gives a 2-minute recorded message about current activities and events in the Phoenix metropolitan area; (602) 252–5588.

The Valley Reservation System, also operated by the Visitor's Bureau, enables visitors to make *one* toll-free call for reservations at over 100 hotels, inns, and resorts in the Phoenix-Scottsdale area, as well as the Grand Canyon National Park lodges. Reservations also can be made for car rentals, apartments, and condominiums, bus and air tours, plus mule rides into the Grand Canyon. Call (800) 528–0483, in Arizona (602) 257–4111.

However, if your tastes encompass an area beyond metropolitan delights, contact the *Arizona Office of Tourism,* Suite 180, 1480 E. Bethany Home Rd., Phoenix, 85014; (602) 255–3618. They can send brochures on the state's many natural wonders.

There are six national forests in Arizona. Call (602) 225–5296 for a recorded Forest Service information message and campground update. Contact specific headquarters for more information:

Apache-Sitgreaves National Forest, Box 640, Springerville 85938; (602) 333–4372.

Coconino National Forest, 2323 E. Greenlaw Ln., Flagstaff 86004; (602) 527–7400.

Coronado National Forest, Federal Building, 300 W. Congress, Tucson 85701; (602) 629–6483.

Kaibab National Forest, 800 S. 6th St., Williams 86046; (602) 635–2681.

Prescott National Forest, 344 S. Cortez, Prescott 86303; (602) 445–1762.

Tonto National Forest, Box 5348, Phoenix 85010; (602) 225–5200.

If your travel plans include a trip to the Grand Canyon, keep in mind that there are many ways to explore this imponderable abyss other than just gaping at it from the rim. Contact *The Grand Canyon National Park Lodges,* Box 699, Grand Canyon 86023; (602) 638–2631, for information on hiking, mule rides, bus tours, helicopter and air tours, and smooth-water rafting. *Wilderness River Adventures,* Box 717, Page 86040; (602) 645–3296, will provide information on white-water rafting in the canyon. Rafting trips start in mid-May and cost from $400 to $1,800 per person depending on the length and type of trip. Trips run 3, 4, 9, and 14 days, most beginning and ending in Las Vegas, Nevada. Six months' advance booking is recommended and a deposit of $100 per person is required.

The influence of the early Spanish settlers lives on in the southern half of the state. In the towns of Tubac, Nogales, and Tucson, you can tour 17th-century Spanish missions and some of the earliest buildings in America.

Arizona is rich with natural history museums. Among them the Arizona Sonora Desert Museum in Tucson houses a tremendous variety of wildlife and plant life found in the Sonora Desert. Call (602) 883–2702 for hours and information on special exhibits. Tucson also is home to many historic buildings that can be seen during a walking tour of the city. See what the Tucson area has to offer by writing or calling the *Metropolitan Tucson Convention & Visitors Bureau,* 130 S. Scott Ave., Tucson 85701; (602) 624–1889.

Arizona has many downhill and cross-country ski areas located throughout the state. Near Flagstaff: Arizona Snow Bowl, Bill Williams Ski Area, Mormon Lake Ski Touring Center, and Montezuma Ski Nordic; in the White Mountains: Greer Ski Area and Sunrise Ski Area; and outside Tucson: Mount Lemmon Ski Valley. Ski areas are generally open fron November to April and most offer instruction, food, and ski rental.

TIPS FOR BRITISH TRAVELERS. Passports and Visas. You will need a valid, 10-year passport (cost: £15). You do not need a visa if you are staying for less than 90 days, have a return ticket, and are flying with a participating carrier. Ask your travel agent or call the U.S. Embassy (01–499–3443) for details.

No vaccinations are required for entry into the U.S.

Customs. If you are 21 or over, you can take into the U.S.: 200 cigarettes or 50 cigars or 3 lbs. of tobacco (combination of proportionate parts permitted); and 1 U.S. quart of alcohol. In addition, every visitor, including minors, is allowed duty-free gifts to a value of $100. No alcohol or cigarettes may be included in this gift exemption, but up to 100 cigars may be. Be careful not to take in meat or meat products, seeds, plants, fruits, etc. Avoid narcotics like the plague.

Returning to Britain you can bring home: (1) 200 cigarettes *or* 100 cigarillos *or* 50 cigars *or* 250 grams of tobacco; (2) two liters of table wine with additional allowances for (a) one liter of alcohol over 22% by volume (most spirits), (b) two liters of alcohol under 22% by volume (fortified or sparkling wine), or (c) two more liters of table wine; (3) 50 grams of perfume and ¼ liter of toilet water; and (4) other goods up to a value of £32.

Insurance. We recommend that you insure yourself to cover health and motoring mishaps, with *Europ Assistance*, 252 High St., Croydon CRO 1NF (01-680 1234). Their excellent service is all the more valuable when you consider the possible costs of health care in the U.S. It is also wise to insure yourself against trip cancellation and loss of luggage.

Airfares. We suggest you explore the current scene for budget flight possibilities—standby, APEX, and other fares offer considerable savings over the full price. Quite frankly, only business travelers who don't have to watch the price of their tickets fly full price these days—and find themselves sitting right beside APEX passengers! At press time, APEX round-trip fares to Phoenix or Tucson cost from £409. You may want to look into available fly-drive programs offered by firms such as *Kuoni, Thomas Cook,* and *Trans World Airlines.*

WHEN TO GO. The climates of the northern high-country and the low, central, and southern deserts are quite different, so when to go depends on what part of the state you plan to visit. As a rule, the state is at its best during the spring and autumn seasons.

Winter. From mid-September through April, central and southern Arizona experience mild, sunny weather. At this time of year, the deserts teem with life and the cities and towns bustle with tourists. The winter months sparkle with festivals, art shows, plays, parades, and rodeos.

The best lodging rates at the Grand Canyon occur during the winter. There are fewer crowds because of the cold weather. If you are willing to brave the bitter climate, you may discover the unique beauty of the canyon draped in snow. But bundle up—winter in northern Arizona is a serious business. Temperatures can drop below zero and snow and freezing rain are not uncommon.

Summer. It is oppressively hot in the desert regions during June, July, and August. However, air-conditioning is ubiquitous, so one remains comfortable by staying indoors. Summer in the high-country is mild and pleasant—the most favorable weather for exploring the canyons and natural monuments of northern Arizona.

A word of caution to those planning any type of summer activity in the desert: Always remember to take along enough drinking water—one gallon per person per day, minimum. It really does get hot.

CLIMATE. Arizona is a state of diverse climates. Phoenix is sunny about 300 days of the year and receives only seven inches of precipitation annually.

The northern half of the state—Flagstaff, Prescott, and Sedona—gets more rain during the year. During the summer, you can expect temperatures during the day to be 10 degrees cooler up in the pines and 20 to 25 degrees cooler at night. And in the winter, when people in Phoenix are going about in shirtsleeves, Flagstaff might very well be blanketed in snow.

At the Grand Canyon, temperatures can be cool on the rim and 20 degrees warmer at the bottom. During the winter, it snows most on the

North Rim (6–12 inches), while the South Rim generally gets less than six inches.

In the southern half of the state, the winter temperatures (October through March) average highs of 70 degrees and lows of 43 degrees. Summer temperatures range from average highs of 91 degrees to average lows of 54 degrees.

The largest southern city—Tucson—gets about 11 inches of rain yearly, and most of that occurs July through September and December through March.

Following are the average yearly temperatures in Phoenix, as provided by the U.S. Weather Service:

	Jan.	Feb.	Mar.	Apr.	May	June	July	Aug.	Sept.	Oct.	Nov.	Dec.
High	65	69	74	84	92	101	105	102	98	88	75	66
Low	38	41	45	52	60	68	77	76	69	57	45	38

WHAT TO TAKE. When trying to decide what to pack, remember that Arizona is an easygoing state. That means casual. There are some clothes that will work well in winter or summer, such as jeans, T-shirts, sneakers, boots (depending on whether you plan on a lot of horseback riding or hiking) slacks, and blouses. Winter wear should also include a sweater or jacket for cool morning hours.

Because the temperature soars during the summer, the comfort factor becomes harder to maintain. The most comfortable summer attire includes skirts, sundresses, shorts, and lightweight shirts and trousers. Swim suits, hats, and sandals are necessities.

Restaurants in the metropolitan areas require the correct attire. Women may want to take several basic dresses that can be varied with an easy change of accessories. Men will probably want to take a sports or dinner jacket, dress shirt, and tie.

Throughout the year, it is wise to use a sunblock when spending time outdoors. Don't forget to take a camera—this is some of the most photogenic scenery in the world. Always carry an extra pair of glasses, including sunglasses, especially if they are prescription lenses. A traveling iron is a good idea, as are large and small plastic bags for wet items and laundry.

Of course, there's plenty of shopping opportunity in Phoenix and Tucson. From real Western garb to stylish new fashions, the local stores carry just about everything.

WHAT IT WILL COST. During the tourist season—September through April—you can expect to pay $75 to $275 for a double-occupancy room in one of the better hotels, motels, inns, or resorts. During this time of year, those hotels and motels that cater to the budget-minded will also have raised their rates, but generally only by $15 to $20.

Some travelers may prefer the relative economy of bed and breakfasts to resorts and motels. There are over 240 B&Bs in Arizona. For information or reservations, contact *Bed and Breakfast in Arizona,* Box 8628, Scottsdale 85252; (602) 995–2831; or *Mi Casa–Su Casa Bed and Breakfast,* Box 950, Tempe 85280; (800) 456–0682, (602) 990–0682 in Arizona. *B&B Scottsdale and the West,* Box 3999, Prescott, 86302; (602) 776–1102 lists B&Bs in Scottsdale, throughout Arizona, and in other western states.

Budget Tips

If you don't mind intense—but dry—heat, it might be worth your while to look into the summer bonus season (May through September). Hotel and resort rates are at their lowest then, offering gigantic savings often of 50 percent or more. Outdoor activities such as tennis, horseback riding, and golf are played year-round and are generally less expensive during the summer. Mountain climbing and waterskiing are also popular summer-time sports.

HINTS TO THE MOTORIST. While driving Arizona highways, observe the speed limit. The highway police use sophisticated speed detection devices, including aircraft, to spot speeding motorists.

Many of the state roads pass through one of the 20 Indian reservations in Arizona and these roads are patrolled by highway police. However, if you do any driving within any of the reservations, on roads owned by the reservation, take precautions. Observe all signs. These roads are under the jurisdiction of reservation police.

The major routes through Arizona running east–west are Interstate 40, 10, and 8; U.S. 60, U.S. 70; north–south, U.S. 666, U.S. 89, and U.S. 93; Interstate 17 and 19; and State 95.

A free Arizona State road map is available from the Arizona Department of Transportation by writing to *Arizona Highways Magazine,* 2039 West Lewis Ave., Phoenix 85009. If you are planning an extended stay, consider calling the *Arizona Department of Motor Vehicles* at (602) 255-7011 for a free copy of driving rules and regulations. It can make driving in Arizona a less confusing experience.

Traveling by car is a wonderful way to see all that Arizona has to offer. By taking some precautions, you can make your trip safe and enjoyable.

It is typical for intense dust storms to occur prior to thunderstorms in the monsoon months–mid-July to mid-September. These dust storms can cause very low visibility. If you are on the road during a dust storm, it is best to pull far off the road, turn off your headlights, and wait the 15 or 20 minutes required for the storm to pass. Radio station KTAR (620 AM, an all-news frequency) carries weather and road-condition reports.

During both the summer monsoon and winter rains, flash floods occur over low-lying areas. Especially susceptible are the numerous dry washes that run throughout the state, which can fill up with running water immediately after a storm. Do not attempt to cross them. Watch for posted areas and listen to your radio for weather information.

If you are hoping for some all-terrain vehicle or four-wheeling adventures, keep in mind that it is strictly illegal to drive off established roadways. Also remember that desert temperatures can soar or plummet dramatically, and water is scarce. It is easy to become disoriented. So inform someone of what area you plan to be in. If you do become lost, or a problem develops with your vehicle, do not attempt to walk out. Wait for help to arrive.

Rental Cars

All of the major and several small, independently owned car-rental companies operate within the state. The national companies generally offer similar rates and services from city to city. Some of the smaller local agencies offer late-model used cars with low rates but not as many services. In Phoenix, most of the rental agencies have desks in Sky Harbor Airport and a few have offices at the major resorts. Several agencies provide free airport pickup as well as a ride to the airport.

The *Phoenix & Valley of the Sun Convention & Visitors Bureau;* 505 N. 2nd St., Phoenix 85004, (602) 254–6500, can send you a listing of car rental agencies. Many of those listed offer a toll-free reservation number. And if you are planning your trip during the tourist season, make car reservations before your actual arrival in town.

Pulling a Trailer

If you plan on pulling a trailer (house or boat) on your trip and have not done so before, don't just hook up and take off. Driving with a trailer requires a different set of driving skills—starting, stopping, turning, backing up, and passing—so a certain amount of practice is recommended. Also make a thorough check of your vehicle to see that it can handle pulling a trailer.

• Your automobile rear springs must be of sufficient strength to support the added weight of the trailer while still maintaining your vehicle in an approximately level position.

• It is necessary to increase the pressure in the rear tires of your car to accommodate the extra weight of the trailer. Inflate rear tires approximately six pounds above normal pressure, but do not exceed the pressure limits stamped on your tires.

• State law requires automobiles towing trailers to be equipped with mirrors on both sides. Inadequate side mirrors increase driving hazards by limiting rearward vision.

• Water radiator cooling may be improved by cleaning and refilling the radiator with a commercial coolant solution. Engine oil should be fresh and of the maximum viscosity recommended for your particular engine.

• Engine and transmission heat increase as automobile speed increases. To ensure proper cooling, do not exceed 45 mph regardless of engine size or load.

• Automobile manufacturer's recommended maximum passenger/cargo load is reduced by an amount equal to trailer tongue weight carried on the trailer hitch. Compensate for this extra weight by decreasing the load carried inside the trunk and rear seat areas.

• When you stop at rest areas during your trip, walk around the car and trailer and check the following. It will afford you a better, safer trip. *Load heavier in front. Hitch tight. Chains attached. Lights working. Tire pressure okay.*

There are trailer parks throughout the state where you can park for a day, week, or month. And the more remote parks usually sell gas and groceries.

HOTELS AND MOTELS. Be choosy about your lodgings; don't take pot luck. If you haven't made reservations, you'll undoubtedly waste time looking for a place and often won't be satisfied with it. If you have to look, begin early in the afternoon. If you do have reservations but don't expect to arrive before 5 or 6 P.M., advise the hotel or motel in advance. Some places will not, unless guaranteed payment, hold reservations after 6 P.M.

The Phoenix Visitors Bureau has recently designed a program to end the looking-for-the-right-hotel blues. The **Sunsational Holiday Vacation Package** features 30 hotels and resorts that offer special seasonal rates and amenities packages, including golf, tennis, and car rentals. In Phoenix, there are eight hotels and motels listed. Contact the *Phoenix and Valley of the Sun Convention and Visitors Bureau* at 505 N. 2nd St., Phoenix 85004, (602) 254–6500.

Most of the hotels and motels have pools; some are heated during the winter season.

Hotel and Motel Chains

In addition to the independent hotels and motels throughout Arizona, there are dozens of national or regional chains. An advantage of the chains is the ease of making reservations. If you are a guest at a member hotel or motel, management will be happy to secure you a room at an affiliated hotel or motel at your next destination. Most chains also have a toll-free number to allow you to make reservations on your own.

Because lodging is the single biggest expense of your trip, take a little time to compare prices and amenities offered. The price might include amenities that you have no use for.

In the case of such chains as *Ramada, Holiday Inn,* and *TraveLodge,* prices will vary depending on the location, season, and area, but the amenities stay the same. In metropolitan Phoenix, two adults may pay $70, but in a suburban location of the same hotel, they might pay $60.

Hotel and Motel Categories

Hotels and motels in this guide are divided into five categories, arranged primarily by price but also taking into consideration the degree of comfort you can expect, the amount of service you can anticipate, and the atmosphere of the establishment. Our ratings are flexible and subject to change.

We should also point out that limitations of space make it impossible to include every establishment. We have, therefore, listed those *we* recommend as the best within each price range.

Although the names of various hotel and motel categories are standard throughout this series, the price ranges listed under each category vary from area to area to reflect local price standards. What might be considered a moderate price in a large urban area could be expensive in a rural area. In every case, however, the dollar ranges for each category are clearly stated after the name of the establishment.

Super Deluxe: This category is reserved for only a few hotels. In addition to giving the visitor all the amenities discussed under the deluxe category (following), the super deluxe hotel has a special atmosphere of glamour, good taste, and dignity.

Deluxe: As a rule of thumb, we suggest that the minimum facilities must include bath and shower in all rooms, valet and laundry services, suites available, a well-appointed restaurant and a bar, room service, TV and telephone in room, air-conditioning and heating, and an atmosphere of luxury, calm, and elegance. In a deluxe motel, there may be less service rendered by employees and more by machine or automation (such as refrigerators and ice-making machines in or near your room), but there should be a minimum of do-it-yourself in a truly deluxe establishment.

Expensive: All rooms must have bath or shower, valet and laundry service, restaurant and bar, with at least some room service, TV and telephone in room, attractive furnishings, heating and air-conditioning. Although decor may be as good as that in deluxe establishments, hotels and motels in this category are frequently designed for commercial travelers or for families in a hurry and are somewhat impersonal in terms of service. As for motels in this category, valet and laundry service will probably be lacking; the units will be outstanding primarily for their convenient location and functional character, not for their attractive or comfortable qualities.

Moderate: Each room should have an attached bath or shower, there should be a restaurant or coffee shop, TV available, telephone in room, heating and air-conditioning, relatively convenient location, clean and comfortable rooms, and public rooms.

Inexpensive: Motels in this category do not necessarily have attached bath or shower, nor a restaurant or coffee shop (though one is usually nearby), and, of course, may have no public rooms to speak of. Nearby bath or shower, telephone available in office, and clean rooms are the minimum.

BED & BREAKFASTS. Arizona Bed & Breakfasts run the gamut from a working ranch in Camp Verde to a 24-room Phoenix estate owned by a former movie actress. The rates are comparable to moderately priced hotels and motels, but such advantages as home cooking, good company, and a soft bed sometimes outweigh staying at a motel. Hosts are also a storehouse of information on what to do and what to see locally.

For a listing of bed and breakfasts in Arizona, write or call: *Bed & Breakfast in Arizona,* Box 8628, Scottsdale 85252; (602) 995–2831. They list 240 homes, ranches, and guest houses statewide, many of them in Tucson. *Mi Casa—Su Casa Bed and Breakfast,* Box 950, Tempe 85280; (800) 456–0682 or (602) 990–0682, has metropolitan and rural listings for guest rooms, suites, guest houses, and ranches statewide. *B&B Scottsdale and the West,* Box 3999, Prescott 86302; (602) 776–1102, lists B&Bs in Arizona and other western states. Most doubles begin at $35.

GUEST RANCHES. Arizona has a variety of guest ranches, from luxury 100-unit resorts, where your every whim is catered to, to small family-run ranches where you are expected to help with the chores. Located in rugged, scenic settings, they emphasize outdoor recreation, especially horseback riding. For a list of Arizona guest ranches, contact the *Arizona Office of Tourism,* Suite 180, 1480 E. Bethany Home Rd., Phoenix 85014; (602) 255–3618.

HOSTELS. American Youth Hostels were established to provide clean, inexpensive lodging for young people traveling by foot or bike. Nowadays, however, increasing numbers of people traveling by bus, train, and car use the hostel system. And don't let the *youth* in American Youth Hostel scare you off. It refers to a state of mind rather than an age.

So what can you expect when staying at a hostel? Facilities vary, but most hostels have dormitories segregated by sex, and in the standard hostel, each dorm includes at least 30 square feet of floor space per bed. The hostel also includes hot running water, showers or tubs, and comfortable dining area, kitchen, and common rooms. There is no maid service at hostels; everyone is expected to do some chore to help keep the place clean. Beds are equipped with mattresses and pillows only; each visitor must bring her or his own sheet or sleeping bag or rent one there.

Hostels may be used by members only; an AYH card costs $20 for adults. Maximum length of stay is three days without special permission. Lights out and bunkdown time is from 11 P.M. to 7 A.M., but the individual house parents may vary these hours. They also may collect double fees for violation of quiet time. Alcoholic beverages and illegal drugs are not permitted on hostel property, and smoking is usually not permitted inside the hostel. Rates average around $8 per person per night for most hostels; for those in the Superior rating, expect to pay a little more.

Arizona's hostels are spread out, many being more than a comfortable day's bicycle ride apart, but for bus or car travel, they are just fine.

Arizona's American Youth Hostels include: *Flagstaff's Weatherford Hotel,* 23 N. Leroux, Flagstaff 86001; *The Grand Canyon International Hostel,* Box 270, Grand Canyon 86023; *Rancho Motor Lodge,* corner of Apache Drive and 57 Tovar Street, Box 698, Holbrook 86025; *White Mountain Youth Hostel,* Route 1, Box 210K, Lakeside 85929; *Valley of the Sun International Hostel,* 1026 N. 9th Street, Phoenix 85006; *Old Pueblo,* 411 E. 9th Street, Tucson 85705; *Williams International Hostel/Grand Canyon Hotel Annex,* 134 W. Bill Williams Ave., Williams 86046. For more information, write to the Arizona State Council of the American Youth Hostels, 1026 N. 9th St., Phoenix 85006; (602) 254–9803.

DINING OUT. During high tourist season—late November through April—restaurants stay busy. When possible, make reservations. If a restaurant does not accept reservations, ask what time would be best to avoid the rush. Most hotels, dude ranches, and farm vacations have set dining hours. Dress codes are strict at many finer restaurants, especially in the evenings and in the cities. When in doubt, call ahead and ask about standards.

Restaurant Categories

The restaurants we list that are in large cities are categorized by price as well as by cuisine: American, Mexican, French, "natural," etc., with general fare listed as American-international. Restaurants in smaller towns are categorized by price only: Super Deluxe, Deluxe, Expensive, Moderate, and Inexpensive. The price ranges for each category are given in the restaurant section for each area. Prices in metropolitan areas tend to be higher, but many ethnic food restaurants are surprisingly inexpensive.

TIPPING. A good rule for restaurants and bars is 15 percent of the bill before taxes for good service, 20 percent for excellent service, and anything you want to leave for less than adequate service. For bellmen, 50¢ per bag is the going rate, and a dollar minimum is standard. If you really load him down, you may want to give more. One night's stay in a hotel or motel requires no tip, but if you stay longer, leave the maid $1 to $1.50 per day, $7 per person per week. If you stay under the American plan (meals included in the price), leave $1.50 per person per day for the waiter at the end of your stay. If there have been a number of waiters, leave the tip with the captain or the maître d'hotel and ask him to distribute it.

Here is a list of appropriate tips for other services you may require at a large hotel or resort: doorman, 25¢ for a taxi, 50¢ for baggage handling; bellman, 50¢ per bag, more for heavy loads; parking attendant, 50¢; bartenders, 15 percent of the bill; room service, 15 percent of each bill; laundry or valet, 15 percent; pool attendant, 50¢ per day; snack bar attendant at pool or golf course, 50¢ plus 15 percent of the beverage bill; locker attendant, 50¢ per person per day or $2.50 per person per week; masseur or masseuse, 20 percent of the bill; golf caddies, $2 to $3 per bag or 15 percent of the greens fee on an 18-hole course, $3 on a free course; barbers, 50¢; shoe shine attendants, 50¢; hairdressers, $1.50; manicurist, $1.

Transportation: taxi cab, 15 percent; limousine, 20 percent. Car rental, nothing. Buses, porters, 25¢ per bag; drivers, nothing. (On charter and package tours, drivers usually get $5 to $10 from the group; be sure to check if this is included in the price. On short sightseeing runs, you may tip the driver/guide a dollar, more if he or she has been especially helpful.) Airport buses, nothing. Redcaps, 50¢ per bag. Tipping at curbside check-in is unofficial but same as given. On the plane, no tipping.

On trains, leave 15 percent of the bill for waiters, but nothing for the steward who seats you. Sleeping-car porters get $1 per person per night. The station baggage porter gets 25¢ to 50¢ per bag *over and above* the 25¢ to 35¢ they charge per bag (they turn in the 25¢ per bag with each ticket they collect).

DRINKING LAWS. The legal drinking age in Arizona is 21. Liquor can be served legally from 6 A.M. to 1 A.M. (except Sundays, when hours are noon to 1 A.M.), and all glasses and bottles served in bars and restaurants must be behind the bar by 1:15 A.M. Arizona has stiff drunk driving laws. Driving while intoxicated carries a penalty of a $550 fine, a mandatory 24 hours in jail, and a 90-day suspension of driver's license.

TIME ZONE. Since most of Arizona's population lives in the desert, saving daylight in summer was not of great concern. Most desert dwellers can't wait for the sun to go down in the summertime so things can cool off a little. For this reason, the state elected to stay on *Mountain Standard Time* year-round, except for the Navajo Indian Reservation in the northeastern part of the state, which is on *Mountain Daylight Time.*

TELEPHONES. All Arizona is within area code 602. Directory assistance is 1411. Pay telephone calls cost 25¢. **Emergency telephone numbers:** *Poison Control,* 800–326–0101; *Emergency Assistance,* 911; *FBI,* 279–5511; *Department of Public Safety* (Highway Patrol), to report an accident, 262–8011; outside Phoenix, (800) 525–5555.

BUSINESS HOURS. *Banking hours* may vary slightly from town to town, but usual hours are 10 A.M. to 4 P.M., weekdays. (Currency exchanges are transacted at banks.) *Post office hours* are 8:30 A.M. to 5 P.M., weekdays. *Government and municipal office hours* are 8 A.M. to 5 P.M., weekdays.

Business hours for *retail stores* vary greatly. The majority are open daily from 9 or 10 A.M. to 6 or 7 P.M. and Thursday nights until 9. During the Christmas season, from mid-October to Christmas, most stores are open from 9 to 9.

SENIOR CITIZENS' PROGRAMS AND DISCOUNTS. Arizona is especially solicitous to vacationers and residents who are 55 years old and over. Sun City, Youngtown, Leisure World, and Green Valley are a few of Arizona's retirement communities. These communities are self-contained, offering shopping, entertainment, dances, concerts, and a variety of sport and hobby activities.

If you have always had the urge to travel, the opportunity is certainly available. For those travel-oriented senior citizens, seven Arizona campuses are part of the Elderhostel program.

Elderhostel offers a study program for older adults (people 60 or over or couples of which one partner is at least 60). The enrollees take specially designed one-week courses at colleges and universities. They live in dormitories, dine in campus cafeterias, attend classes taught by regular faculty members, and take field trips.

The seven Arizona campuses active in the program are the University of Arizona, Arizona State University, Northern Arizona University, Cochise College, Yavapai College, The College of Ganado, and Eastern Arizona College at Thatcher. Areas of study include Native American archaeology, the Navajo, astronomy, history of the Pueblo Indians, folk dancing, cowboys and the Old West, the geology of the Grand Canyon, and the flora and fauna of the Sonora Desert.

Arizona is only one of the 50 states involved in Elderhostel, which began in 1975 in New Hampshire. If you are interested in obtaining a catalog of course offerings in Arizona or any other state, call (617) 426–8056, or write Elderhostel, 80 Boylston St., Suite 400, Boston, MA 02116.

The parks and recreation departments of the larger cities sponsor activities geared specifically toward seniors' interests. Unless otherwise indicated, admission is walk-in and free of charge. Some of the activities are special-interest classes, dinners, tours, discussion of great books, and exercise and crafts classes. Many older travelers avail themselves of the cities' senior centers. Most centers are open seven days a week and provide a gathering place for seniors to play bridge, darts, bingo, and shuffleboard, as well as holding coffee hours and special events. For information, call (602) 262–6861 in Phoenix; (602) 994–2408 in Scottsdale; (602) 791–4865 in Tucson.

Phoenix's *Adult/Senior Centers* offer hot meals and a relaxed atmosphere with lounges, card and game areas, volunteer-operated libraries, and classes and field trips. For information call 262–7379.

The centers also have a variety of activities, including workshops, potluck dinners, trips, and weekly dances. Along with the extensive ongoing programs, they offer recreational and educational classes four times a year to anyone 18 years or older. These classes include painting, exercise, personal development, and languages. The fees are low, and because they are popular, registration is necessary. Class brochures are available at the centers prior to registration.

Senior-citizen discounts are common throughout Arizona, but there are no set standards. Some discounts apply to people over 55; others to people over 65—you can never be sure. To be eligible for some discounts, you must fill out a card and register. The best bet is simply to ask whether there is a senior citizen discount available on your ticket or meal or hotel stay. Most municipal, county, state, and federal agencies (national and state parks, city bus lines, state hunting and fishing licenses) offer some sort of price break to the elderly, but definitions vary.

PHOTOGRAPHY AND CAMERA CARE. In the high altitude and low humidity of the mountain ranges of Arizona, the air is thin and extremely clear, with an abundance of ultraviolet (UV) light. While UV light is invisible to the human eye, it is picked up on color film as a blue haze. A skylight filter on your camera will cut the haze and make your photographs look normal. Light at these altitudes is very bright. Pictures taken in full sunlight require one-half to a full stop less exposure than you would normally use at lower altitudes. One way to be sure you've gotten the right exposure is to "bracket," exposing one frame over and another frame under the first exposure. Professional photographers often use this technique.

Particularly in the warmer months, leaving camera and film in a car is a sure way to ruin every shot you've taken. The extreme temperatures inside a car will cause the color to shift, giving pictures a red cast.

A wide-angle lens is almost a must in photographing Arizona. It will enable you to capture the wide panoramas of this vast open land and get both the sky and the canyons' bottoms within a picture.

CAMPING. Given Arizona's variety of altitudes and climates, nearly every type of camping can be found within the state at any time of year—warm deserts where cactus blossoms greet the morning sun, cool mountain glades brushed by pine-scented breezes, and high snowcapped mountains with panoramas of hundreds of miles. Arizona has a wide range of facilities, from private recreational vehicle parks and campgrounds with electric and water hookups, to deluxe U.S. Park Service and Arizona State Park campgrounds featuring showers and running water, to U.S. Forest Service Wildernesses where no vehicles are allowed and the only access is on foot or horseback.

Most high-country camping areas are open from May through October, while desert campgrounds are open year-round. During peak seasons (June, July, and August in the mountains and January through April in the desert), reservations may be necessary, so contact the facility where you plan to stay at least two weeks in advance of your arrival.

For a directory of camping facilities contact: *Arizona Office of Tourism,* Suite 180, 1480 E. Bethany Home Rd., Phoenix 84014; (602) 255–3618.

INDIAN RESERVATIONS. Remember that you are a guest when visiting any of the Indian reservations in Arizona. This land was given to the Indians by the United States government, and the individual Indian tribes own the land. Respect their privacy and ask permission before trespassing or venturing off the main roads on the reservation.

Oftentimes tribal festivities such as some of the Hopi dances are actually sacred religious ceremonies. You may be allowed to watch the ceremonies, but cameras, tape recorders, and sketch pads are forbidden at these gatherings.

Many Indians on the reservations are sensitive about having their pictures taken, as modeling is a source of income for them. Always ask permission before photographing them, and if they require a modeling fee, they will tell you then.

Commercial photography is restricted on some reservations, and you will be required to purchase a permit from the tribal governments.

ARIZONA'S FRAGILE DESERT. Much of Arizona is desert—a dry, harshly beautiful land of rock and cactus, sand and sun. And although the country is filled with jagged mountains, sheer-walled canyons, and miles of grassy plains that appear rugged and indestructible, the desert environment is surprisingly fragile and easily damaged.

Some areas of Arizona receive as little as three inches of rain in a year's time, most of it falling within the short late winter rainy season. With this sparse amount of water, not much vegetation covers the rocky desert floor, and the winds blow away what little organic matter the growing plants produce. This creates the extremely sensitive, easily scarred skin of the desert that takes centuries to heal. The damage wrought by unauthorized motor vehicles and careless human interlopers is irreparable. Bear in mind that fire hazard in these arid regions is much greater than in moister forests. Campfires are illegal except in designated areas. Smokers beware. Live cigarette ashes cause brush fires.

Intaglios, huge figures etched into the desert floor by Indians hundreds of years ago, are as strikingly visible today as they were the day they were made. The tank tracks left by General Patton's troops when they trained in the Arizona desert in the early 1940s look as if the tanks had just left for Africa yesterday. The tracks will probably remain for a thousand years. So special care must be taken by off-road enthusiasts in the desert. Four-wheel-drive vehicles and all-terrain cycles leave tracks that will last as long as the intaglios and Patton's tank tracks. When driving off the main highways in the desert, it is unlawful to leave established roadways.

PROTECTED PLANTS. Most desert plants grow very slowly. By the time the stately saguaro cactus towers 25 feet above the desert floor, it is between 75 and 100 years old. Saguaros usually must reach nearly 50 years of age before they sprout the waxy white flower and produce the tiny seeds that begin the next generation. Other desert plants have similar growth patterns. So when they are removed from the desert or destroyed, it takes years for another plant to take its place. Most desert plants are protected by state law in Arizona, and theft or destruction of them carries a $500 fine and possible imprisonment.

PARTICIPANT SPORTS. Arizona's natural beauty and mild climates draw people out of doors. However, strenuous activity during the hot summer months in the desert should be limited to morning and evening hours.

Write for visitor's guides, which contain lists of sports facilities and sports-related services. For the Phoenix-metro area, write the *Phoenix & Valley of the Sun Convention and Visitors Bureau,* 505 N. 2nd St., Suite 300, Phoenix 85004; for the Tucson area, write the *Tucson Convention & Visitors Bureau,* 130 S. Scott Ave., Tucson 85701.

Swimming. Most hotels and apartments have swimming pools, and nearly all cities have public pools. Many are heated for year-round comfort and in cooler climates are indoors.

Tennis and racquetball. From free public courts at nearly every municipal park to posh athletic clubs to luxurious tennis resorts, Arizona caters to the racquet set. Check with your hotel for facilities. Many have them on the property, while others have clubs nearby where guests can play for a nominal fee.

Golf. Arizona, home of the Phoenix and Tucson opens, is a golfers' paradise. Top-ranked courses, both municipal and private, green the desert by the hundreds, and for summer golf, the high country offers some terrific fairways under the pines. Northern courses close for the winter, but the desert courses are open year-round, with real bargain greens fees during the summer months. For a free brochure on all the golf courses in Arizona, write to the *Arizona Golf Association,* Box 13236, Phoenix 85002; or call (800) 458–8484, 264–7607 in Phoenix.

Hiking. A hiker need never be bored in Arizona. More than a thousand miles of hiking trails braid the mountains and deserts beyond the cities and towns, and many towns and cities have municipal and county parks or national forests nearby where you can be in wilderness within a few minutes. For information, contact the city parks and recreation departments and the national forest offices in the area. The *Sierra Club* leads group treks, of various degrees of difficulty, into the Arizona wilderness. Phone (602) 267–1649 for schedules and information.

Boating and waterskiing. For a state known mostly for its desert areas, Arizona has a surprising number of lakes, all but one of them man-made. Many are near the major cities and boat and ski rental is available. For information, contact the *Arizona State Parks Department,* 1688 W. Adams, Phoenix 85001; 255–4174.

River rafting and kayaking. For real adventure, try a raft trip down the Colorado River through the Grand Canyon. One-day to 14-day trips run all summer long. For information, contact *Grand Canyon National Park,* Box 129, Grand Canyon 86023; 638–2411. The Salt and Verde rivers near Phoenix make for exciting rafting, too. Check with the *Visitors Bureau,* (800) 528–0483, 252–4111 in Phoenix.

Mountain climbing. Climbers "rope up and go," scaling soaring cliffs on desert mountains and snow-covered slopes. Check with local park services for conditions and hazards before setting off. Inexperienced climbers should note that getting down off a mountain is often a far more difficult task than getting to the top. The air mountain-rescue squads keep busy all year round removing stranded—and, frequently, injured—novices.

Horseback riding. Arizona still retains much of its Old West flavor, and stables where you can rent horses, gentle or spirited, are everywhere. Check local telephone directories under "Horse Rentals & Riding" or look for the "Riding Stables" listing in the visitor's guides.

Bird-watching. Arizona also is a bird-watcher's paradise. Rare Central American birds are often sighted along the state's southern border. Several areas in southern Arizona are set aside as sanctuaries. For information, contact: *Arizona Game and Fish Department,* 2222 W. Greenway Rd., Phoenix 85023; 942–3000.

Ballooning. Arizona is second only to New Mexico in the number of balloons per capita. And in Phoenix and Tucson, there are a number of balloon rental services where, during the cooler months, you can rent a piloted balloon and see the area as is possible no other way. Check the local directory under "Balloons."

Soaring (also know as sail planing). Take a ride in a glider. As with balloons, you can charter a ride. Contact Arizona Soaring, 568–2318.

Skydiving. Arizona fields the best skydiving teams around, and, thanks to its climate and wide-open spaces, it is a great place to learn. Check telephone directories under "Parachute Jumping."

Four-wheeling. Arizona has thousands of miles of rugged roads leading across scenic wide-open country. You can drive your own, or some rental agencies offer four-wheel-drive vehicles. *Stay on existing roadways* to keep from destroying the fragile desert environment.

Skiing. In the high, snowy mountains of Arizona, both downhill and cross-country skiing are popular at a number of facilities ranging from beginner to expert. It's a great way to see a part of Arizona unknown to most. In Flagstaff, contact the Fairfield Snowbowl, 774–0562; in the White Mountains, contact Sunrise Ski Resort, (800) 772–7769; and in Tucson, contact Mount Lemmon Ski Valley, 576–1400.

HUNTING AND FISHING.

You can hunt duck, goose, grouse, quail, dove, deer, antelope, elk, javelina, mountain lion, rabbit, and even desert bighorn sheep and buffalo in Arizona, although some of the less populous species can be hunted only by residents.

Fish are plentiful in the mountain streams, a half-dozen major rivers, and hundreds of man-made lakes in the state. Trout, bass, pike, catfish, and crappie are the predominant species. Hunting and fishing licenses are required; contact the *Arizona Game and Fish Department,* 2222 W. Greenway Rd., Phoenix 85023; 942–3000.

ROCKHOUNDING.

Rock hounds will find an unbelievable variety of rock formations and minerals scattered across the deserts and mountains. And collectors gather at rock and gem shows year-round in Arizona to display, sell, and swap. The largest show, at Quartzsite in late January, attracts tens of thousands from all over the West. For more information, contact: *Arizona Department of Mineral Resources,* Mineral Building, State Fairgrounds, Phoenix 85007; 255–3791.

HINTS FOR THE DISABLED TRAVELER.

Arizona is making the great outdoors—and indoors—more accessible to the disabled.

The most comprehensive guide to the valley is *Access Valley of the Sun,* Arizona Easter Seal Society, 903 N. 2nd St., Phoenix 85004; (602) 252–6061. The information contained in the booklet includes Phoenix and the surrounding cities. For a guide to Tucson and the northern half of the state, the Easter Seal Society also publishes *Access Tucson & Green Valley* and *Access Northern Arizona* (SASE requested).

Another source of information is the *Visitors Bureau,* 505 N. 2nd St., Phoenix 85004; (602) 254–6500. The staff can supply the disabled visitor with a listing of hotels and motels throughout the state that are equipped with facilities for the handicapped. Also, the *Arizona Hotel and Motel Association,* 110 E. Missouri, Suite 720, Phoenix 85014; (602) 264–6081, publishes a free yearly *Arizona Accommodations Directory* that lists those member hotels and motels that cater in some way to the disabled.

Some areas of Arizona's outdoors that are now accessible to the handicapped include four "barrier-free" rest areas along Interstate 17.

In the Grand Canyon, some South Rim overlooks are wholly accessible or in part. All North Rim overlooks are wholly or partially accessible.

Canyon de Chelly National Monument provides audiovisual programs and interpretive talks at the visitor center.

If you enjoy touring with a group of people, the *Arizona Recreation Center for the Handicapped* schedules regular trips for handicapped persons. Contact them at 1550 W. Colter St., Phoenix 85029, (602) 230–2226, for more information.

For a more complete list of handicapped facilities at Arizona's state parks, write or call *Arizona State Parks,* 800 W. Washington, Suite 415, Phoenix 85007; (602) 542–4174.

If your travels cover more than Arizona, a handy U.S. guide for those restricted to wheelchairs is *The Wheelchair Traveler,* by Douglas R. Annand, Ball Hill Road, Milford, NH 03055. The guide lists accessible restaurants, hotels, motels, and attractions.

Many of the nation's national parks have special facilities. These are described in *National Park Guide for the Handicapped,* available from the U.S. Government Printing Office, Washington, DC 20402. A central source of free information is the *Travel Information Center,* Moss Rehabilitation Hospital, 12th St. and Tabor Rd., Philadelphia, PA 19141. Or pick up some good traveling tips from *Travel Tips for the Handicapped,* a free brochure from Consumer Information Center, Pueblo, CO 81009.

TWA publishes a free 12-page pamphlet entitled *Consumer Information About Air Travel for the Handicapped* to explain available special arrangements and how to get them. Also, Congress allows airlines to give reductions to disabled individuals. Your travel agent can explain whatever regulations pertain to this discount. If anyone requires a special diet, the agent will notify the airline.

Bus companies also assist the disabled. *Greyhound's Helping Hand* program and *Trailways' Good Samaritan* program allow the disabled person and the attendant to travel together for the price of one fare. A doctor's certificate is necessary to prove that the person absolutely could not travel without an attendant. Your local bus company has the details, or contact Greyhound Lines, Director of Customer Relations, Greyhound Tower, Phoenix 85077, and Continental Trailways, 1512 Commerce St., Dallas, TX 75261.

For the blind person, *Sheraton Inns and Hotels* and the *McDonald's* hamburger chain have menus printed in Braille.

HEALTH AND SAFETY HINTS. Arizona's deserts may seem a hostile place to visitors from cooler climates, but it just takes common sense and a little preparation to be very comfortable in the warmth and dryness the area is famous for.

The most common ailment of newcomers to Arizona is sunburn. Sure you want to go back home with beautifully bronzed skin, but take it easy. You can't do it all in one day. It is better to start with small amounts of sun—maybe 15 minutes the first day—then soak up the rays for increasingly longer periods of time each day. If you overdo and burn the first day, you'll feel miserable. You'll also be peeling within a week.

The time of day governs the strength of the sun's rays on your skin. The hours from 11 A.M. to 1 P.M. are when the sun is strongest. Also altitude affects how quickly you will burn. There is a lot less atmosphere to screen out the sun's rays at 7,000 feet near Flagstaff than at 1,000 feet in Phoenix, so you'll want to take that into consideration also.

If you must be in the sun for any length of time, wear protective clothing and a hat, or use a suntan product that contains a sun block. If you do get sunburned, there are several preparations available at drugstores that will ease the pain.

Another common ailment of visitors to Arizona's deserts in the summer is heatstroke, and it can be serious. It is not uncommon for the summertime high temperatures each day to exceed 110 degrees Fahrenheit. And if you are outside in that temperature, you had better take it easy. No one's body functions well at that temperature. (For some people, walking in that temperature can be overexertion.) If you do find yourself outside in the heat and you start to feel nauseous, you may be experiencing one of the early signs of heatstroke. Other symptoms include lightheadedness and fainting, flushed or pale skin, headache, fever with no sweating, and general weakness. The intense sunshine can turn cars into ovens within a few minutes, and every year several children and dozens of pets die because they were left trapped in unventilated vehicles. It is illegal to leave a child or pet in a motor vehicle unless the windows are fully down.

The best way to treat heatstroke is to get the victim cooled down fast. Get the person to a hospital or doctor. If that is not possible, get the victim out of the sun and heat and sponge her or him with water or alcohol to reduce body temperature.

Poisonous creatures. Arizona has a number of poisonous snakes, one poisonous lizard (the Gila monster), and several poisonous bugs. Some bites and stings can be fatal, others merely irritating. Although your chances of seeing a snake are slim, you may encounter one if you journey into the back country. Snakes are to be respected wherever you encounter them. Often the poisonous ones resemble the nonpoisonous, so be safe and stay clear of all of them. If you should meet a snake, stop and retreat slowly. The snake is strictly a defensive reptile, and if you back off, so will it. If you stumble onto one and are bitten, try to stay calm and restrict your movement as much as possible. Rattlesnakes envenomate 30 to 60 percent of the time, but there's no way to tell immediately after being bitten if you've been poisoned. If you have ice handy, apply it to the bitten area to slow the effects of the venom, and get to a hospital or doctor as quickly as possible.

Pollution. As the Phoenix metropolitan area expands, the air quality deteriorates. Phoenix has a few days between November and January when the smog is thick enough to pose a danger to persons with breathing difficulties or lung disease.

Protection from vacation crooks. Urban areas everywhere are haunts for petty crooks. Arizona's major cities are no exception. Here are a few tips to prevent ripoffs from ruining your travels.

Keep a close eye on luggage, especially in and around airports, hotel lobbies, and parking areas. Check with your hotel manager for safe and unsafe areas of the city, and stay in well-lighted areas. Always check the back seat before getting into your car to be sure no one is hiding there. Carry as little cash as possible. Prepay as many expenses as you can. Carry only one or two credit cards. Use safe deposit boxes at the hotel for valuables. Buy traveler's checks; they're as good as cash, and safer. Destroy carbons of charge card forms. To reduce chances of having your pocket picked, wrap a thick rubber band around your wallet, it will keep it from slipping out easily.

PHOENIX

Phoenix, Arizona's capital, is the nation's ninth largest city, with a population of approximately 950,000. It also ranks among the largest in land areas, with 393 square miles of territory.

Incorporated in 1881, Phoenix began as a farming community whose biggest crop was hay for the cavalry horses at Fort McDowell, some forty miles to the northeast. Its name comes from the mythological phoenix bird, which was destroyed by fire, then rose from its own ashes. The name was given to it by Darrell Duppa, an English remittance man who had been a world traveler and was knowledgeable in the classics as well as a connoisseur of good whisky.

Phoenix did in effect rise from the ashes of another civilization—that of the Hohokam Indians, who disappeared in the fifteenth century. The Hohokams, whose name means "the people who have gone," had large settlements here. Archeological digs have established that theirs was an advanced civilization with a system of irrigation canals to water crops with diversions from the Salt River.

A former lieutenant in the Confederate Army, Jack Swilling, formed an irrigation company in 1867 and used some of the Hohokams' canals in his system. This launched Phoenix and the Salt River Valley on its way to becoming an agricultural empire.

When Theodore Roosevelt Dam was built in the mountains northeast of Phoenix, the expansion of agriculture received another giant boost. The dam made it possible to store water from the summer and winter rains and thus stabilize the year-round supply. Roosevelt and other dams, added later, also supply some of the domestic water for Phoenix and other valley cities.

As Phoenix continued to grow because of its salubrious climate (it was recommended for people with lung problems) and its agriculture, it also became a trade center and a distribution point. By 1889, its population had grown so much that it had enough legislative clout to be made the capital. Previously the capital had been Prescott, then Tucson, then Prescott again.

As the seat of state government, Phoenix attracted more population and more and more of the amenities of civilization. Even though it started as a rowdy town and a national crossroad, it matured into a modern city and began to be known as a fine place to spend the winter.

However, in summertime in pre-air-conditioned days, everyone who could fled either to the mountains or the "seaside," as the Pacific Coast was known. The family breadwinners who had to brave Phoenix's scorching summers worked in the early morning hours, kept in the shade as much as they could, and slept outside at night. Screen porches were a necessity.

Nowadays, of course, Phoenix is cooled mostly by refrigeration, although new systems using a "swamper" supplement are coming into use because of higher energy costs. A common boast in Phoenix in summer is, "I go from my air-conditioned house (or apartment) in my air-conditioned car to my air-conditioned office."

Because of its warm climate—summer lasts from early May into October—dress is mostly informal. In recent years, with the arrival of more Eastern people and Eastern-based companies, people do dress up more. Even so, they tend to wear as little as the law will allow in the hot months during their leisure time.

World War II brought explosive growth to Phoenix and changed its image as an agriculture and tourist center. (Tourism ranks second—after manufacturing—in the economy.) And Camelback Road, which was known as a resort area, rapidly is being transformed into a street of business and office complexes. Such famous hostelries as the Biltmore and Camelback Inn are being boxed in on every side by residential developments of virtually every density.

Phoenix has become national headquarters for a variety of businesses. Many high-tech firms have moved in, especially in the Southeast Valley area.

Phoenix is a modern, airy, attractive city where the bulk of growth has been outward rather than upward. However, high-rise apartments and office buildings now are part of the city whose skyline previously was a network of surrounding mountains with landmarks like Squaw Peak and Camelback Mountain.

Camelback Mountain

Camelback Mountain is a spectacular, inimitable landmark. You can see Camelback from almost any point in the city, and almost everyone looking at it for the first time remarks about how much it really does look like a reclining camel.

Up close on Camelback Road, you find that it is indeed a sizable "rock." For the record, its peak is 1,800 feet high. You reach Camelback Road by going north from downtown on almost any main north-south street.

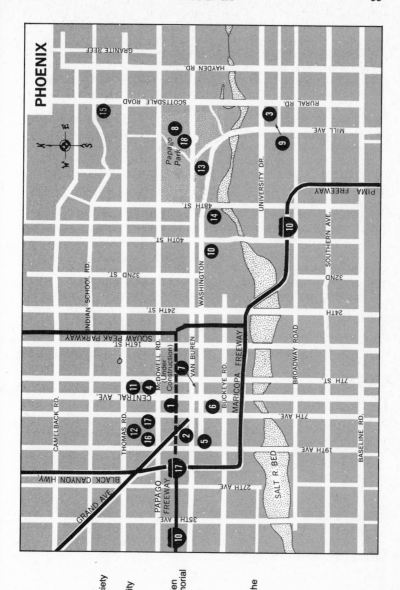

Points of Interest

1) Arizona Historical Society Museum
2) Arizona Museum
3) Arizona State University
4) Art Museum
5) Capitol Building
6) City-County Complex
7) Civic Plaza
8) Desert Botanical Garden
9) Grady Gammage Memorial Auditorium
10) Greyhound Park (Dog Racing)
11) Heard Museum
12) Mineral Museum
13) Municipal Stadium
14) Pueblo Grande
15) Scottsdale Center for the Arts
16) State Fairgrounds
17) Veteran's Memorial Coliseum
18) Phoenix Zoo

A City of Parks

The city's green appearance contrasts sharply with the arid brownness of desert land around the valley. Nowhere is this more vivid than in the recently renovated Encanto Park, a midtown section of winding, palm-shaded lagoons, golf courses, tennis courts, pool, gardens, band shell, picnicking, and recreation from boating to shuffleboard.

A few blocks west, the Arizona State Fairgrounds is the site of the huge Arizona Veterans Memorial Coliseum. Built in 1965, it hosts year-round attractions in addition to the annual county and state fairs each autumn.

South Mountain Park, whose nearly 15,000 acres make it the nation's most extensive city-owned park, is a great place for hiking and rock-scrambling. You'll also find desert-mountain picnic sites and an unparalleled view of the valley.

On the east side of Phoenix, Papago Park, marked by eroded red sandstone hills, is a tourist lodestone. Hiking and riding trails thread through desert terrain that overlooks the city. An 18-hole municipal golf course challenges the average golfer. The Phoenix Zoo features both native and foreign birds, reptiles, and animals in a 125-acre park. And the Desert Botanical Garden, covering more than 150 acres, offers hundreds of species, easily admired along paved paths, of desert flora from all over the world. Pottery shards from former Hohokam homesites can still be found in the park.

Squaw Peak desert mountain park lies in the northeast part of the valley. The somewhat strenuous hike to the top attracts hundreds of people on weekends.

A Sports Town

Since it is an outdoor-oriented climate, Phoenix is extremely sports-minded. With the relocation of the NFL Cardinals to Phoenix from St. Louis for the 1988 season, the Valley of the Sun truly moved into the sports big leagues. In addition, the Phoenix Suns are crowd-getters on the NBA circuit, and the Phoenix Firebirds play in the Triple A Baseball League. The Cardinals take the field at Arizona State University's Sun Devil Stadium in Tempe during the fall. The Suns' home base is the Veterans Memorial Coliseum, from October through March; and the Giants play at Phoenix Municipal Stadium from May through August.

Baseball fans can take in spring training games at moderate prices from February through April, featuring the following teams at these locations: Chicago Cubs, Hohokam Stadium, Mesa; Oakland Athletics, Phoenix Municipal Stadium; San Francisco Giants, Scottsdale Stadium, Scottsdale; Milwaukee Brewers, Compadre Stadium, Chandler; and the Seattle Mariners at Tempe Diablo Stadium, Tempe.

For auto racing fans, there is Phoenix International Raceway at 115th Avenue and West Southern; Manzanita Speedway, 35th Avenue and Broadway; and Firebird International Raceway, 20000 N. Maricopa Road. Take I-10 south to the Maricopa Road exit. Beginning June 1990, Phoenix plays host to a Grand Prix auto race.

Horseracing is offered on varying schedules each week at Turf Paradise, 19th Avenue and Bell Road, October through May. Take 19th Avenue north to Bell Road, or turn east on Bell from I-17. The dogs run at Phoenix Greyhound Park, 3801 E. Washington, year-round, and at Apache Greyhound Park, 2551 W. Apache Trail, Apache Junction, from October to May.

Golfers have a virtual smorgasbord—more than 70 courses to choose from—in the Phoenix area. In addition, there are 4 large municipal courses. Almost every resort of any size has at least a putting green.

Tennis, too, is a favorite in Phoenix and the Salt River Valley. Courts can be found at almost any resort, park, and recreational facility. There are 140 parks in the Phoenix parks system. Racquetball, too, is popular, and many of these courts are located outdoors.

Joggers will find that Phoenicians do a lot of their running along city streets, as they do elsewhere, although there are many jogging tracks at city parks. One favorite place for running is along the canal banks. Each November, there is a 10 kilometer run down Central Avenue, the east-west dividing line in Phoenix's street numbering system.

Boating, waterskiing, and sailing are available at six major lakes, all within a sixty-mile radius of Phoenix.

Another water sport that attracts many Phoenicians is tubing. In spring and summer, you can rent inner tubes and go for a leisurely float on the Salt River north of Mesa. Shuttle buses are available.

Hiking is big in Phoenix, too, and many mountain parks around Phoenix have trails.

Civic Plaza

Phoenix Civic Plaza is host to a variety of activities, including conventions and exhibits of almost every description. At the nearby Symphony Hall, the Phoenix Symphony Orchestra presents concerts featuring many world-renowned artists such as Itzhak Perlman, Henry Mancini, Doc Severinsen, and Joel Grey.

Just east of the Civic Plaza is the Rosson House, a carefully restored turn-of-the-century mansion, where tours are available.

The State Capitol

Another interesting old-timey tour is the state capitol at 17th Avenue and Washington. Although a new capitol and other office buildings have been built around it, the old capitol, dedicated in 1901, still stands, lovingly restored to almost original condition.

Constructed of tufa stone, a native material, the old capitol has a rotunda four stories high with a copper dome. Inside the rotunda, each floor is open in the middle and has a railing around the opening. For decades, lobbyists operated "off the rail" as they tried to importune legislators to favor their causes.

A special staff conducts several tours daily. The tour provides a good look at the history of Arizona lawmaking over nearly a hundred years.

On the third floor of the old capitol is the State Department of Library and Archives, which includes an Arizona section with old manuscripts, maps, and pictures going back to territorial days; a section devoted to genealogy, with records of land titles from many states; and sections on American history, geography, political science, and geology.

In front of the capitol is a statue of Frank Luke, Jr., famous "balloon buster" of World War I, and other monuments to Arizona war heroes.

Across the street east from the capitol is Wesley Bolin Plaza, where the anchor from the U.S.S. *Arizona* has been emplaced. The *Arizona* was sunk at Pearl Harbor with 1,104 crewmen aboard.

Seeing More of Phoenix

Phoenix is finally emerging. As the nation's ninth largest city, it is a twinkling, sophisticated metropolitan area, while underneath, it is committed to the casual life-style of the Old West. A young city, Phoenix offers cultural opportunities—museums, performing arts—that rival America's older cities.

Besides being a metropolitan city with all the amenities. Phoenix is also a major jumping off point to recreation adventures that are usually just a short distance away in beautiful desert/mountain country, where the outback is just a step off the paved highway.

There's more. The city has the cleanest thoroughfares, the prettiest lawns and gardens—not to mention incredible numbers of backyard swimming pools and beautiful homes tucked into pleasant byways. To see more of the beauty of the town, try an auto tour north on Central Avenue to Lincoln Drive, then east on Lincoln Drive through the foothills of the Phoenix Mountains to Scottsdale Road. From there, turn south to Camelback Road and then west on this major east-west boulevard back into the heart of Phoenix.

A word about Phoenix's people. You'll find them friendly, chatty, and happy to meet you. It's the relaxed climate that does it—plus a touch of genuine Southwestern hospitality.

PRACTICAL INFORMATION FOR PHOENIX

HOW TO GET THERE. By air. Phoenix Sky Harbor International Airport is one of the busiest in the nation and is served by most of the nation's and the world's major airlines. Because of the usually clear weather in Phoenix, Sky Harbor often is where air traffic is diverted when West Coast landing fields are locked in.

All the major domestic carriers serve Phoenix. *PSA, Skywest,* and *Southwest* provide regional service.

By train. *Amtrak* serves Phoenix. Call Amtrak toll-free at (800) 872-7245.

By bus. *Greyhound-Trailways* buses serve Phoenix. Contact your local Greyhound-Trailways office for information and reservations. Special tours of Arizona are offered in addition to travel discounts and special children's fares, so check for specific information. Check also with your travel agent for special motor coach tours to Phoenix; many include points in northern Arizona like the Grand Canyon, Lake Powell, and the Painted Desert. Greyhound-Trailways Charter and Tour Service can be reached at 246-4341.

The area between Phoenix and Show Low via Payson is served by the *White Mountain Passenger Line,* 275-4245. From Las Vegas via Lake

Havasu, use *Sun Valley Gray Line,* 254–4888. From the southwest corner
and Yuma, *Arizona Bus Lines* comes in from Ajo and Gila Bend; call
254–5451. From Yuma itself, ride *Greyhound-Trailways.* If Mexico is your
starting point, *Citizen Auto Stages* connects Nogales with Tucson,
287–5628. *Greyhound-Trailways* has a Phoenix-Tucson-Douglas route;
also Phoenix to Nogales.

By car. Phoenix is served by a fine highway system—state, U.S., and
interstate—that permits both easy access and exit. Main east-west routes
are U.S. 60 and I-10; north-south ones are I-17 and 10, and U.S. 89. Other
routes include State Routes 85, 87, and 93.

IMPORTANT TELEPHONE NUMBERS. Although no one wants to
think about it, there are times during a trip when a doctor or a visit to
the hospital may be necessary. The following list will provide a Phoenix
visitor with vital numbers, as well as phone numbers for bus services, highway conditions, parks and recreations, libraries, and senior citizens and
youth programs. *Note:* Some phone numbers are subject to change. For
any emergency in metropolitan Phoenix, dial 911.

Airport Paging for Passengers, Sky Harbor International Airport,
273–3455.

Ambulance Services: Southwest Ambulance Service, 267–8991; Metro-
Care Ambulance Service, 242–3263; Professional Medical Transport,
263–8563.

Air Ambulance Services: AirEvac, 247–3822.

Bus Service: Schedule Information, 253–5000; Sunday Dial-a-Ride,
243–7755.

Civic Plaza, 262–6225; Box Office, 262–7272.

Community Information and Referral, 263–8856 (24 hours a day).

Crisis Intervention (24 hour), 258–8011.

Fires, to report fires, 911.

First Aid Emergencies ("Lifeline"), 911.

Highway conditions around the state, recorded message, 256–7706.

Department of Public Safety, 223–2000.

Hospitals: St. Joseph's Hospital and Medical Center, 350 W. Thomas
Rd., 285–3000; Good Samaritan Medical Center, 1111 E. McDowell Rd.,
239–2000; Phoenix General Hospital, 1950 W. Indian School Rd.,
279–4411; Phoenix Children's Hospital, 1111 E. McDowell, 239–2400;
Humana Hospital Phoenix, 1947 E. Thomas Rd., 241–7600; John C. Lincoln Hospital and Health Center, 9211 N. 2nd St., 943–2381; St. Luke's
Medical Center, 1800 E. Van Buren, 251–5183; Scottsdale Memorial Hospital, 7400 E. Osborn Rd., 994–9616; Arizona Heart Institute, 2111 E.
Highland Ave., 955–0868.

Information (City Switchboard), 262–6011.

Libraries, general information, 262–6451.

Parks and Recreation: Arts and Crafts, 261–8774; Cultural Activities,
262–4627; Desert Mountain Parks, 276–2221; Golf Classes and Clinics,
262–6542; Performing Arts Building, 262–4627; Recreation Program Information, 262–6412; Sports activities, men, 262–6483, women, 262–6483.

Phoenix & Valley of the Sun Convention and Visitors Bureau; 254–6500.

Police: Crime Stop (Emergency Calls, 24-hour service) 262–6151; Silent
Witness (24-hour service) 261–8600.

Scottsdale Center for the Arts: 994–2787.

Senior Citizens Programs: 262–7379; Reserve-A-Ride, 262–4501; Golden Senior Discount Card, 262–7379; Los Olivos Adult Center, 256–3130; South Phoenix Adult Center, 262–4874; Washington Adult Center, 262–6971.

HOTELS AND MOTELS. Phoenix is a sprawling city, so location should be a primary consideration in your choice of where to stay. Most of the shopping and gallery viewing is in the east side of town and Scottsdale. The Convention Center and government offices are in the center of town, or downtown, and the west side and Sun City are the focal points of the retirement community. In Phoenix, hotels and motels usually come equipped with swimming pools, sun patios, cabanas, and poolside service. Principal types of lodging: resorts; small inns or guest lodges; resort hotels; guest (dude) ranches; motor hotels or motels; trailer parks. Costs are for in season rates and double-occupancy rooms, with reductions of 25 to 50 percent out of season. Some resorts and dude ranches operate on the American plan (meals included with price of room), though there is a trend away from strict AP rates lately. Listings are in order of price categories. A lodging tax, which varies, is added to all accommodation bills.

The price categories in this section, for double occupancy, will average as follows: *Deluxe,* $150 and up; *Expensive,* $90–$150; *Moderate,* $60–$90; *Inexpensive,* under $60. For a more complete description of those categories, see *Facts at Your Fingertips.*

Deluxe

Arizona Biltmore Hotel. 24th St. and Missouri, 85002; 955–6600 or (800) 528–3696. The grand dame of Arizona resorts, designed by architect Frank Lloyd Wright. Thirty-nine landscaped acres; five restaurants; pools; golf; tennis. Close to hiking, riding, shopping, and Scottsdale. Handicapped facilities.

Hotel Westcourt. 10220 N. Metro Parkway E., 85021; 997–5900. A luxury conference center surrounded by shopping and entertainment. A good place to stay if you plan to concentrate on north Phoenix or Sun City. Handicapped facilities.

The Pointe at Squaw Peak. 7677 N. 16th St., 85020; 997–2626. Rambling, Spanish-mediterranean-style architecture. Built on a cliffside. All rooms are suites or villas. Complimentary breakfast and cocktails. Two other valley locations. Tennis, golfing. Handicapped facilities.

The Pointe at Tapatio Cliffs. 11111 N. 7th St., 85020; 866–7500. Out-of-the-way desert resort. Complimentary breakfast buffet, cocktails daily. All rooms mountainside suites. Golf privileges.

Ritz-Carlton Hotel. 2401 E. Camelback Rd., 85016; 468–0700. Elegant corporate hotel with unparalleled service. Basic rooms are small, but all have views. Close to shopping, Scottsdale, and business district. Two restaurants; afternoon tea; tennis; pool; exercise room. Handicapped facilities.

Royal Palms Inn. 5200 E. Camelback Rd., 85018; 840–3610. Thirty-two acres on the south slopes of Camelback Mountain. Golf; tennis; handicapped facilities.

Sheraton Phoenix. Box 1000, 85001; 257–1525. N. Central and Adams. Mobil 4-Star Award, 4-Diamond Award. Downtown, within walking distance of government buildings and Civic Plaza. Rooftop pool; exercise room.

Expensive

Doubletree Suites, Phoenix. 320 N. 44th St., 85008; 225–0500. All suites. Complimentary breakfast and cocktails included. Four minutes to airport. Handicapped facilities.

Embassy Suites Biltmore. 2630 E. Camelback Rd., 85016; 955–3992. All suites, complimentary breakfast and cocktails included. Adjacent to Biltmore Fashion Park.

Executive Park Hotel. 1100 N. Central Ave., 85004; 252–2100. Lovely, spacious rooms. Restaurant. Shuttle service.

Holiday Inn & Holidome Phoenix Corporate Center. 2532 W. Peoria Ave., 85029; 943–2341 or (800) 843–3663. In northwest Phoenix. Indoor/outdoor heated pools, complete indoor recreation and exercise center.

Hyatt Regency Hotel. 122 N. 2nd St., 85004; 252–1234 or 800–228–9000. Mobil 4-Star Award, AAA 4-Diamond Award. Tastefully appointed rooms. Revolving rooftop restaurant. Exercise facilities; pool.

Inn Suites. 3101 N. 32nd St. 85018; 956–4900. All suites. Complimentary breakfast. Free airport transfer.

Les Jardins. 3738 N. 4th Ave., 85013; 234–2464. An elegant garden hotel with exercise room, spa, and kitchenettes. Convenient to museums.

La Mancha Resort Hotel. 100 W. Clarendon Ave., 85013; 279–9811 or 800–422–6400. Centrally located hotel-cum-athletic club. Health spa; racquetball and basketball courts. Near museums.

Moderate

Airway Inn. 124 S. 24th St., 85034; 244–8221 or 800–5AIRWAY. Near airport, five minutes from downtown Phoenix. Free airport transportation. Café; bar; pool; and other facilities.

Crescent Hotel. 2620 W. Dunlap Ave., 85021; 943–8200 or 800–423–4126. In northwest Phoenix. Large rooms. Restaurant; tennis.

Days Inn, Camelback. 502 W. Camelback Rd., 85013; 264–9290. Centrally located. Meeting and banquet facilities. Lounge with live entertainment.

Days Inn, San Carlos. 202 N. Central Ave., 85004; 253–4121 or 800–528–5446. Historic building in downtown Phoenix. Within walking distance of Civic Center. Restaurant; free breakfast; pool.

Fountains Suite Hotel. 2577 W. Greenway Rd., 85023; 375–1777 or 800–527–7715. Restaurant. Tennis; racquetball; handball; health spa; putting green.

Heritage Hotel. 401 N. 1st St., 85004; 258–3411. Specialty suites.

Holiday Inn-Phoenix Airport. 2201 S. 24th St., 85034; 267–0611. Heated pool; laundry room; airport transportation.

Kings Inn at Turf Paradise. 1711 W. Bell Rd., 85023; 866–2089. Next to Turf Paradise horse racing. Close to shopping; handicapped facilities.

Park Central Motor Hotel. 3033 N. 7th Ave., 85013; 277–2621 or 800–528–0368. Kitchenettes. Apartment-size suites. Close to shopping, golf, and tennis; handicapped facilities.

Phoenix Best Western Inn Suites and Resort. 1615 E. Northern, 85020; 997–6285 or 800–842–4242. Free continental breakfast; unlimited cocktails; in-room refrigerator.

La Quinta Motor Inn. 2725 N. Black Canyon Hwy., 85009; 258–6271. Nonsmoker rooms; senior citizen discounts; complimentary morning coffee; handicapped facilities.

Rodeway Inn-Grand Avenue. 3400 Grand Ave., 85017; 264–9164 or 800–228–2000. Children under 18 free with adult; weekend rates; free satellite color movies.

TraveLodge at Terminal One. 2901 Sky Harbor Blvd., 85034; 275–3634. Part of national chain. Twenty-four-hour limousine service; gift shop; restaurant; tennis.

Inexpensive

Airporter Inn of Phoenix. 2501 E. Van Buren St., 85008; 275–6211 or 800–854–3380. Entirely renovated. Spa; kitchenettes available; laundry facilities; children under 12 free.

American 6 Motel. 4021 N. 27th Ave., 85017; 277–6661. In west Phoenix. Clean rooms; heated pool, pets; laundry.

Arizona Ranch House Inn. 5600 N. Central Ave., 85021; 279–3221. Kitchenettes; complimentary continental breakfast; Jacuzzi; pets.

Comfort Inn Airport. 4120 E. Van Buren, 85008; 275–5746 or 800–228–5150. Spanish-style eastside hotel, convenient to Tempe and Scottsdale. Nice rooms; pets allowed; coffee shop; pool.

Days Inn. 2735 W. Sweetwater Ave., 85029; 993–7200. Located just off I-17. Clean rooms; pool; restaurant.

Desert Rose Motor Hotel. 3424 E. Van Buren, 85008; 275–4421. Ten minutes by car from Tempe and Scottsdale. Clean rooms; pool; coffee shop.

International Villa Motor Inn. 4526 N. Black Canyon Hwy., 85017; 242–7088. Studios, one-and two-bedroom apartments; kitchens; coin laundry; pool.

Phoenix Airport Travelodge. 2900 E. Van Buren, 85008; 275–7651. Plain, but clean rooms. Pool; coffee shop nearby.

Phoenix Sunrise Motel. 3644 E. Van Buren., 85008; 275–7661. Small pets allowed; heated pool; HBO.

Quality Inn-Airport. 1820 S. 7th St., 85034; 254–9787 or 800–228–5050. Close to a convention center; free airport shuttle; tennis.

Quality Inn Desert Sky. 3541 E. Van Buren, 85008, 273–7121 or 800–228–5151. Ten-minute drive to Tempe and Scottsdale. Free HBO; heated pool; cocktail lounge; pets; direct-dial phones.

Quality Inn West. 2420 W. Thomas Rd., 85015; 257–0801. Spa; shuffleboard; horseshoes; in-house movies; golf; and tennis. Kitchenettes and studio rooms available.

Sandman Motel. 2120 W. Van Buren, 85008; 258–8357. Pool; guest laundry; free transportation to airport.

Spanish Oaks. 4221 E. McDowell Rd., 85008; 267–7917. Convenient to east valley. Fully equipped kitchens; pool; spa; tennis court; cable TV.

Super 6. 938 E. Van Buren St., 85006; 258–5540. Kitchenettes available. Small pets allowed; near Phoenix Convention Center; airport pickup.

TraveLodge Civic Plaza. 965 E. Van Buren, 85006; 252–6823. Good central location. Pool; restaurant.

HOW TO GET AROUND. By taxi. Taxis in Phoenix are not regulated, and mileage fees and waiting charges vary *greatly*. Don't feel shy about establishing the fare before you go. Taxis do not cruise the streets, so you must call for one. It's wise to check the hotel and resort limousines for complimentary service. *Air Courier,* 244–1818; *Supershuttle* to and from airport, 244–9000; *Yellow Cab,* 252–5071.

By bus. Phoenix is an automobile city; public transportation can be inefficient. *Phoenix Transit* is working to upgrade bus service; however, buses run from 6 A.M. to 7:30 P.M. (with major lines running until 9:15). Mondays through Fridays, 6:30 A.M. to 7:30 P.M. on Saturdays. There is no bus service on Sundays. Express routes bring commuters from outlying areas into town. Call 253–5000 for route information. Exact fares are required; as of this writing, adult fares are 75¢, and 35¢ for elderly, handicapped, and children under 12. Children under six ride free. Phoenix Transit bus No. 2 runs from the airport to downtown every 30 minutes from 6 A.M. to 6:40 P.M. (from the last terminal).

Grayline offers bus tours of Greater Phoenix, a great way to orient yourself to the area. Grayline of Phoenix, Inc., Box 2471, Phoenix 85002, 254–4550, toll-free outside Arizona, (800) 241–3521. *Destination West,* 7434 E. Stetson, Scottsdale 85251, 947–7211, specializes in airport transfers and local tours.

By car. You can't beat having your own car to see this large metropolis packed full of intriguing things to see and do. Rental agencies include *Hertz,* (800) 654–3131; *Avis,* (800) 331–1212; *Enterprise,* 225–0588; *General,* 273–0991; *Payless,* 275–5701; and myriad more listed in the *Phoenix Visitor's Guide.* Several companies have offices at or near Sky Harbor Airport.

Phoenix streets are laid out in an uncomplicated grid system, the center of which is Central Avenue (north-south) and Washington (east-west). From there, all roads running north and south are either numbered streets and places (east of Central) or avenues and drives (west of Central), commencing with 1st Street all the way out to 70th Street. Major east-west arteries are situated at one-mile intervals; for example, Camelback Road is five miles from the heart of the city and is in the 5000 block of North Central Avenue. The only complication in the grid is going around mountains and crossing waterways, but streets resume their logical pattern on the other side.

If you are a staunch believer in driving yourself, a word to the wise: Because of Phoenix's phenomenal growth in the past ten years, traffic can sometimes become congested, especially during the morning and afternoon rush hours. To somewhat alleviate the problem, a parkway and expressway additions are being constructed at various points throughout the city.

Parking meters downtown are free weekdays after 5 P.M. and on Saturdays and Sundays, but street parking spaces can be difficult to find during the week. You're usually better off with one of the office buildings' parking garages.

Speed limit is 25 mph unless otherwise posted.

TOURIST INFORMATION. For information on the Greater Phoenix metropolitan area, contact the *Phoenix & Valley of the Sun Convention and Visitors Bureau,* 505 N. 2nd St., Suite 300, Phoenix 85004; 254–6500. In addition, *visitor information centers* are located in terminals 2 and 3 at Phoenix Sky Harbor International Airport and on the northwest corner of Adams and Second streets in downtown Phoenix.

The Arizona Office of Tourism's main office is in Phoenix at 1480 E. Bethany Home Rd., Phoenix 85014; 255–3618. Either they or the Convention and Visitors bureau will have information on any community attraction or event in the Valley of the Sun.

Note: See also "Useful Telephone Numbers," above.

RECOMMENDED READING. Like to know a little more about Phoenix and Arizona before you visit? Or has the visit been so memorable you'd like something to read to remind you of your stay? Try these:

A Guide to the Architecture of Metro Phoenix. James W. Elmore. Central Arizona Chapter of the American Institute of Architects, Phoenix Publishing, Inc., 1983, 201 pp. Significant architecture in the Metro Phoenix area is documented in this guide. This is a picture book, organized to facilitate tours of many of the award-winning, historical, or unique buildings in the area. Included are works by Frank Lloyd Wright and Paolo Soleri.

Phoenix: Valley of the Sun. G. Wesley Johnson, Jr. Continental Heritage Press, Tulsa, Okla., 1982, 240 pp. Johnson traces the development of Phoenix from prehistory to the present-day metropolis in this informative book. There are many historic and contemporary photographs, capturing forever the life and times of Phoenicians.

Phoenix: 1870–1970, in Photographs. Herb and Dorothy McLaughlin. Arizona Photographic Associates, Phoenix, 1970, 208 pp. This photographic documentary depicts the first century of Phoenix's history. Included are essays about early settlement in the valley, Spanish contact, the impact of World War I.

I, Jack Swilling: Founder of Phoenix, Arizona. John Myers. Hastings House Publishers, New York, 1961, 308 pp. This first-person narrative reconstructs the adventures of Jack Swilling, the man responsible for rebuilding Phoenix's prehistoric irrigation canal system, bringing agriculture once more to the valley.

Hashknife Cowboy Recollections of Mack Hughes. Stella Hughes. University of Arizona Press. It's an intriguing look at growing up on the northern Arizona range. The book is an authentic look at cowboying as it really was. *Hashknife Cowboy* is illustrated with 29 original drawings by cowboy artist Joe Beeler.

Arizona Memories. Edited by Anne Hodges Morgan and Rennard Strickland. University of Arizona Press. In this anthology of memoirs and recollections, Arizona's history from the mid-19th to mid-20th century is captured in the words of the people who lived it. The 28 selections have been chosen to convey the breadth of Arizona's cultural heritage.

SEASONAL EVENTS. Many of Arizona's sun-filled days come complete with some type of activity. Listed here are the monthly highlights, with phone numbers to call for dates and times. **January.** *Arizona National Boat Show,* held at the Phoenix Civic Plaza, 277–4748. *The Arizona Livestock Show,* held at the State Fairground, 19th Ave. and McDowell, 258–8568. *The Phoenix Open Golf Tournament,* held at the Tournament Players Club of Scottsdale, 263–0757, is the PGA at its best, with a $200,000 purse. *The Phoenix City Marathon,* 244–0121.

February. *Annual Metropolitan Travel Show,* 271–8411. *Aid to Zoo National Horse Show,* 264–5691.

March. *Heard Museum Indian Fair,* 252–8848. *Phoenix Jaycee Rodeo of Rodeo's Parade and Rodeo,* 264–4808. *Maricopa County Fair,* 252–0717. *Major League Baseball Spring Cactus League Training,* 829–5555. *Hello Phoenix Festival,* 262–7272. *Samaritan Turquoise Golf Classic,* 495–GOLF.

April. *Desert Botanical Garden Cactus Festival,* 941–1225. *Desert Wildflower Viewing,* wildflower hotline 941–1239. *Checker 200 Indy Car Race,* 252–3833. *All Indian Days Annual Pow-Wow,* 244–8244. *Scottsdale Culinary Festival,* 994–2301.

May. *Cinco De Mayo Fiesta.* Traditional Mexican celebration of Mexico's 1863 victory over France, 254–6500.

October. *Greek Festival* at the Greek Orthodox Church, 1973 E. Maryland. The festival grows yearly with exhibits, Greek food, dancing, and music, 264–7863. *Annual Western States Karate Championships,* 262–7272. *Arizona State Fair,* State Fair Grounds, is overflowing with entertainment, rides, game booths, exhibits, livestock, art shows, 4-H exhibits, and much more, 252–6771. *Cowboy Artists of America Sale and Exhibition,* 257–1880. This internationally known sale and exhibition began with a nucleus of four artists in Sedona in 1965. The first CAA exhibition of a dozen charter artists sold a total of $49,000 in works. Today, with 25 active members, their works go for six-figure prices.

November. *Phoenix 10 Kilometer Run,* 241–0995. *Annual Gem and Mineral Showcase,* Arizona State Fairgrounds, 255–3791. *The Heard Museum Native American Art Show,* 252–8848. *Annual Holsum Olympic "Bun Run,"* 10,000 meters, 252–2351. *Christmas Tree Lighting Ceremony,* at the Phoenix Art Museum, 257–1222.

December. *Luminaria Night,* Desert Botanical Gardens. The walks through the garden are lined with luminarias, small paper sacks partially filled with sand. A small candle is placed in the center and lighted. Music, food, and festivities, 941–1225. *Annual Clay Show and Sale,* Heard Museum, 252–8848. *Annual Indian Market,* Pueblo Grande Museum, 275–3452. The market offers a wide selection of handmade dolls, jewelry, clothing, and much more. *Fiesta Bowl events,* golf tournaments, parade, parties, exhibits, 952–1280.

TOURS. While Arizona's outdoors have so much to offer, so do the indoors. Capture man's best works with a **State Capitol Walking Tour.** In the vicinity of the State Capitol, you'll find many interesting sights to fill your day. For information on the tour, contact the Arizona State Capital Museum, 1700 W. Washington, Phoenix 85007; 255–4675.

The tour encompasses the Confederate Monument, erected by the Daughters of the Confederacy to honor Arizona's confederate dead. Frank Luke Memorial, erected in honor of Arizona's World War I Ace; Capitol Museum, located on the four floors of the Capitol, along with the Arizona Library and Archives; David Swing Murals, found at various locations throughout the Capitol, depict some of Arizona's outstanding scenic and historical attractions; Lon Megaree Paintings, displayed in the Capitol and senate, created to decorate the Arizona exhibit at the 1915 Panama–Pacific International Exposition in San Francisco; Jay Datus Murals, featured in Department of Library and Archives, painted in 1939 to depict

"The History of Arizona Progress"; U.S.S. *Arizona* Anchor, east of the state capitol, a monument to the 1,100 men entombed aboard the vessel at Pearl Harbor.

Grayline offers bus tours of Greater Phoenix, a great way to orient yourself to the area. Grayline of Phoenix, Inc., Box 2471, Phoenix 85002, 254–4550, toll-free outside Arizona, (800)241–3521.

Rainbow Tours, 8518 N. 82nd St., Scottsdale 85260, 998–7669, offers personalized van tours of the metro area and outlying points.

PARKS. The fog hangs low, hugging slabs of granite and sandstone alike. In the distance, you hear the sweet trill of a mourning dove. And look at those unusual tracks in the sand, as though someone had gone mad with a cookie cutter. Beautiful wilderness? No. It's one of Phoenix's many city, county, or state parks. There are five mountain preserves that encircle Phoenix, strung together with the **Sun Circle Trail,** or Arizona Trail Number One, a 110-mile loop for hiking, camping, and horseback riding. The trail was officially mapped and opened in 1964. Parts of the trail are still being marked as money becomes available.

Although the mountains are not far from the city, remember it is desert. And the preserve trails are rugged and remote. Be sure to wear sturdy shoes and a hat. Also take enough water—a gallon a day per person, minimum—and take a friend. And whenever planning a desert activity, let someone know your destination and when you plan to return. Following are some of the parks you can visit along this trail.

The trail begins at *Granite Reef Dam.* Follow it south through the city of Mesa along canal banks to the town of Gilbert.

And 12 miles due west, following the banks of the Western Canal, is **South Mountain Park.** The trail meanders along the crest of the mountain for 12 miles, then teams up with the Gila River on the other side of the park. It is the world's largest municipally owned park, with 16,000 acres of hikable desert.

As all around Arizona, remnants of past Indian civilizations can be found in the parks. These remnants can be petroglyphs (pictures pecked into rocks using a stone implement) or an occasional tiny speck of pottery. But please, these treasures are for all to enjoy. Stiff penalties have been adopted for vandalizing or removing artifacts.

The park also offers picnic sites and special areas for dancing and skating. And if you don't have your own horse in tow, there is the *South Mountain Stables* at 10005 S. Central Ave., 276–8131.

Getting back on track, Sun Circle Trail skirts the boundary of the *Gila River Indian Reservation* to the edge of **Estrella Mountain County Regional Park.** The trail does not enter Estrella, but there are many smaller trails winding through the park that are wholly accessible.

From there, the Circle Trail continues to where the Salt and Agua Fria rivers meet. Nineteen miles north of the confluence, you come to the *Arizona Canal.* Just above where the trails hangs east along *Skunk Creek,* Olive Avenue introduces you to the beautiful **White Tank Mountains County Preserve.**

The White Tanks is the largest park under Maricopa County jurisdiction, and the least developed. The mountains took their name from stone depressions found in the creekbed. When it rains, these "tanks" fill with water, offering desert wildlife a refreshing drink.

If you continue on the Circle Trail, it will eventually lead you back to Granite Reef Dam. But it passes more mountain parkland that sits on the edge or in the very heart of Phoenix.

The weatherbeaten red sandstone faces of the *Papago Buttes* is a popular picnic spot in Phoenix and part of the Phoenix Mountain Preserves. The 888-acre **Papago Park** is the most developed of the city parks. On its grounds lie an *18-hole golf course,* the *Phoenix Municipal Stadium,* the *Desert Botanical Garden,* and the *Phoenix Zoo.*

The Phoenix Mountain Preserve is all one range and includes: *North Mountain, Shaw Butte,* and the *Papago Buttes.* The city of Phoenix began buying land for the preserves in the 1950s, and acquisition continues today.

Shaw Butte was also once inhabited by Hohokam Indians, who may have used it as a seasonal home while hunting bighorn sheep on their annual migration. Today the butte is a popular place to see various birds of a feather, including an occasional hawk, and hang gliders.

Squaw Peak, right in the heart of Phoenix, is probably the most heavily used park. Hardy joggers and walkers brave the almost vertical ascent to the peak at a brisk pace.

Its close neighbor is **Camelback Mountain,** well known for the "praying monk" rock formation. Although there is a trail on the mountain, there have been adventurous types who would rather make their own trail and wound up with broken legs. Camelback Mountain has many steep precipices and slide areas. Enjoy all that the mountain has to offer, but stay on the trail.

Also located in the valley area is **North Mountain Park.** It has always been a very popular spot for picnics and leisurely hikes. Sitting in one of the many cabanas that dot the foothills, one can view the city all the way to South Mountain. The park's entrance is on 7th Street, past Hatcher.

South Mountain has a paved scenic drive to the top. The view of the valley is breathtaking. In addition to the many picnicking sites, there are a number of hiking trails that are relatively easy to walk and do not take a great amount of time to complete.

Now, if you were standing on the top of South Mountain right near sunset, you would notice a red-hued mountain range to the northeast. This is **McDowell Mountain Regional Park.** Located 15 miles northeast of Scottsdale, this park encompasses 21,099 acres. Access to the park entrance road is from Rio Verde Dr., 10 miles east of Pinnacle Peak.

McDowell Mountain Park rates as one of the most scenic parks, with an abundance of vegetation and majestic mountain views. The park elevations range from 1,500 feet at the southeast corner to 3,000 feet along the park's west boundary. Park facilities include picnic areas, a horse staging area, campsites, and several trails.

Altogether, the Desert Mountain Parks encompass approximately 23,640 acres, or 37 square miles. Of this total, 6,520 acres are in the Phoenix Mountain Range alone.

For those who enjoy a walk among tree-lined paths, **Encanto Park,** 15th Avenue and Encanto, can offer just that. It has a tree-lined lagoon, a bandshell, a newly renovated red-brick clubhouse, a refreshing swimming pool, a creative play area, lighted racquetball and tennis courts.

Other Phoenix community parks include:

Arcadia Park, 56th St. and Osborn. This park has picnic facilities, ball-fields, a shuffleboard court, and a playground. **Madison Park,** 16th St. and Glenrosa, is every kid's dream. It has ball fields, basketball courts, soccer, shuffleboard, volleyball, a swimming pool, tennis courts, and, of course, a playground. **Los Olivos Park,** 28th St. and Glenrosa, has an exercise course and a Senior Center. **Cielito Park,** 3402 W. Campbell, is the only park like it in the Phoenix area. It's approximately 40 acres in size, has the usual ballfields and basketball courts, but also includes a handicapped exercise course.

PARTICIPANT SPORTS. Dependable sunshine and great weather make outdoor sports a way of life in the Valley of the Sun. Phoenix offers endless activities to choose from. Enjoy waterskiing, hydroplaning, fishing, backpacking, soaring, bicycle riding, jogging, racquetball, ballooning, exercise courses, and, of course, horseback riding.

Golf. Few places in the United States can offer the avid golfer the variety of course designs and the ideal year-round weather that can be enjoyed here. More than 60 courses, ranging from less demanding nine-hole "pitch-and-putt" to the challenging 18-hole championship courses, are available. Some of the courses are even illuminated for night play.

The Arizona Biltmore, 24th St. and Missouri, 955–6600, has 36 holes of PGA-rated championship semi-private golf, pro shop, lessons, clinics, food and beverage service.

Encanto 18-hole Golf Course, 2705 N. 15th Ave., 253–3963, is in the heart of Phoenix. *Encanto Golf Course II* is down the street at 2300 N. 17th Ave., 262–6870.

Ahwatukee Lakes Country Club, 13431 S. 44th St., 275–8099, is a public par 60, 18-hole, 4,083-yard executive course with four large lakes.

Papago Golf Course, 5595 E. Moreland, 275–8428, a desert course surrounded by purple rock mountains.

Royal Palms Inn, 5200 E. Camelback, 840–3610, semi-private, par 34, 9-hole, 2,110 yards. Rental clubs available.

Tatum Ranch Golf Course, 4410 E. Dixileta Dr., 252–1230, a scenic desert course.

Villa de Paz Golf Course, 4220 N. 103rd Ave., 877–1171, on the west side of town; par 72.

For **tennis,** the *Phoenix Tennis Center,* 6330 N. 21st Ave., 249–3712, has 22 lighted public courts. They are inexpensive, and court reservations are accepted. The *Arizona Biltmore,* 24th St. and Missouri Ave., 955–6600, has 17 private courts of various surface types. *The Pointe at Tapatio Cliffs,* 11111 N. 7th St., 866–7500, offers 17 private lighted courts.

If you don't mind a possible short wait, many of the city parks are equipped with courts, and they are free. An example is *Encanto Park,* on 15th Avenue and Encanto. The park has just built some nicely maintained public courts.

Because of Arizona's fair weather, **hot-air ballooning** has become very popular in the valley. A number of ballooning companies in the Phoenix area offer rides, champagne flights, and flight instruction. Arizona also is the site for several balloon races throughout the year.

Want an uplifting experience? *Xanadu Balloon Adventures,* 3745 W. Columbine Dr., offers balloon rides with experienced commercial pilots. They also provide gourmet picnics.

Hot Air West, 2632 E. Mountain View Rd., 992–7414, has a champagne fun flight. And if you are swept away by the experience, they also sell balloons and will provide flight instruction.

An Aeronautical Adventure, 2433 E. Dahlia Dr., 992–2627, features spectacular sunrise and sunset flights.

For more information on ballooning activities in Phoenix and the state, contact the *Arizona Balloon Club.* The commander is Karen Bagwell, who can be reached at 242–3626.

Horseback riding. Forgot your horse and you'd like to see some of Phoenix the way the pioneers did? Phoenix is full of horse-rental and riding stables that can saddle you up for an hour, a day, or a weekend.

Arizona Country Outfitters. 4700 N. Litchfield Rd., 846–9777, offers sunset and steak rides, breakfast rides, and trail rides.

North Mountain Stables. 12633 N. 7th St., 581–0103. This stable has been in existence since 1964. In addition to renting horses, they provide group trail rides and hay rides and give Western riding lessons.

Hole in the Wall Stables. 7677 N. 16th St., 997–1466. Located at the Pointe Resort near Squaw Peak and the Phoenix Mountain Preserves, Hole in the Wall rents horses for one to two hours, half-day, or all day. They have evening hay rides, breakfast rides, and cookouts.

Several stables near South Mountain offer guided trail tours in South Mountain Park, hay rides, riding lessons, and steak fries. They accommodate all skill levels: *Ponderosa Stables,* 10215 S. Central Ave., 268–1261; *All Western Stables,* 10220 S. Central Ave., 276–5862; *South Mountain Stables,* 10005 S. Central, 276–8131.

SPECTATOR SPORTS. For the sports enthusiast, the year begins with the *Fiesta Bowl Football Classic* on January 1. It is the fifth largest college bowl game in the country. Call 840–2693 for information and tickets. From September through May, you can enjoy other college football teams as they compete with the *Arizona State University Sun Devils* at the ASU campus in Tempe, 965–2381.

New to ASU's Sun Devil Stadium for the 1988 season were the *NFL Cardinals,* formerly of St. Louis. Call 967–1402 for ticket information.

Or maybe basketball is your game. Then cheer on the *NBA Phoenix Suns* at Veteran's Memorial Coliseum, 263–7867. In March, eight major league baseball teams come to Arizona for the *Cactus League* spring training season. For tickets call the box offices: *California Angels,* (619) 327–1266; *Chicago Cubs,* 964–4467; *Milwaukee Brewers,* 821–2200; *Oakland Athletics,* 220–0896; *San Francisco Giants,* 994–5123; *Seattle Mariners,* 438–8900. Then on to January again for the $200,000 *Phoenix Open Golf Tournament;* call 263–0757 for information. And in March, witness the $150,000 women's *LPGA Samaritan Turquoise Classic;* call 495–4483 for information.

HISTORIC SITES AND HOUSES. Between August, 1983, and March, 1984, the Junior League of Phoenix conducted a survey of all commercial properties more than 40 years old in the central Phoenix area. Its purpose—to identify buildings of historic or architectural significance that may be eligible for the National Register of Historic Places. From this survey, 70 properties were found to be eligible for listing on the Register. For more information, contact the Junior League at 234–3388.

Before Columbus even dreamed of sailing west, those industrious Hohokam Indians lived and prospered in the Salt River Valley. More than a thousand years ago, they built a community we now call **Pueblo Grande** ("large or great town").

This community included homes, storerooms, a platform mound, and a ball court. But much more significant, the inhabitants learned to live in this desert and to farm crops through a system of canals.

The Pueblo Grande Museum, 4619 E. Washington, 275–3452, lets you walk among ruins thought to have been occupied from 200 B.C. to A.D. 1400. The museum was created in 1929 to house the materials excavated from the site. Its purpose is to preserve and interpret the Hohokam culture.

The museum, which has been designated a National Landmark and is on the National Register of Historic Places, is operated by the City of Phoenix Parks, Recreation, and Library Department. The excavation of the site is under the direction of the city archaeologist. The museum is open 9 A.M. to 4:45 P.M. Monday through Saturday, 1 to 4:45 P.M. Sunday. Admission charge.

Another very livable form of desert architecture is evident at **Taliesin West,** the Western architectural school and winter home of the late architect Frank Lloyd Wright. It is located off Shea Blvd. on 108th St. in northeast Scottsdale. For information on hours, tours call 860–8810.

Or visit houses that were once home to Arizona pioneers. **Heritage Square,** located downtown at 6th and Monroe streets, is one city block of restored homes dating from the late 1800s that have been placed on the National Register of Historic Places. It is the only remaining group of residential structures from the original town site of Phoenix. For information on the square, call 262–5029.

The focal point of the square is the *Rosson House,* built in 1895 by Dr. and Mrs. Roland Lee Rosson. The cost: $7,525.00. It was one of the most prominent homes in Phoenix. It is a beautiful example of the Victorian Eastlake style popular in San Francisco at the turn of the century.

The house was purchased by the city in 1974 and has been authentically restored through the contributions of many individuals, groups, and businesses. Open from 10 to 4 Wednesdays through Saturdays, noon to 4 Sundays. (Last tour at 3:45.) Closed Mondays and Tuesdays. Admission charge.

Other restored buildings on the block include: The *Burgess Carriage House.* It is the only building that has been moved to the square. Built some time before 1901, it originally rested at Second Street and Taylor. Now it houses a gift shop and information center (262–5070) that serves as a starting point for the Rosson House Tours.

The Carriage House, located in the center of the square, was built around 1900. It originally sheltered horses, vehicles, harnesses, and a groom. Today it houses the Duck & Decanter, a popular sandwich/imported foods shop.

The Lath House Pavilion, completed in 1980, serves as a community meeting area. Its design was influenced by such nineteenth-century Phoenix architectural styles as gazebos, botanical conservatories, beer gardens, and shopping arcades. The structure was designed by architect Robert Frankeberger and can be rented for many events, including weddings and banquets. For more information, call 262–5071.

The Duplex, built in 1923, is the most typical of Arizona architecture. It features canvas and wood-paneled sleeping porches and currently houses communications exhibits sponsored by local television stations, radio stations, newspapers, and Mountain Bell.

The Stevens House was constructed in 1901 and today features a belled, hipped roof and a double pyramid roof. Its maintenance is sponsored by Arizona State University.

The Stevens-Haustgen House is a turn-of-the-century California-style structure that is home today to the Arizona chapter of the American Institute of Architects. Exhibits show future urban planning for Phoenix.

The Bouvier-Teeter House was built in 1899 in a midwestern-style architecture. It is sponsored by the Central Arizona Museum and holds changing historical exhibits.

What a greeting you'll receive when you enter the *Silva House.* A talking mannequin of Theodore Roosevelt is seated at a desk within the main room, a replica of the first Salt River Valley Water Users' Association office. This early-1900s home is decorated with a turn-of-the-century flair that includes a Victrola and overstuffed chairs. Restored by Salt River Project, this house has handicapped facilities. These houses are open from 10 to 4 Tuesays through Saturdays, 12 to 4 Sundays. Admission is free.

Another wonderfully preserved house is the *Duppa-Montgomery Homestead* at 116 W. Sherman St. The homestead, part of the Central Arizona Museum of History, is a two-room adobe structure thought to have been built between 1868 and 1872. Although a concrete floor has been laid because of heavy foot traffic, the house remains much as it was. Inside are utensils that were common kitchen aids in the 1800s, including a hand-forged iron cot, a potbelly stove, hickory chairs, kerosene lanterns, and an 1876 kitchen cabinet.

The homestead acquired its name from Bryan Duppa, who owned the land (he is credited with naming Phoenix and Tempe), and from John Montgomery, a Maricopa County sheriff. The museum is open from 2 to 5 Sundays through Tuesdays, November through May.

Visitors are transported back to the nineteenth century at the *Pioneer Arizona Living History Museum,* off Black Canyon Freeway on Pioneer Rd., 993–0210. Tour a faithful replica of a pioneer town, complete with blacksmith, barnyards, an old schoolhouse, and a staff dressed in period costumes.

MUSEUMS. The Valley of the Sun has many sights to offer, both indoors and out. History and art at their finest are on display at valley museums and galleries. Listed here are a great number of Phoenix's museums, but because of limited space, we are unable to detail all the museums the city has to offer.

Displays at **The Arizona Museum** at 1002 W. Van Buren (253–2734) span 1,500 years of central Arizona history. Founded by the first families of Phoenix, this museum is a collection of "firsts" for the state. For instance, it is the first building constructed in Arizona to be used specifically as a museum.

The museum also contains the first territorial infantry flag from U.S. Volunteers in 1864, religious artifacts from some of Phoenix's first churches, and the first motorcycle invented in the United States happened in Phoenix in 1883. Other exhibits include relics from various Indian tribes and specimens of Indian art. Open 11 A.M. to 4 P.M., Wednesday through Sunday. Closed national holidays. Free admission.

The Heard Museum of Anthropology and Primitive Art, 22 E. Monte Vista Rd. (252–8848/0). Founded in 1928 by Dwight and Maie Heard, the museum offers over 75,000 Indian artifacts, including blankets, pottery, basketry, and jewelry.

The Heards began their collection of Indian artifacts in 1895. Since then, other large collectors, such as Barry Goldwater and Fred Harvey, have added their artifacts to the constantly growing museum collection.

The museum recently opened a new permanent exhibit, "Native Peoples of the Southwest." This exhibit spans from 15,000 B.C. to the present.

The Heard wants to make its treasures open to everyone, and to achieve that end, several museum guides have taken special training from the Phoenix School for the Blind. Open 10 to 5 Mondays through Saturdays; 1 to 5 Sundays. Closed major holidays. Admission charge.

The Arizona Historical Society Museum, 1242 N. Central Ave. (255–4479), gives a glimpse of Arizona's early days as seen through the eyes of her pioneers. Exhibits include toys, a discovery room where visitors can use branding irons, jump onto a saddle, or use a telegraph. One hallway in the museum has been converted to house three turn-of-the-century stores, complete with old-time bottles, storage barrels, and scales. Open 10 to 4 Tuesdays through Saturdays, closed Sundays, Mondays, and holidays. Free admission.

The Phoenix Art Museum, at 1625 N. Central Ave. (257–1222), has a permanent collection of more than 10,000 paintings, sculptures, costumes, and other works of art from the fifteenth through the twentieth centuries. The main level emphasizes Asian art, graphics, and Western American paintings by such notables as Remington and Russell. The second floor contains eighteenth-century French paintings, Old World European masterpieces, and works of other nineteenth- and twentieth-century painters and sculptors. A real treat for pint-size visitors are the Thorne Miniature Rooms. The one-inch-to-one-foot rooms are designed in 16 different periods of world history. Open 10 to 5 Tuesdays through Saturdays, 10 to 9 Wednesdays, 1 to 5 Sundays. Closed Mondays and major holidays. Admission charge (no admission fee on Wednesday).

The Shemer Arts Center, 5005 E. Camelback Rd. (262–4727), displays the works of Arizona artists. Exhibits change from month to month, so call for information and hours.

Arizona Mineral Museum, State Fairgrounds, 1826 W. McDowell (255–3791), is a many-faceted display of everything from crystallized minerals and precious gems to fluorescent minerals exhibited under ultraviolet light. The more than 11,000 catalogued specimens have all been donated to the museum by private individuals. Open 8 to 5 Mondays through Fridays, 1 to 4 P.M. Saturdays and Sundays. Free admission.

If you are curious about how things work, you will enjoy the approximately 140 hands-on comprehensive science exhibits at the **Arizona Museum of Science and Technology,** 80 N. 2nd St. (256–9388). The museum allows the curious to examine life sciences, energy, and human development. The *Energy Theatre* alone has four different areas. In one area, visitors can activate wind, volcano, and solar displays through the use of a touch sensor.

Also learn how the human body works through an exhibit that allows visitors to measure their lung capacity and respiration rate and take their blood pressure. A *Young People's Discovery* area lets youngsters test their coordination and measure their size and height in comparison to various animals. Open 9 to 5 Mondays through Saturdays, 1 to 5 Sundays. Closed national holidays. Admission charge.

The Desert Botanical Garden Living Museum, 1201 N. Galvin Pkwy. (941–1225), in Papago Park, houses many types of desert plants. Cactus can be as tiny as a thimble or as tall as 40 feet and more than 150 years old. In addition to a living collection of over 4,000 species of plants from arid regions, the garden maintains an ethnobotany trail which depicts how Indians and settlers have adapted to and lived in the desert over the last 10 centuries. On the second and fourth Sundays of each month, from September to May, the garden hosts musical recitals (free with admission). The garden is home to half of the world's 1,800 different species of cacti, all shown in natural settings. The museum also offers classes and workshops throughout the year for cactus lovers. Open 9 to sunset from September through June; open 7 to sunset July and August. Admission charge.

Anyone who has ever owned a home can appreciate **The Hall of Flame Museum** at 6101 E. Van Buren St. (275–3473). This memorial to man's attempt to fight the most feared of nature's forces has over 90 firefighting vehicles, all in operating order. Of particular interest to visitors from the Midwest is the Rumsey fire engine, used in the Chicago Fire of 1871. Thousands of related articles that make up a fire fighter's life hang on walls and are displayed in cases. It is the world's largest firefighting museum. Open 9 to 5 Mondays through Saturdays. Closed Sundays, Thanksgiving, Christmas, and New Year's Day. Admission charge.

Have you wondered what medical treatment was like in the early years of the country? After a tour through **the Medical Museum** in the lobby of Phoenix Baptist Hospital, 6025 N. 20th Ave. (249–0212), you'll see that the treatment was sometimes worse than the ailment. The museum contains cases upon cases of historic medical instruments, some dating from the American Revolutionary period; herbal, patent, and quack remedies; sickroom equipment; and apothecary jars. An English leech jar with bleeding bowl is a grim reminder that medical science has come a long way. Open 8 A.M. to 9 P.M. daily. Free admission.

Ever wonder what it would have been like to see territorial Arizona behind bars—bank teller's bars, that is. Now is your chance. The **Arizona History Room,** First Interstate Bank Plaza Lower Level, 100 W. Washington (271–6879), has an authentic 1877 bank teller's cage, complete with inkwell, ledgers, and gold scales on display. Other exhibits within the History Room deal with mineral specimens that are on permanent loan from the Stephen Congdon Earth Sciences Center of the Arizona–Sonora Desert Museum in Tucson. Open 10 to 3 Mondays through Fridays. Closed weekends and holidays. Free admission.

A different type of science, military science, has been studied as long and even longer than earth sciences. **The Arizona Military Museum** on the Papago Park Military Reservation, 5636 E. McDowell Rd. (273–9700), displays memorabilia from battles lost and won, beginning with Spanish armor, remnants of Spain's attempted control of the New World. Next are uniforms and weapons from the American Indian wars era, followed by photographs of the Border Incident of 1916–1917 involving Pancho Villa and the Mexican Revolution. In chronological order are items from World War I, World War II, Korea, and Vietnam.

The museum also houses a library of military history and a photo collection. Open 10 to 4 weekends. Closed Mondays through Fridays. Free admission.

How can a desert with less than seven inches of rainfall per year and only one natural lake be transformed into a home for more than one million residents? **The Salt River Project History Center,** at 1521 Project Dr. (236–2208), has the answers. Located off the main lobby of the SRP administration building, the center explains how the prehistoric Hohokam Indians were the first to bring Salt River water to the valley via their 250-mile canal system. To acquaint visitors with today's system of garnering electricity and water, the center displays the workings of power plants and includes photos depicting the building of Roosevelt Dam. The center has handicapped facilities.

The Phoenix Zoo, 5810 E. Van Buren (273–7771), in Papago Park, maintains a collection of over 1,200 animals and has a special Arizona exhibit comprised exclusively of animals native to the state. The zoo recently opened a 5-acre African veldt exhibit.

MUSIC. The **Phoenix Symphony** (264–4754) performs, with noted guest artists, from October through May at Symphony Hall in the Civic Plaza, Gammage Auditorium in Tempe, and Scottsdale Center for the Arts.

The **Arizona Opera** (264–1664) is under the direction of General Director Glynn Ross. Their performances are also held at Phoenix Symphony Hall.

The **Phoenix Boys Choir** (264–5328) has gained international recognition in its 37 years of active performance.

Ballet Arizona (381–0184) performs October through April at Phoenix Symphony Hall, Gammage Auditorium, and Scottsdale Center for the Arts.

STAGE AND REVUES. Residents and visitors grab all the entertainment gusto that Phoenix has to offer, from down-and-dusty rodeos to sophisticated theater productions. Capacity crowds always flock to both types of events. And with more than 20 companies, you can have your choice of amateur, professional, children's, family, or adult experimental theater.

Phoenix Little Theatre/The Cookie Co. (254–2151), founded in 1920, is the longest continuously running community theater in North America. It mixes drama, comedy, musicals, and children's productions.

The City of Phoenix Performing Arts Theatre (965–3434) performs comedies, musicals, theater productions, and drama from September through May. Dance productions include jazz, modern, and ballet. The season runs from October through June.

The Arizona Theatre Company (234–2892), a resident company, began in Tucson in 1967 and came to Phoenix in 1978. Their productions range from musical revues to Shakespearean tragedy. Performances are held at Phoenix College Theatre.

The **Black Theatre Troupe** (251–8128) has presented local talent in a variety of performances for more than a decade. The season runs from September through May. Each season comedy, musical, classical, and strong contemporary plays are produced.

A unique theater experience comes from **Alwun House** (253–7887). The productions are often multimedia with a single focus. Media used include mime, photography, art, music, and dance.

And for every child who dreams of seeing her or his name up in lights, the **Phoenix Children's Theatre** (484–7252) provides "theater for children by children." The 25-year-old institution helps make those dreams come true for children 6 through 18 by offering working positions both onstage and backstage. Workshops on various theater techniques are also held throughout the year.

A la Carte Players, 8955 N.W. Grand Ave. (979–7200), offers musical events on Friday and Saturday nights at the 110-seat Northwest Phoenix Grand Inn. Well-known melodies by famous composers accompany stories written by the A la Carte group.

Actors Theater of Phoenix, 320 N. Central Ave. (254–3475), is a limited-equity house that presents a wide variety of classic plays with an occasional foray into the avant-garde.

Musical Theater of Arizona works closely with Arizona State University, with performances held at Gammage Auditorium (965–3434) in Tempe and the Sundome (975–1900) in Sun City West.

For Broadway shows and professional theater there is the **Herberger Theater Center** (254–7399).

GALLERIES. Phoenix and Scottsdale have become among the leading visual art centers of the country, with world-famous art galleries featuring top-rated displays of contemporary, Western, and Indian art and sculpture. Phoenix's fine galleries include:

The **Craftsmen's Cooperative Gallery** at Heritage Square (253–7770) shows original works by local artisans.

Gallery-McGoffin, 902 W. Roosevelt (255–0785), is the only working studio/gallery of batik in the country.

Shorr-Goodwin Gallery Ltd., Biltmore Fashion Park, 2474 E. Camelback Rd., has the valley's largest selection of graphics by Miró, Erte, and Dali, as well as contemporary impressionist paintings.

SHOPPING. Shopping is comfortable year-round in Phoenix, with enclosed, air-conditioned shopping malls. Some of the popular malls include: **Christown Mall,** 19th Ave. and Bethany Home Rd. Major stores within the complex are the *Broadway Southwest, Bullock's, J.C. Penney,* and *Montgomery Ward.*

Biltmore Fashion Square, 24th St. and Camelback. Seventy-two stores, including *Saks* and *Gucci,* as well as six restaurants.

Metro Center, Peoria Ave. and Black Canyon Highway. It is the state's largest mall and includes these major stores: *Dillard's, Broadway Southwest, Goldwaters,* and *Sears.*

The Colonnade, 20th St. and Camelback. Major stores include *Marshall's, Mervyn's,* and *Sears.*

Outlet Mart, 33rd St. and Thomas. The entire mall is made up of outlet stores selling merchandise at reduced prices.

Park Central, Central Ave. and Osborn. Major stores include *Goldwater's* and *Dillard's.*

Town and Country Shopping Center, 20th St. and Camelback. Boutiques, restaurants, UNICEF store.

Some **shopping gems** include: *Banana Republic,* Biltmore Fashion Center, 24th St. and Camelback. All the latest in 100% cotton safari wear.

Christopher Collection, Biltmore Fashion Park, 24th St. and Camelback. Oriental and contemporary gifts and furnishings.

Jutenhoops, 1803 E. Camelback Rd., in Colonnade Mall. Unique party goods, cards, and novelty items.

The Country Goose, 9415 N. 7th St. Southwestern and country style crafts and antiques.

Frontier Boot Corral, 403 E. Van Buren. Western outfitters a few blocks away from the Convention Center.

Gilbert Ortega, 1803 E. Camelback Rd. Colonnade Mall. Large collection of Indian arts and crafts. Also stores at Park Central and Christown malls.

Stockman, 4648 N. 16th St. Extensive collection of real cowboy clothes.

But if you're the type that really likes to look for a bargain, hundreds of Phoenix residents hold *carport, garage,* and *yard sales* Fridays through Sundays. A list of sales can be found in the want ads of the Arizona *Republic/*Phoenix *Gazette* newspapers.

Or visit the *state's largest yard sale,* held each weekend at the Phoenix Greyhound Park parking lot, Washington and 40th St. People rent a space and display their wares, reusables, or crafts.

Do you have a food fetish? There are many *ethnic and specialty food stores* located in Phoenix. Several of the more popular include: *Luigi's,* 6505 N. 16th St. Serving a bevy of Italian food products and ingredients.

La Tolteca, 1205 E. Van Buren St. Offers Mexican food products, pastries, and imported spices.

Middle Eastern Bakery and Deli, 3052 N. 16th St. Sells Arabic, Greek, and Armenian foods and ingredients.

Lee Hing Oriental Food Center, 1510 W. McDowell. A real grocery shopping experience. The center offers many food products and spices from China and south Asia.

Sees Candy, 132 E. Camelback and branches throughout Phoenix. An Arizona institution for old-fashion confections.

Sphinx Date Ranch, 4401 E. Thomas. Enormous, succulent *medjool* dates grown in local neighborhoods.

DINING OUT. *Haute cuisine* does not a cultural capital make, but Phoenix's standing among the cities of North America has certainly been enhanced by the surprising variety and quality of its restaurants. The city's famed resorts have had the wherewithal to lure some of the finest American and European chefs out into the middle of the Sonora desert, and affluent immigrants to the state have brought with them a taste for their native cuisines.

But Phoenix has thrived gastronomically in a way that cannot be explained by mere economic influence alone. California, with its variety of experimental cuisines and top-quality wines, has a preponderant influence on the state's diners, and Phoenix is not short of nouvelle-yogurt emporia. The variety of Mexican cuisines south of the border have given native

Phoenicians a taste for the exotic, the adventurous, and the spicy. Meanwhile, the real native cuisine of the place—hearty, Western-style steaks and barbecues—thrives in a number of unpretentious, swinging-doors-type places.

Restaurant price categories are as follows: *Deluxe,* $30 and up; *Expensive,* $20 to $30; *Moderate,* $10 to $20; and *Inexpensive,* under $10. Prices are for salad or soup, entrée, and beverage, exclusive of drinks, tax, and tip.

American

Expensive

Bobby McGee's. 8501 N. 27th Ave., 995–5982. Costumed waiters deliver entertainment along with well-prepared steaks and seafood.

Chaps Ribs & Whiskey. 24th Street and Camelback, Town and Country Shopping Center, 957–1796. Contemporary Western atmosphere. A small menu dominated by big portions of ribs.

Chubb's. 6522 N. 16th St., 279–3459. Pubby, masculine interior. Adept staff serves up excellent steaks and prime rib.

Oscar Taylor. 2420 E. Camelback Rd., 956–5705. Looks like an exclusive club. The menu runs to standard favorites. Ribs and onion rings shine.

Timothy's. 6335 N. 16th St., 277–7634. An attractive, refurbished cottage. The menu features steaks, seafood and well prepared Cajun specialties. Good jazz on weekends.

Moderate

Cork 'n Cleaver. 5101 N. 44th St., 952–0585. Relaxing Southwestern ambience, professional service, good steaks, and an above-average salad bar.

Durant's. 2611 N. Central Ave., 264–5967. A perennial favorite. The red-and-black interior evokes the '50s. Service and food can't be faulted.

My Mother's. 4130 N. 19th Ave., 279–7225. An eclectic menu includes prime rib, barbecue, and pizza. Portions are huge, service friendly.

Stuart Anderson's Black Angus. 2125 E. Camelback Rd. and five other valley locations, 955–9741. Super-reliable chain featuring all-American beef and seafood selections. The blend of rustic and contemporary decors is especially inviting.

Inexpensive

Ed Debevic's. 2102 E. Highland Ave., 956–2760. Fun 1950s diner atmosphere. A competent short-order menu stars.

The Good Egg. 906 E. Camelback Rd., 274–5393. Serving breakfast and lunch with an emphasis on cackleberries.

Original Hamburger Works. 2801 N. 15th Ave., 263–8693. Big, juicy burgers served with choice of works.

Patty Ann's Drive Inn. 3517 W. Camelback Rd., 973–6279. Archetypal drive-in (counter service inside) with all the old standbys; BLTs, patty melts, fried-egg sandwiches, and some fine fried catfish.

Pugzie's. 4700 N. 16th St., 279–3577. Sandwich shop with a perky jungle atmosphere. Good soups, sandwiches, and desserts.

R.J.'s Osborn Cafe. 2333 E. Osborn Rd., 956–4420. The place has a likeable small-town feel and a down-home menu. The fried foods are remarkably light and fresh-made pies are great.

Real Texas Bar-B-Que. 2415 W. Bethany Home Rd., 249–9985. Rustic building and down-home ambience. The spicily sauced, wood-smoked meats are as good as they get.

French

Expensive

The French Corner. 50 E. Camelback Rd., 234–0245. Wonderful all-purpose bistro serving all the way from breakfast to late night. Staff is on the ball; food is country-French and terrific.

Greek

Expensive

Bacchanal. 3015 E. Thomas Rd., 224–9377. Subtle renditions of Greek specialties, smooth service, and traditional bouzouki music add up to a memorable experience.

Greekfest. 1219 E. Glendale Ave., 265–2990. Attractive Mediterranean atmosphere. Food is uncompromisingly authentic.

Mykonos. 4110 N. 49th St., 952–1958. An exciting addition to the ethnic scene. The food is delicious, the music divine. Patio dining in good weather.

Inexpensive

The Golden Greek. 7126 N. 35th Ave., 841–7849. Comfortable tavern, family-owned and operated with a Greek cook at the helm. Try taramosalata, fried squid, and succulent lamb.

Indian

Moderate

Delhi Palace. 5050 E. McDowell Rd., 244–8181. Tiny and clean with an ultra-polite staff. The food is spicy and superb.

Jewel of the Crown. 5029 N. 44th St., 840–2412. The food is the thing here—tandoori preparations, well-handled vegetarian entrees, and sweet, gooey, traditional desserts. Negligible decor and a semi-skilled staff are the downside.

International

Deluxe

The Restaurant at the Ritz-Carlton. 24th St. and Camelback Rd., 468–0700. Just as fine as the Ritz-Carlton name suggests, with rich, ornate surroundings and smooth-as-silk service. A compelling menu combines elements of Southwestern, Oriental, Mediterranean, and nouvelle Californian cuisines.

Moderate

The 1895 House. 362 N. 2nd Ave., 254–0338. One of the new fine dining spots in the downtown area. It's a revamped Victorian mansion; the limited menu is exciting and well-prepared.

Razz International. 13831 N. 32nd St., 867–8638. Chef owner Erasmo (Razz for short) is one of the best around. His product is imaginative, delicious, and changes seasonally.

Italian

Expensive

Allegro. 1301 E. Northern Ave., 861–1391. Colorful, cozy environs, perfectly prepared food, and proper service. A winning combination.

Pronto. 3950 E. Campbell Ave., 956–4049. Elegant, if slightly cluttered. The service is professional and the food is Italian-Swiss.

Moderate

Grandinetti's. 1957 W. Dunlap Ave., 870–4565. Family-owned and operated. No one is a stranger at Papa Joe's place. Robust Southern Italian cuisine.

Michelina's. 3241 E. Shea Blvd., 996–8977. Romantic and softly lit. The young chef/owner turns out a remarkably consistent product. Seafood dishes are fabulous.

Inexpensive

Pizza by Angelo. 6224 N. 43rd Ave., 934–8906. No frills, just good service, great food, and cold beer.

Red Devil. 3102 E. McDowell Rd., 267–1036. An old-time, red-checked-tablecloth kind of place. The walls are imbued with the odor of garlic and the pizza is crusty and good.

Mexican

Moderate

Aunt Chilada's. 7330 N. Dreamy Draw Dr., 438–0992. The best of the "Americanized" Mexican spots. It's spacious and cheery, with a real Aunt C. patting out tortillas. The menu includes some unusual regional offerings.

Inexpensive

Don Jose. 3734 E. Thomas Rd., 955–7870. Plain little place with just-adequate service. The steaming-hot Mexican food is out of this world.

Fina Cocina. 130 N. Central Ave., 258–5315. Close to downtown hotels. The cafeteria set-up moves fast. Check out the machaca burros and the changing exhibit of Hispanic artworks.

La Parilla Suiza. 3508 W. Peoria Ave., 978–8334. A nice change from the usual Sonoran-influenced Mexican food. This mild Central Mexican cuisine is savory and delicious.

Rosita's Place. 2310 E. McDowell Rd., 244–9779. Authentic Sonoran-style food with hard-to-find specialties like *mole* and *menudo.* Be careful of the deep-red hot sauce, which will take paint off a barn wall.

Oriental

Expensive

Ayako of Tokyo. 2564 E. Camelback Rd., 955–7007. A recent refurbishing makes this Benihana-style restaurant shine. If communal dining and showy chefs aren't your cup of *oolong,* join the local cognoscenti at the sushi bar.

Shogun. 12615 N. Tatum Blvd., 953–3264. Attractive contemporary Japanese dining with arguably the best sushi bar in town.

Moderate

Banzai. 7811 N. 12th St., 944–2291. Just about the best tempura around. Good sushi, too. Clean, sedate surroundings and good service.

China Gate. Colonnade Mall, 1815 E. Camelback Rd., 264–2600. An unusually pretty restaurant. The menu is lengthy and the spicier dishes have some real zing.

China Village. 2710 E. Indian School Rd., 956–9840. An extremely able staff makes this one of the most pleasant places in town to dig into moo shu pork and scallops in garlic sauce.

Mr. Sushi. 8041 N. Black Canyon, 864–9202. Forget that silly name. The nice people who run this restaurant dish up superlative sashimi, crisp tempura, and other, more exotic Japanese dishes.

Thai Lahna. 3738 E. Indian School Rd., 955–4658. Tiny place that turns out some explosive Thai food.

Vietnam Restaurant. 803 E. Van Buren St. in the Sundancer Motel, 252–7266. Though it looks like a coffee shop, this family-owned and operated eatery turns out the best Vietnamese food in town. Freshness and delicacy are a hallmark.

Inexpensive

Blue Fin. 1401 N. Central Ave., 254–3171. Open for lunch and early dinner. Justly popular for inexpensive and excellent Japanese fast food. No atmosphere and little seating.

Seafood

Expensive

Rusty Pelican. 9801 N. Black Canyon Freeway, 944–9646. Not much in the way of atmosphere, but the fresh catch is faultless and prepared just as it should be.

Top of the Market. The Fish Market, 1720 E. Camelback Rd., 277–3474. Bypass the noisy, cavernous downstairs restaurant for the upscale effort on the second floor, which resembles the famed San Francisco seafood grills. The product is marvelous.

Moderate

Tug's. 7575 N. 16th St., 997–0812. Clubby, turn-of-the-century atmosphere. Competently prepared seafood.

Inexpensive

Taylor's Chowder House. 3540 W. Calavar Rd., 978–1815. A bit out of the way but worth seeking out for fresh New England-style seafood.

Steak

Deluxe

Ruth's Chris Steak House. 2201 E. Camelback Rd., 957–9600. They bill themselves as the home of serious steaks, and with reason. These monster chunks of prime meat (with monster sides to match) are absolutely succulent.

Moderate

Lone Star Steaks. 6003 N. 16th St., 248–7827. A rustic, country-western-flavored slice of Texas. All the steaks are good and the chicken-fried version would make a cowboy weep for joy.

Stockyards. 5001 E. Washington St., 273–7378. The area used to be the largest feed lot in the world. All that's left is the interesting deco-stucco building (nicely renovated) and some great beef.

T-Bone Steak House. 10037 S. 19th Ave., 276–0945. One of the best of the cowboy steakhouses. No-nonsense service and grub plus a great view of the city from the slopes of South Mountain.

Southwestern

Deluxe

Vincent Guerithault's. 3930 E. Camelback Rd., 224–0225. Still the shining star in the local restaurant firmament. The talented young chef/owner has melded French technique and Southwestern ingredients in a way that is most intriguing. Glorious desserts.

Expensive

Cafe Sonora. Arizona Biltmore Hotel, 24th St. & Missouri, 954–2518. Bright and breezy restaurant featuring a mixed bag of mesquite-grilled meats and Mexican-influenced dishes.

NIGHTLIFE. Phoenix's fast-paced nightlife is a contradiction to the city's usual daytime easy going pace. Some of the more popular night spots in Phoenix include:

Finney Bones. 504 W. Camelback. The country's top comedians, as well as a few up-and-comers, perform five nights a week. Reservations suggested.

The Gold Room. The Arizona Biltmore, 24th St. and Missouri. Big-band music with occasional name performers. Tuesdays through Saturdays.

Malarkey's. 4701 N. 16th St. This massive nightclub features ongoing partying with nightly free buffet and dance and lip-synch contests.

Mr. Lucky's. 3660 Grand Ave. This split-level monster property has both country-western and contemporary live music and dancing.

Royal Palms Inn. 5200 E. Camelback Rd. Big-band–style entertainment with both dancing and easy listening.

Studio West. 4029 N. 33d Ave. The hottest thing on the west side for those who crave loud music, fast dancing, and plenty of excitement.

Timothy's. 6331 N. 16th St. The lounge features nightly jazz performances.

Vinnie's. 2210 E. Highland. Popular nightclub with disc jockey spinning the discs nightly.

Zazoo's. 909 E. Camelback Rd. Huge and glitzy; where the beautiful people hang out. Free buffet. Disk jockey.

EXPLORING OUTSIDE PHOENIX

The Valley of the Sun in Maricopa County is the heart of Arizona—politically, economically, demographically, and in almost every other way. It includes Phoenix and its gracious suburbs, the more interesting of which are Scottsdale, Tempe, Cave Creek/Carefree, Mesa, and the popular Sun City and Sun City West retirement communities. This sun-blessed section of the land also is fabulous winter resort country, famed not only for the sun but for mild desert temperatures in season as well.

Scottsdale

Scottsdale is Arizona's art capital, and is second only to Santa Fe in its concentration of outstanding southwestern art galleries. Scottsdale is also the place to go for sophisticated fashions, western memorabilia, souvenirs of every sort, and some of the state's best restaurants.

For shopping, try Fashion Square, a huge complex of upscale shops and department stores located at Scottsdale Road and Camelback. Intersecting Scottsdale Road a half-mile south is Fifth Avenue, a popular winding street of boutique shops, restaurants, and galleries—all with an individual quality. The Borgata, between McDonald and Lincoln drives on Scottsdale Road, is comprised of pricey, elegant shops set in a replica of a medieval Italian village. On Main Street and Marshall Way, galleries line the streets, one against the other. There's a Thursday Night Art Walk in season, when the galleries are open till 10 P.M. and serve wine to passersby and browsers. Among the most prominent galleries are the Elaine Horwitch Galleries, 4211 N. Marshall Way; the Suzanne Brown Gallery, 7160 E. Main St.; and Hand & the Spirit Gallery, 4222 N. Marshall Way.

Across Scottsdale Road, two blocks east, is the Civic Center, which includes a beautiful park, the Scottsdale Center for the Arts, a visual and performing arts center owned and operated by the city, the city hall complex, Chamber of Commerce, a Doubletree Inn complete with Rotisserie bar and grill, shops, a sculpture garden, and more, all of which help preserve the unique character and life-style of the exciting downtown area.

Back to Scottsdale Road, then north to Indian Bend Road, and a turn to the east (right) and on to Hayden Road and another right turn. This brings you to a marvelous bit of greenbelt along Indian Bend Wash.

The U.S. Army Corps of Engineers had proposed back in the 1960s to construct a concrete-lined ditch through town as a check against floods. But citizens had a better idea, and community spirit won the day. Today,

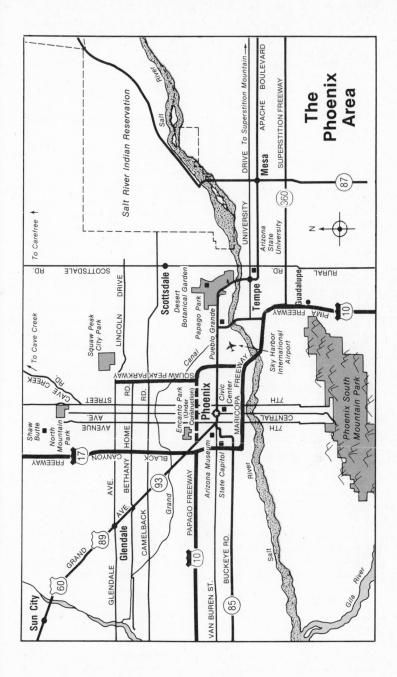

The Phoenix Area

instead of an unsightly culvert, Scottsdale has a superb seven-mile park with bike paths, golf links, walking trails, boating and fishing lakes, picnic spots, and more.

Scottsdale is so closely wrapped up in the Phoenix resort picture as to be an integral part of it. In fact, many of the so-called Phoenix resorts are actually in Scottsdale, where city lines meet around Camelback Mountain. A short motor swing around the landmark lets you see a majority of the posh and varied resorts catering to many winter vacationers. Scottsdale, in addition, is a thriving arts and crafts center. The downtown section retains a pseudo–Old West appearance, but the rest of town reflects newer ideas in smart stores, art galleries, crafts shops, and outstanding restaurants. Many of the homes are luxurious.

Carefree and Cave Creek

No tour of the northeast suburban area of Phoenix would be complete without including the Carefree–Cave Creek area. To get there, go north on Scottsdale Road, past posh hostelries, residential complexes, and the Borgata.

Farther north on Scottsdale Road, you come into high desert. Scottsdale city fathers (and mothers) have passed many ordinances to preserve the desert plant life and the Western Way. As a matter of fact, they recently bucked the trend of more intensive development by rezoning a 19½-square-mile area from one home per acre to one home per 2½ to 5 acres. That's why Scottsdale is Scottsdale.

Carefree, which sits like a crown on some low hills, is home base for some high achievers like Hugh Downs, Joe Garagiola, and country-western singer Glen Campbell. It's also home to an interesting variety of shops and restaurants and thoroughfares with names like Easy Street, Elbow Bend, and Wampum Way, where the bank is situated.

Going on downhill around the bend to your left, you come to Cave Creek, which used to be an outpost for cowboys and miners. Nowadays its flavor is still cowboy and miner, but Cave Creek has been modernized, with attractions and watering places with names like The Horny Toad. You can get back to Phoenix by following Cave Creek Road on through town.

Tempe

Another community of interest to visitors is Tempe, south of Scottsdale. From Phoenix proper, take Van Buren Street east. From Scottsdale, take Scottsdale Road south. Mill Avenue in Tempe has been restored to better than old-time appearance, with colorful shops, excellent bookstores, and special attractions.

Continue on Mill Avenue to the campus of Arizona State University. Its enrollment is the third-largest in America. (Stop at Memorial Union and pick up a visitor's guide.)

Where Mill Avenue turns into Apache Boulevard is Grady Gammage Auditorium, the last public building designed by the late architect Frank Lloyd Wright. Its exterior design includes contoured curtains and globe-lighted ramps.

Mesa

Farther east on Apache Boulevard is Mesa, founded in 1878, and long a haven for retirees and winter visitors. Today the town has so many young families that the median age is only 28.1. Current population is approximately 270,000. A beautifully landscaped area off the right of Apache Boulevard—past the business district—frames a Mormon temple. Also see Centennial Hall, Mesa Amphitheater, the downtown district, Fiesta Mall, and Mesa Community College.

Superstition Mountain

In another 15 miles, along Apache Boulevard, you'll see Superstition Mountain looming ahead. This brooding, much-photographed range is where Jacob Walz, dubbed "the Dutchman" by his friends, had a gold mine. But he never told anyone where it was, taking his secret with him to the grave. Since then, dozens of people have died searching for it. Because of its close proximity to Phoenix, the Superstition Mountain range is the most popular recreation site around.

On the way back to Phoenix, visit the Champlin Fighter Museum at 4636 Falcon Circle. There you'll find a huge collection of fighter planes from World War I through the Korean Conflict.

Guadalupe

One more attraction on the way back to town is Guadalupe, where you can experience a microcosm of Old Mexico. Settled by a group of Yaqui Indians in 1916, the village has a square, a restored church, and adobe houses. Recently a colorful new Mexican shopping mall, the Mercado, has been added.

Sun City

Sun City, about 10 miles west-northwest of Phoenix on U.S. Routes 60 and 89, is a showcase retirement community. Its 11 golf courses wind through the residential areas, and golf carts account for most of the traffic. The community also has seven recreational complexes that offer every kind of sports activity; 72 shuffleboard courts; studios for almost every kind of hobby or craft; card and meeting rooms; exercise rooms; therapy pools; the 7,500-capacity Sun Bowl; Sun City Stadium, where national league baseball teams train; 10 shopping centers; 20 fine restaurants; 35 houses of worship representing every major faith; banks; brokerage houses; and Walter O. Boswell Memorial Hospital.

Sun City West, about two miles west of Sun City, offers seven 18-hole golf courses; Sundome Center for the Performing Arts; the R. H. Johnson Recreation Center, which offers swimming, shuffleboard, lawn bowling, miniature golf, running track, 15 tennis courts, handball, racquetball, arts and crafts rooms, a 40,000-volume library, a 1,200-seat social hall, and card-playing and meeting rooms.

Sun City now has a population of 47,000, and its younger sister, only seven years old, has more than 13,000 residents.

Phoenix's other suburbs also are popular with tourists: Chandler, home of the famous San Marcos Hotel; Gilbert, a quiet, friendly farming community; Glendale, home of the American Graduate School of International Management; Litchfield Park, a pretty town built around the famed Wigwam Resort Hotel; plus the friendly west side farm communities of Tolleson, Cashion, Avondale, and Goodyear. All are special in their own way.

PRACTICAL INFORMATION FOR
OUTSIDE PHOENIX

HOW TO GET TO AND AROUND THE PHOENIX SUBURBS. By bus. Phoenix Transit has routes to most of Phoenix's suburbs. For route information write to 101 N. 1st Ave., Phoenix 85003; 253–5000.

By taxi. Cabs can take you almost anywhere in the Valley of the Sun but due to the spread-out nature of the area it is quite expensive. Try *Air Courier Cabs,* 244–1818; *Checker Cab,* 257–1818; or *Yellow Cab,* 252–5252.

By car. You can't beat having your own car to see the Phoenix suburbs. Rental agencies include *Hertz,* (800) 654–3131; *Avis,* (800) 331–1212; and myriad more, in the Phoenix Yellow Pages.

HOTELS AND MOTELS. The cities surrounding Phoenix provide everything possible in accommodations, from budget to several four star resorts. Expect to pay an average of between $50 and $80 per night for double occupancy. Rates vary with the season, and you can expect a drop of $5 to $15 from June to October. All hotels listed accept MasterCard and Visa, most accept American Express, and some accept Diners Club and Carte Blanche.

The price categories for double occupancy are: *Deluxe,* $120 and up; *Expensive,* $90 to $120; *Moderate,* $60 to $90; and *Inexpensive,* under $60.

Scottsdale

The Cottonwoods. *Deluxe.* Stouffer Resort, 6160 N. Scottsdale Rd., 85253; 991–1414. Hot tub, spa, jogging course, two heated pools, tennis, restaurant, lounge.

La Posada. *Deluxe.* 4949 E. Lincoln Dr., 85253; 952–0420, 800–547–8010. A 30-acre resort with pool, tennis courts, putting green, exercise facilities. Three restaurants and little shopping complex.

Marriott's Camelback Inn. *Deluxe.* 5402 E. Lincoln Dr., 85253; 948–1700, 800–228–9290. Scottsdale's oldest resort. Golf Club, pools, tennis courts. Dining and entertainment.

Marriott's Mountain Shadows. *Deluxe.* 5641 E. Lincoln Dr., 85253; 948–7111, 800–228–9290. Sandwiched between Camelback and Mummy mountains with views all around. Pool, spa, golf, tennis, restaurants.

The Sheraton Scottsdale Resort. *Deluxe.* 7200 N. Scottsdale Rd., 85253; 948–5000. Newly renovated with expanded meeting space, restaurant, cocktail lounge, poolside cafes, and bars. Racquetball and tennis courts, weight and game rooms.

Camelview Radisson. *Expensive.* 7601 E. Indian Bend Rd., 85235; 991–2400. Spa, pool, tennis, restaurant, lounge.

Doubletree Inn at Scottsdale Mall. *Expensive.* 7353 E. Indian School Rd., 85251; 994–9203. Restaurant, lounge, Jacuzzi, tennis, par course, pets allowed.

The Inn at McCormick Ranch. *Expensive.* 7401 N. Scottsdale Rd., 85253; 948–5050. Lighted tennis courts, putting green, paddleboats, sailing, sauna, Jacuzzi, restaurant, lounge, condominiums available.

Ramada Pima Golf Resort. *Expensive.* 7330 N. Pima, 85253; 948–3800, 800–344–0262. Newly renovated suites with kitchens and private patios. Pool, spa, golf, restaurant.

Scottsdale Embassy Suites. *Expensive.* 5001 N. Scottsdale Rd., 85253; 949–1414, 800–528–1445. Suites with kitchens. Free breakfast and cocktails. Golf privileges, pool, spa, tennis.

Holiday Inn of Scottsdale. *Moderate.* 5101 N. Scottsdale Rd., 85253; 945–4392. Coffee shop, cocktail lounge, dining room, pets allowed.

Hospitality Inn. *Moderate.* 409 N. Scottsdale Rd., 85257; 949–5115. Close to Tempe. Suites with kitchens. Free breakfast and cocktails. Pool and tennis.

Roadway Inn. *Moderate.* 7110 E. Indian School Rd., 85251; 946–3456. HBO, pets allowed.

Tempe

Westcourt in the Buttes. *Deluxe.* 2000 Westcourt Way, 85282; 225–9000. Nestled in the mountain, with every precaution taken to preserve the environment. Breathtaking views from the upscale restaurant.

Embassy Suites. *Expensive.* 4400 S. Rural Rd., 85282; 897–7444. A short drive from ASU and Old Town. Suites equipped with microwaves and full kitchens. Free breakfast and cocktails. Pool, spa, restaurant.

Sheraton Tempe Mission Palms Hotel. *Expensive.* 60 E. 5th St., 85251; 894–1400. In Old Town. Pool, spa, tennis courts, exercise room, restaurant.

Woolley's Petite Suites. *Moderate.* 1635 N. Scottsdale Rd., 85281; 947–3711. Pool, pets allowed, laundry, complimentary breakfast and cocktails.

Fiesta Inn. *Moderate.* 2100 South Priest Dr., 85282; 967–1441. On the corner of Broadway and Priest. Lighted tennis courts, restaurant, cocktails, sauna, Jacuzzi, pool, health club.

Holiday Inn. *Moderate.* 915 E. Apache Blvd., 85281; 968–3451. Heated pool, spa, HBO, dining room, entertainment in the lounge, pets allowed.

La Quinta Motor Inn. *Inexpensive.* 911 S. 48th St., 85281; 967–4465. HBO, pool, pets allowed, no-smoking rooms.

Franciscan Inn. *Inexpensive.* 1005 E. Apache Blvd., 85281; 968–7871. Pool, pets allowed.

Royal Tempe Motor Lodge. *Inexpensive.* 1020 E. Apache Blvd., 85281; 967–8981. Within walking distance of ASU. Newly renovated, clean rooms. Pool.

Vagabond Inn. *Inexpensive.* 1221 E. Apache Blvd., 85281; 968–7793, 800–522–1555. Recently refurbished. Close to ASU, shopping. Pool. Pets allowed.

Sun City

Best Western Inn of Sun City. *Inexpensive.* 11201 Grand Ave., 85372; 933–8211. TV, pool, small pets allowed.

Grand Inn. *Inexpensive.* 8955 Northwest Grand Ave., 85345; 979–7200. Pets allowed, coffee shop, putting green, dining room, dinner theater, cocktails, entertainment.

Windmill Inn of Sun City West. *Inexpensive.* 12545 W. Bell Rd., 85374; 583–0133, 800–547–4747. Close to Sundome, freeways. Golf, pool, kitchenettes.

Carefree

The Boulders. *Deluxe.* Box 2090, 85377; 488–9009. At 34631 Tom Darlington Road. Scenic, remote desert setting. All units are *casita*-style cottages. Four restaurants, pool, coffee shop, dining room, cocktails, golf, tennis. Closed June 1 through October 1.

Litchfield Park

The Wigwam. *Deluxe.* Box 278, 85340; 935–3811. Litchfield and Indian School roads. One of the oldest resorts in the state. Riding and western activities. Suites, bungalows, heated pools, tennis courts, three 18-hole golf courses, pets allowed, men's and women's health clubs. Open September 18 through May 31.

Mesa

Arizona Golf Resort. *Expensive.* 425 S. Power, 85206; 832–3202, 800–528–8282. Kitchenettes, one-and two-bedroom condo suites, complimentary greens fees, 18-hole golf course, lighted tennis courts, pool, Jacuzzis, coffee shop, restaurant, lounge.

Hilton Pavilion. *Expensive.* 1011 W. Holmes Ave., 85202; 833–5555. Pool, pets allowed, coffee shop, dining room, cocktails, golf, tennis.

Best Western Mesa Inn. *Moderate.* 1625 E. Main St., 85204; 964–8000. Color TV, HBO, heated pool, whirlpool, pets allowed, coffee shop, no-smoking rooms, complimentary coffee and cocktails.

Best Western Dobson Ranch Inn. *Moderate.* 1666 S. Dobson Rd., 85202; 831–7000. Restaurant, lounge, patio dining.

Courtyard by Marriott–Mesa. *Moderate.* 1221 S. Westwood, 85201; 461–3000, 800–228–9290. New hotel next to the Fiesta Mall. Courtyard, pool, spa, exercise room.

Ramada Renaissance. *Moderate.* 200 N. Centennial Way, 85201; 898–8300. In Mesa's historic downtown. Exercise room, pool. Special weekend rates.

Maricopa Inn Motor Hotel. *Inexpensive.* 3 E. Main St., 85202; 834–6060. Combination baths, pool, pets allowed, coffee shop.

Rodeway Inn. *Inexpensive.* 5700 E. Main St., 85205; 969–3561. Pool, pets allowed, coffee shop, dining room, cocktails, golf.

CAMPING. November through May are the best months for camping in the Valley of the Sun, as summers are rather uncomfortable without air-conditioning. Camping space near the metropolitan area is at a premium at this time of year, so reservations are recommended. For more information on camping in the valley call the Maricopa County Parks and Recreation Department, 272–8871.

Paradise Valley Park. North Phoenix at the corner of 40th Street and Union Hills Drive (971–1160). Open year-round. Water and restrooms. RVs and tents allowed.

Palisades McDowell Mountain Regional Park (471–0173). Fifteen miles northeast of Scottsdale. Open September through May; 14-day limit; fee; restrooms; RVs and tents allowed.

Usury Mountain Park. Twelve miles northeast of Mesa (986–2310). Open September through May; restrooms; RVs and tents allowed.

TOURIST INFORMATION. For information on the greater Phoenix metropolitan area, contact the *Phoenix and Valley of the Sun Convention and Visitors Bureau,* 505 N. 2nd St., Suite 300, Phoenix 85004; 254–6500. In addition, *visitor information centers* are located in terminals 2 and 3 at Phoenix Sky Harbor International Airport and on the northwest corner of Adams and Second streets in downtown Phoenix.

The *Arizona Office of Tourism's* main office is in Phoenix at 1480 E. Bethany Home Rd., 85014; 255–3618. Either they or the Convention and Visitors Bureau will have information on any community attraction or event in the Valley of the Sun.

The *Scottsdale Chamber of Commerce,* 7333 E. Scottsdale Mall, Scottsdale, 85253; 945–8481, will provide information about places to stay and things to do in the east valley.

SEASONAL EVENTS. There's something interesting or exciting going on in the Valley of the Sun nearly every weekend throughout the autumn, winter, and spring, from arts fairs to rodeos to concerts and more. Here are a few of the fun events scheduled around Phoenix.

November. *Fountain Hills Festival of the Arts.* All-day celebration and sale of arts and crafts. Live entertainment and food are part of the fun. Drive northeast of Scottsdale and see the world's largest man-made fountain while getting an introduction to Southwestern-flavored art.

Thunderbird Invitational Balloon Race. Colorful race with an international flair at the American Graduate School of International Management in Glendale. Nearly 100 balloons compete. Also offers international food booths.

Day of the Dead Festival. Latin American festival of performing arts with crafts and food booths, in Mesa.

December. *Tempe Old Town Festival.* One of the larger arts and crafts festivals in the West. Tempe closes its restored downtown district to traffic, and the 12-block-square festival fills the town for three days. Arts, crafts, music, food, and more.

January. *Fiesta Bowl Football Classic.* One of the top ten college bowl games attracting sellout crowds to Tempe's Sun Devil Stadium each New Year's Day.

February. *Wickenburg Gold Rush Days.* Northwest of Phoenix, the Old West town of Wickenburg relives its past with a rodeo, dances, gold panning, mineral show, and more.

Scottsdale's Parada del Sol Rodeo and Parade. One of the more popular tourist attractions in the state. The parade runs down Scottsdale Road complete with beautiful floats, high-spirited horses, handsome cowboys, pretty cowgirls.

Lost Dutchman Days—Apache Junction. Bluegrass music festival, carnival, rodeo.

March. *Scottsdale Center for the Arts Festival.* A large, well-run festival on beautiful Scottsdale Mall, with arts, crafts, music, and food.

Tempe Spring Festival of the Arts. Arts, crafts, food, and music. A bit campier than Scottsdale's arts festival.

TOURS. Bus tours of the suburbs surrounding Phoenix can be arranged through:

Sun Valley-Grayline Tours, Box 2471, Phoenix 85002, 254–4550, toll-free outside Arizona, (800) 241–3521.

Champagne Cowboy Tours, 4002 N. 85th St., 85252; 998–1020.

Grand Canyon Tours, 1436 E. McNair, Tempe, 85283; 820–9068.

Vaughn's Personalized Southwest Tours, Box 31312, Phoenix, 85046; 971–1381.

MUSEUMS. Champlin Fighter Museum, 4636 Falcon Circle, Falcon Field, Mesa. Open 10 to 5 daily. Admission, $4 for adults; $2 for children. This fine museum features 28 restored World War I and World War II fighter planes, a gift shop, and an art gallery.

Scottsdale Center for the Arts, 7383 Scottsdale Mall, Scottsdale. Open daily 10 to 5. Free exhibitions of major works of art. Traveling exhibits in the gallery, and sculptures around the Scottsdale Mall. Also the finest in performing arts. A classic cinema series is part of what is offered.

ASU Art Museum, Matthews Center, ASU, Tempe; 965–2874. Hispanic and North American art, ceramics, and prints.

AMUSEMENTS AND SCENIC ATTRACTIONS. Apacheland Movie Ranch, off U.S. 60 7 miles east of Apache Junction. Open daily, but call for hours. Old movie set where Westerns and commercials are still being made. Saloon, restaurant, horse rentals, live entertainment on weekends.

Big Surf, 1500 N. Hayden Road, Tempe. Open 11 to 6 Tuesdays through Thursdays, 11 to 10 Fridays and Saturdays, closed Mondays. Man-made beach and wave machine provide swimming, surfing, and other water sports. Also occasional nighttime entertainment. Fee $5, adults; $3, children and seniors.

Rawhide, 23023 N. Scottsdale Road. Open summers, 5 P.M. to midnight, winters, 12 noon to midnight. Replica of an 1890s Western town, complete with blacksmith shop, jail, corral, restaurant, general store, and other shops.

Taliesin West, on 108th Street north of Shea Boulevard, Scottsdale. Open from 10 to 4 October through May, 9 to 10:30 A.M. May through October. Former residence of architect Frank Lloyd Wright, now Wright's Fellowship School of Architecture. Fee $5, adults; $2, children.

Arizona State University, University Drive east of Mill Avenue, Tempe. *Grady Gamage Center for the Performing Arts,* designed by Frank Lloyd Wright at the largest university in the Rocky Mountain area.

PARTICIPANT SPORTS. Tennis. In the Valley of the Sun tennis is played year-round, and many hotels feature tennis courts. Also, every municipality in the valley has free public courts. Contact the local parks and recreation department.

Golf. More than 70 lush resort, private, and public golf courses dot the Valley of the Sun. Some of the better ones in the outlying areas include: *Gold Canyon Ranch,* Apache Junction, tel. 982–9090; *Orange Tree Golf Club,* Phoenix, tel. 948–6100; *San Marcos Country Club,* Chandler, tel. 963–3358; *Fountain Hills Golf Club,* Fountain Hills, tel. 837–1173; *Estrella Mountain Golf Course,* tel. 932–3714; *Tournament Players Club,* Scottsdale, tel. 585–3600; *McCormick Ranch Golf Course,* Scottsdale, tel. 948–0260; *Continental Golf Course,* Scottsdale, tel. 941–5521.

Hiking. A number of mountain parks ring the Valley of the Sun. For information on exploring these unique desert wildernesses, contact the City of Phoenix Parks and Recreation Department, 125 E. Washington, Phoenix, tel. 262–6861, and the Maricopa County Parks and Recreation Department, 4701 E. Washington, Phoenix, tel. 272–8871. Also Tonto National Forest, 2324 E. McDowell Road, Phoenix, tel. 225–5200.

Fishing. Six major lakes are within 60 miles of the Greater Phoenix area, the closest two being Saguaro Lake and Lake Pleasant. For fishing information and licenses, contact the Arizona Game and Fish Department, 2222 W. Greenway Rd., tel. 942–3000.

Hunting. Dove, quail, rabbit, javelina, and other desert animals can be hunted in the areas surrounding the Valley of the Sun. For information and licensing, contact the Arizona Game and Fish Department at the address just given.

Horseback riding. More than 50 stables rent horses in and around Phoenix. Check the Yellow Pages under "Riding Stables" or visit *Horsemen's Park,* 16601 N. Pima Rd., Scottsdale, 85260; 585–3844. A 350-acre equestrian facility with a four-mile cross-country course.

Boating and waterskiing. All nearby lakes have marinas with fishing and pontoon boat rentals, but only Apache Lake Marina rents ski boats. *Lake Pleasant,* 974–1388; *Canyon and Saguaro Lake,* 986–5546; *Apache Lake,* 467–2511; *Roosevelt Lake,* 467–2245.

Ballooning. Several Phoenix area companies offer balloon rides, champagne flights, and instruction for balloon pilot's license throughout the cooler months of the year. *Balloon Voyage,* Tempe, 838–4444, will pick you up, take you to the lift-off site, and drop you off at your hotel after landing. *Unicorn Balloon Company,* Scottsdale, 991–3666, offers sunrise and sunset trips. *Balloon Experience,* Scottsdale, 820–3866, specializes in champagne flights.

Shooting. One of the top ranges in the Southwest, Maricopa County's *Black Canyon Shooting Range and Recreation Area,* just west of the intersection of Black Canyon and Carefree highways, offers air rifle, small bore, high power, pistol, skeet, trap, silhouette, running boar and deer, and archery shooting. Adjacent to the range are 110 camping sites with running water. 582–8313.

Inner tubing. Spend a leisurely day floating down the Salt River northeast of the Greater Phoenix area. The cool blue waters of the Salt sweep you through stunning desert scenery while tubers bask under the warm Arizona sun. During summer months a shuttle bus service takes tubers upriver from their cars and lets them float down. For more information, contact *Salt River Recreation Inc.,* Box 6568, Mesa 85206; 984–3305.

Bicycling. The Valley of the Sun is ringed by bike paths, and over 25 bicycle shops rent by the hour, day, or week. For information on rentals, check the Yellow Pages under "Bicycles." For information on bike paths, contact the Maricopa County Parks and Recreation Department, 272–8871.

Running. The fleet-of-foot favor Indian Bend Wash and the banks of the Grand Canal for jogging. A 10-k run is held nearly every weekend from October through May in the valley. Also two marathons are held during the winter season. For information, call the *Arizona Road Racers Club,* 954–8341.

SPECTATOR SPORTS. Arizona State University Sun Devil intercollegiate sports. In Tempe. For information, call 965–6592.

Parada Del Sol Parade and Rodeo. In Scottsdale each February. For information, call the Scottsdale Jaycees, 990–3179.

Major League baseball spring training. A number of the big league teams train in the Phoenix area February through April. Game time is 1 P.M. For information on game dates, locations, and tickets, call: *Chicago Cubs* at Mesa's Hohokam Park, 964–4467. *Oakland A's* at Phoenix Stadium, 220–0896. *San Francisco Giants* at Scottsdale Stadium, 994–5123. *Milwaukee Brewers* at Compadre Stadium, Chandler, 821–2200. *Seattle Mariners* at Tempe Diablo Stadium, 438–8900.

SHOPPING. The Valley of the Sun is a shopper's paradise for nearly anything at a variety of prices. The valley has thousands of stores and shops in scores of shopping centers and malls. Most are open from 9 or 10 in the morning to 6 or 7 at night, and some until 9 at night, especially on Thursdays. Some of the larger and more interesting shopping areas around the valley include:

The Borgata of Scottsdale. 6166 N. Scottsdale Rd., Scottsdale. Arizona's answer to Rodeo Drive. The most exclusive and elegant shopping in the state, set in a renaissance Italian village.

Camelview Plaza. 6900 E. Camelback Rd., Scottsdale. Rich assortment of specialty shops plus *Sakowitz* and *Bullock's.*

Fiesta Mall. 1445 W. Southern, Mesa. *Sears, Broadway, Goldwaters,* and 140 specialty stores set in a bright, well-organized mall.

Los Arcos Mall. 1315 N. Scottsdale Rd, Scottsdale. Over 80 delightful stores, including *Sears* and *Broadway Southwest,* set in a Southwestern-style mall.

Scottsdale Fashion Square. Scottsdale and Camelback roads. A good variety of top-name stores fill an elegant mall near the heart of Scottsdale.

Downtown Scottsdale: Off Scottsdale Road from Camelback to Osborn roads. On either side of Scottsdale for at least two blocks you will find nearly every type of boutique, craft shop, art gallery, restaurant, and much more. Wear a comfortable pair of shoes.

Valley West Mall. 5719 W. Northern Ave., Glendale. *Boston Store, J. C. Penney, Montgomery Ward, Furr's,* and over 70 other stores.

DINING OUT. Scottsdale benefits from the same influences—proximity to Mexico and a diversity of cuisines brought from other parts of the country—that make Phoenix such a pleasant place to dine, but adds to them an upscale ambience that makes it the premiere area for top-notch cuisine in the Valley of the Sun. Tempe and Mesa offer a few pleasant gastronomic surpises as well.

Our price categories for an average three-course dinner for one, exclusive of drinks, tax, and tip, are: *Deluxe,* $30 and up; *Expensive,* $20 to $30; *Moderate,* $10 to $20; and *Inexpensive,* under $10.

SCOTTSDALE

American

The American Grill. *Expensive.* 6113 N. Scottsdale Rd., 948–9907. As the name suggests, typical grill atmosphere with a fine selection of seafood and regional American dishes.

El Chorro. *Expensive.* 5550 E. Lincoln Dr., 948–5170. Steaks, chateaubriand, rack of lamb served in a comfortable Southwestern dining room by overworked staff.

The Impeccable Pig. *Expensive.* 7042 E. Indian School Rd., 941–1141. Happy amalgam of antique shop and restaurant. The service is amusingly outrageous.

The Other Place. *Moderate.* 7101 E. Lincoln Dr., 948–7910. Good steak and seafood. The adobe decor is uncontrived and the young staff hustles. The no reservations policy can be a problem during peak hours.

International

Chaparral Room. *Deluxe.* Camelback Inn, 5402 E. Lincoln Dr., 948–1700. One of the finest restaurants in the country. Continental cuisine served by a letter-perfect staff.

Palm Court. *Deluxe.* Scottsdale Conference Resort, 7700 E. McCormick Pkwy., 991–3400. Elegant old-world service. Classic Continental dishes with an emphasis on tableside preparation.

Golden Swan. *Expensive.* Hyatt Regency Scottsdale at Gainey Ranch, 7500 E. Doubletree Ranch Rd., 991–3388. This sedate, lovely room is a perfect foil for an exciting bill of fare that mixes international and Southwestern cuisines.

The Terraces at Gainey Ranch. *Moderate.* 7600 Gainey Club Dr., 998–0733. Pretty fancy for a golf club. The inspired food is enough to to make you lay down your 9-iron.

French

La Chaumière. *Deluxe.* 6910 Main St., 946–5115. Warm, intimate, Breton ambience. Sophisticated service and classic French food.

Le Relais. *Deluxe.* 8711 E. Pinnacle Peak Rd., 998–0921. A world-class establishment featuring a million-dollar European art collection and the talents of a chef worth at least that much. Not to be missed.

Chez Claude. *Moderate.* 10339 N. Scottsdale Rd., 951–3056. A charmer in all respects. Small and intimate, with super service and fine country-French cuisine.

Petit Cafe. *Moderate.* 7340 E. Shoeman Ln., 947–5288. Clean, contemporary surroundings. The staff is as consistently warm as the food.

Italian

Ambrosino's. *Moderate.* 2122 N. Scottsdale Rd., 994–8404. Exterior looks like a Vegas casino. It's less gaudy inside, and the menu runs the gamut from soothing Northern specialties to spicy Southern Italian ones.

Mexican

Eduardo's. *Inexpensive.* 4949 E. Lincoln Dr., 840–4650. Looks like a Hollywood stage set for the Alamo. The food is on the mild side and portions are generous.

Los Olivos. *Inexpensive.* 7328 2nd St., 946–2256. Scottsdale landmark. The building is sort of Aztec-deco and the food is remarkably consistent.

Moroccan

The Moroccan. *Moderate.* 4228 N. Scottsdale Rd., 947–9590. Authentic music, belly dancing, exciting food. It's a terrific package for the money.

Oriental

Trader Vic's. *Expensive.* 7111 E. 5th Ave., 945–6341. Local branch of the venerable chain is tightly run. Lodgehouse decor and reliable food. Chinese smoked dishes are a good bet.

Daa's Thai Room. *Moderate.* 7419 E. Indian Plaza, 941–9015. One of the best of the many Thai restaurants in town. It's pretty, the staff will help the uninitiated, and the food will knock your socks off.

Eddy Chan's. *Moderate.* 9699 N. Hayden Rd., 998–8188. Sophisticated Oriental ambience. Food is on the tame side.

Restaurant Fuji. *Moderate.* 9301 E. Shea Blvd., 860–9066. One of the best Japanese restaurants around. Meticulous care goes into every facet of the operation. Sushi is marvelous. The special dinner for two is once-in-a-lifetime stuff.

Seafood

The Salt Cellar. *Expensive.* 550 N. Hayden Rd., 947–1963. Cozy, underground establishment. The seafood is invariably fresh and carefully prepared.

Trappers. *Moderate.* 3518 N. Scottsdale Rd., 990–9256. Extra pleasant atmosphere and staff. Seafood heads the list with beef dishes a close second.

Southwestern

8700 at the Citadel. *Deluxe.* 8700 Pinnacle Peak Rd., 994–8700. Gorgeous, understated Southwestern decor. Imaginative food and good service. An after-dinner drink in the bar upstairs buys a great view.

Coyote Cafe. *Moderate.* 7373 E. Scottsdale Mall, 947–7081. One of a ring of shops surrounding the Scottsdale Center for the Arts. The Coyote offers patio dining and some of the most impeccably prepared food in town from a menu that changes weekly. The service is outstanding.

Steak

The Golden Belle at Rawhide. Scottsdale Rd., four miles north of Bell, 563–5111. Excellent ribs and steaks, as well as mountain oysters and rattlesnake for macho types.

MESA/TEMPE

American

Paradise Bar and Grill. *Moderate.* 401 S. Mill, Tempe, 829–0606. Terrific atmosphere, with everything from snacks to prime rib to seafood.

El Charro. *Inexpensive.* 105 N. Country Club Dr., Mesa, 964–1851. A local favorite, spacious and noisy. The food is reliable.

T.C. Eggington's. *Inexpensive.* 1660 S. Alma School Rd., Mesa, 345–9288. A cutesy breakfast and lunch stop, with egg dishes a specialty.

Mexican

Julio's. *Inexpensive.* 1264 W. University, Mesa, 964–7671. A spacious, family-oriented Sonoran joint.

Oriental

Char's. *Inexpensive.* 45 W. Broadway, Mesa, 833–0515, and 927 E. University, Tempe, 967–6013. The oldest and best Thai restaurants in the Valley.

NIGHTLIFE. Scottsdale is filled with night spots offering a variety of entertainment experiences. A few of the more interesting ones are:

Anderson's Fifth Estate. 6820 5th Ave., 994–4168. New Wave and comedy.

Lonnegan's. 7436 E. McDowell Rd., 947–3304. Fun rock-and-roll with a young crowd.

West LA. 1420 N. Scottsdale Rd., 949–7933. Huge, glitzy nightclub with disco music and a young crowd.

Tempe and **Mesa** attract the college crowd and a little older. Some of the better spots are:

Bandersnatch. 125 E. 5th St., Tempe, 966–4438. Two blocks east of Old Town. A casual, friendly bar and restaurant. Two good house ales are also brewed here.

Chuy's. 310 S. Mill, Tempe, 820–8971. The best jazz club and the best jazz entertainment in the valley. The place cooks seven nights a week.

New Yorker Club. 107 E. Broadway, 967–2941. Great blues in a casual but nice atmosphere.

Studebaker's. 705 S. Rural Rd. (in the Cornerstone Mall), 829–8495. A place for the late 20s to mid-40s group to play. Classic rock and roll and disco with nostalgia thrown in. No one under 25 admitted.

Utopio. 919 E. Apache Blvd., Tempe, 921–9776. Features hot new national acts.

TUCSON

Tucson, one of the rapidly growing cities in the Sun Belt, has managed nonetheless to keep its distinctive Southwestern flavor and preserve some of its colorful history. This picturesque city, whose center was built on a gentle slope, is Arizona's oldest population center occupied by people of European extraction.

The first white man to visit the site was Father Eusebio Francisco Kino, a Jesuit missionary, during his first exploration in 1687. It was the availability of water from the now usually dry Santa Cruz River that made the Spaniards decide to settle there.

In the next century, the Spaniards established a *presidio,* a walled city, to offer protection for the settlers against the marauding Indian tribes. One small section of that wall is preserved under glass on the second floor of the Pima County courthouse in downtown Tucson. In 1776, the Spanish fortified their territory in Arizona by assigning a strong garrison to the presidio.

Tucson's name comes from an Indian word *Stjukshon,* meaning "spring at the foot of a black mountain." The city is virtually surrounded by mountains—the Santa Catalinas to the north, the Rincons on the east, the Santa Ritas on the south, and the Tucson mountains on the west. The main part of the city is at an altitude of 2,410 feet, about 1,100 feet higher than Phoenix.

After Mexicans threw off the yoke of Spain in 1821, Tucson became part of Mexico. It became part of the United States through the Gadsden Purchase in 1854. During the Civil War, it was declared part of the Confederacy but later became federal territory when Union forces arrived from

California in 1863. Thus four flags have flown over Tucson, also known as the Old Pueblo from its days as a presidio.

Tucson served as the capital of Arizona from 1867 to 1877, when it was moved back to Prescott, a move made because pioneer Arizonans thought there was still too much sympathy in Tucson for the Confederacy.

The territorial legislature established the University of Arizona there. For a long time, Tucson residents were miffed about this because they wanted a state prison. The land for the university was donated by a saloon-keeper and two gamblers in 1886. Classes began in 1891, and the university started out as a school of agriculture but added arts and sciences, a college of law, and, most recently, a school of medicine where important research is being done on cancer and heart surgery.

It is because of the university that Tucson has a town-and-gown atmosphere, in contrast with the more commercial tone of Phoenix.

Tucson, which has a slightly cooler climate than that of Phoenix because of its higher altitude, also experienced explosive growth as a result of World War II.

Davis-Monthan Air Force Base was located there, along with other flying training fields such as Marana, where the Solar Challenger, a sun-powered aircraft, made its first successful flight.

Besides the air base, Tucson's economic support comes from tourism; the university; branches of government; industries such as IBM, Hughes Aircraft, and Gates Learjet; plus agriculture and mining. High-tech is Tucson's biggest industry.

Located only 60 miles from the Mexican border, Tucson has a large population of Hispanic and Indian people. In fact, some of the oldest and most influential families in Tucson are of Mexican ancestry. The Mexican and Indian cultures have endured and can be seen virtually everywhere in arts and crafts, architecture, and foods.

Experiencing Tucson firsthand is a visitor's delight. The only difficulties you will have are deciding what to see and finding the time to do it all.

A Walking Tour of Central Tucson

The best way to see this compact city is by walking around it. Begin your tour in the center of town at La Placita Village, which combines modern shops and offices with nineteenth-century historic sites like the Samaniego house, once the residence of civic leader Mariano G. Samaniego; the El Charro building; the Plaza of the Two Fountains; and an 1860s street called Calle de La India Triste (the sad Indian girl).

Southern Pacific Park is a few blocks to the east along Congress Street. Built on this site was the first SP railway station in Tucson.

Next stop is to the north several blocks. Take Granada to Paseo Redondo and see the Manning house, a white adobe mansion with a domed entrance on the south side of the structure—a nineteenth-century classic.

To the west, along Redondo and across Main, in an area scribed by Pennington on the south, Church on the west, Washington on the north, and Main on the east, you enter what once was the original walled city of the Old Pueblo. The past is alive here at every turn.

El Presidio Park is on the southern section of the original walled city site. It was selected as a military garrison by the Royal Spanish Army in 1775.

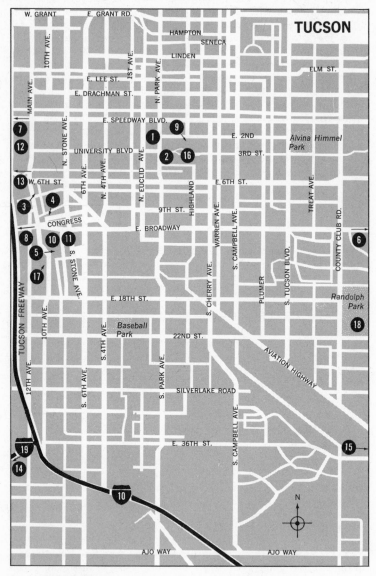

TUCSON

Points of Interest

1) Arizona Historical Society
2) Arizona State Museum
3) Art Center
4) City Hall
5) Community Center
6) Colossal Cave
7) Desert Museum
8) Garden of Gethsemane
9) Mineralogical Museum
10) Music Hall
11) Old Adobe
12) Old Tucson
13) Pima College
14) San Xavier Mission
15) Tucson Botanical Gardens
16) University of Arizona
17) Wishing Well
18) Zoo

In the shaded northwest corner of the Tucson City Hall grounds nearby is the Kino Memorial, dedicated to Father Eusebio Francisco Kino (1645–1711), Jesuit missionary and explorer.

Nearby is the home of Edward Nye Fish and, next door, that of his friend Hiram Sanford Stevens. The Fish house, built in 1868, occupies the site of the old Presidio barracks. The merchant's adobe home has walls two feet thick and a roof supported by huge beams laced with saguaro ribs. For years the Fish and Stevens homes were the social center of town.

The Tucson Museum of Art complex is situated in the northern portion of the Presidio, the Plaza Militar. Included in the complex are a contemporary gallery, art school, and five historic adobe structures.

Part of the complex is what may be the oldest surviving building in Tucson. La Casa Cordova has recently been restored as the Mexican Heritage Museum. The adobe structure is listed in the National Register of Historic Places.

Here, too, is the Romero House, built about 1868 over part of the original Presidio wall. At the corner of Washington and Main is a plaque marking the northwest corner of the wall.

At 182 North Court is another old adobe, this one built in 1874. It has saguaro rib ceilings, corner fireplaces, and, in the patio, a fig tree said to be a century old.

To the south, across Alameda, is the Pima County Courthouse, at the east end of Presidio Park. Its dome is a color-filled mosaic of inlaid tiles. There's also an interior court and fountain.

Immediately north of the Old Wall section is the El Presidio Historic District, where other old Territorial homes drowse in the sun.

The Sam Hughes house, across Washington Street, is currently a series of apartments. The original structure dates back to 1864.

On the west side of Main stands the Albert Steinfeld house, built in 1900. Steinfeld was a well-to-do merchant, and his brick-stucco home, designed by architect Henry Trost, reflects his affluent tastes in a Spanish Mission style.

Nearby, at Main and Franklin, Rosalie Verdugo built her home in 1877. East on Franklin is the McCleary house, constructed in 1880, reflecting Tucson's Mexican-American heritage. To the west, at Franklin and Church, Gustav Anton Hoff, who became a mayor of Tucson, built a home, today little changed from the original except for the roof, which may have been the typical flat style of Territorial adobes.

El Charro, on Court, is constructed of dark stone from Sentinel Peak. It has long been a favorite Tucson restaurant. Created in 1900, its original owner was a French stonemason.

At Church Avenue and Jackson is the Old Adobe Patio, built in 1868. Part of the Charles O. Brown house, the restored Territorial now belongs to the Arizona Historical Society.

About two or three blocks farther south is St. Augustine Cathedral, begun in 1896. The beautiful white adobe covers an entire city block. It is modeled after a cathedral in Queretaro, Mexico.

West and south of the old church is Barrio Viejo (the old neighborhood), now being redeveloped in its original style of the 1880s for contemporary use.

Here, too, is the Montijo house, built during the Civil War (see Practical Information); the Cushing Street Bar and Restaurant, once part of the hundred-year-old Joseph Ferrin house, now furnished in 1880s style; and the America West Gallery, the town home of a Spanish rancher about 120 years ago. (See Practical Information.)

On the north side of Cushing Street, you complete your walking tour at the new $18 million Community Center complex. It includes a sports arena, concert hall, and convention center. The John C. Fremont house, built in the 1850s, is preserved within the complex.

PRACTICAL INFORMATION FOR TUCSON

HOW TO GET THERE. By air. Tucson is served by most major airlines, including *Aeromexico, Alaska, America West, American, Braniff, Delta, Eastern, Northwest, TWA, United* and *USAir.*

By bus. *Greyhound-Trailways* serves Tucson. For reservations and information call toll-free, 800–531–5332.

By train. *Amtrak* serves Tucson. For information and reservations, call Amtrak's toll-free number, 800–USA–RAIL.

By car. *Interstate 10* traverses the southern tier of Arizona from El Paso, Texas, and Las Cruces, New Mexico, through Tucson to Casa Grande, where Interstate 8 takes over for the trip to California via Gila Bend and Yuma. I-10 goes north to the Phoenix area, then west to Blythe, California. *Interstate 19* runs south from Tucson to the Arizona-Mexico border.

IMPORTANT TELEPHONE NUMBERS. To make your stay more pleasant, here is a list of service and information numbers:

Department of Public Safety (weather and road conditions), 294–3113.
Tourist Information, 624–1889.
Fire, Medical or Police Emergencies, 911.
Poison Control, 800–362–0101.
Police Information, 791–4452.
Crime Prevention, 882–7463.
Weather, 623–4000.
Employment Information, 628–5613.
Community Information and Referral Services, 881–1794.
Crisis Counseling, 323–9373.
Chamber of Commerce Information, 792–1212.
City Hall Information, 791–4911.
Marriage Licenses, 882–2710.
Road Conditions, 294–3113.
Animal Control Center Information: Dog Bites, 743–7550.
Travelers Aid of Tucson, 622–8900.
Southern Arizona Legal Aid, 623–9461.
Libraries, Info-line, 791–4010.
Parks and Recreation: City Parks, 791–4873; County Parks, 882–2690.
Senior Citizens: Aging Adult Protective Services, 628–5876; Medicare (Social Security), 800–352–5488.
Hospitals: El Dorado Hospital & Medical Center, 1400 N. Wilmot Rd., 886–6361; Northwest Hospital, 6200 N. La Cholla, 742–9000; Tucson

General Hospital, 3838 N. Campbell, 327–5431; University Medical Center, 1501 N. Campbell, 626–0111; St. Joseph's Hospital, 350 N. Wilmot, 296–3211.

Ambulance: Air Ambulance Network, Inc., 800–327–1966; Kord's Ambulance Service, 795–1211; Metro Medic, 795–5721.

HOTELS AND MOTELS. From the ultimate in luxury to the Western atmosphere of guest ranches, Tucson offers the best in comfort and service. Most of the hotels and motels are equipped with swimming pools and sun patios.

The primary types of lodging are resorts, small inns or guest lodges, guest ranches, resort hotels, and trailer parks. (See information on guest ranches in the *Facts at Your Fingertips* section.)

Cost figures are for in-season rates and double-occupancy rooms, with reductions of 25 to 50 percent out of season. Some resorts and dude ranches operate on the American plan (meals included with price of room), though there is a trend away from strict AP rates lately. Listings are in order of price categories. A lodging tax, which varies, is added to all accommodation bills.

The price categories in this section will average as follows: *Super Deluxe,* $100 and up; *Deluxe,* $80 to $100; *Expensive,* $60 to $80; *Moderate,* $40 to $60; and *Inexpensive,* under $40. For a more complete description of those categories, see *Facts at Your Fingertips.*

Super Deluxe

Arizona Inn. 2200 E. Elm St., 85719; 325–1541. Nicely appointed rooms, suites, and bungalows. Putting green. Pets allowed. Tennis. Children's playground and pool. Handicapped facilities.

Hacienda del Sol Ranch Resort. 5601 N. Hacienda del Sol Rd., 85718; 299–1501. Located in the beautiful Catalina Mountain foothills. Jacuzzi, horseback riding, putting green, exercise center.

Lazy K Bar Guest Ranch. 8401 N. Scenic Dr., 85743; 297–0702. Guests are met at points of arrival. Tennis, horseback riding. Open September through June.

Loews Ventana Canyon Resort. 7000 N. Resort Dr., 85715; 299–2020. Two pools. Dining Room. Lounge. Golf, tennis. Handicapped facilities.

Sheraton Tucson El Conquistador. 10000 N. Oracle Rd., 85704; 742–7000. Spanish/Mexican atmosphere. Coffee shop/dining room. Golf, tennis, horseback riding, health spa. Boutiques. Handicapped facilities.

Tanque Verde Guest Ranch. Route 8, Box 66, 85748; 296–6275. Indoor and outdoor pools. Putting green. Ranch activities. Playground. Horseback riding. Tennis. Whirlpool bath.

Westin La Paloma. 3800 E. Sunrise Dr., 85718; 742–6000. New. Located in the Santa Catalina foothills. Spanish mission design. Twenty-seven-hole golf course designed by Jack Nicklaus. Tennis, racquetball, jogging/cycling trails.

White Stallion Ranch. 9251 W. Twin Peaks Rd., 85743; 297–0252. Three thousand acres of horseback riding. Rodeos, therapy pool, cookouts, hay rides, tennis. Open October through April. No credit cards.

Deluxe

Best Western Inn at the Airport. 7060 S. Tucson Blvd., 85706; 746–0271. Golf and tennis nearby. Guest laundry. Jacuzzi, heated pool.

Airport transportation. Restaurant. Shopping nearby. Handicapped facilities.

Doubletree Hotel. 445 S. Alvernon Way, 85711; 881–4200. Pleasant rooms. Coffee shop/restaurant. Jacuzzi. Pets allowed. Tennis, golf.

Embassy Suites. 7051 S. Tucson Blvd., 85706; 573–0700. Very pleasant surroundings. Nonsmoking rooms available. Pool, Jacuzzi, exercise room. Complimentary breakfast and cocktails. Handicapped facilities.

Embassy Suites. 5335 E. Broadway, 85711; 745–2700. Nice rooms. Complimentary breakfast and cocktails.

Tucson Hilton East. 7600 E. Broadway, 85710; 721–5600. One of Tucson's newest and most luxurious hotels. Access to nearby golf and tennis.

Expensive

Americana Hotel de Tucson. 1601 N. Oracle, 85705; 624–8541. Well-appointed rooms. Golf and tennis nearby. Handicapped facilities.

Best Western Aztec Inn. 102 N. Alvernon Way, 85711; 795–0330. Suites with kitchenettes. Large pool. Dining room. No pets allowed.

Best Western Tucson InnSuites. 6201 N. Oracle Rd., 85704; 297–8111. Kitchenettes. Complimentary breakfast and cocktails. Jacuzzi, tennis. Laundry facilities. Handicapped facilities.

Chateau Apartment Hotel. 1402 N. Alvernon Way, 85712; 323–7121. Daily or weekly rates. One bedroom suites. Kitchens. Pets allowed. Handicapped facilities.

Days Inn Downtown. 88 E. Broadway, 85701; 791–7581. Jacuzzi/saunas. Complimentary golf and tennis. Restaurant.

Holiday Inn-Holidome. 4550 S. Palo Verde Blvd., 85714; 746–1161. Lighted tennis courts, exercise room. Restaurant. Shopping nearby. Airport transportation available. Handicapped facilities.

Holiday Inn-Tucson North. 1365 W. Grant Rd., 85705; 622–7791. Restaurant/cocktail lounge. Pool. Playground. In-room movies.

The Lodge on the Desert. Box 42500, 85733; 325–3366. At 306 N. Alvernon Way. Adobe buildings, some fireplaces. Pool. Dining room. Cocktails. Handicapped facilities.

Plaza Hotel. 1900 E. Speedway Blvd., 85719; 327–7341. Kitchenettes with refrigerators. Garage. Dining room and lounge. Handicapped facilities.

Quality Inn Tanque Verde. 7007 E. Tanque Verde Rd., 85715; 298–2300. Part of chain. Jacuzzi. Complimentary continental breakfast and cocktails.

Quality Inn Airport. 6801 S. Tucson Blvd., 85706; 746–3932. Heated pool. Jacuzzi. Restaurant and lounge.

Ramada Downtown. 404 N. Freeway, 85705; 624–8341. Suites with kitchens. Playground. Pets allowed. Olympic pool. Cafe, bakery, lounge.

Ramada Inn-Foothills. 6944 E. Tanque Verde Rd., 85715; 886–9595. Deluxe rooms and luxury suites. Complimentary cocktails and breakfast. Pool. Spa.

Villa Serenas Apartments. 8111 E. Broadway, 85710; 886–5537. Tennis, golf nearby. Sauna/Jacuzzi. Shopping nearby. Handicapped facilities.

Moderate

Cliff Manor Motor Inn. 5900 N. Oracle Rd., 85704; 887–4000. Spa. Satellite television. Beauty salon. Golf, tennis. Cocktail lounge. Coffee shop.

Continental Inn Tucson. 750 W. 22nd St., 85713; 624–4455. Therapy pool. Coffee shop. Weight room. Handicapped facilities.

La Quinta Motor Inn. 665 N. Freeway, 86745; 622–6491. HBO. Non-smoker rooms. Handicapped facilities.

Skytel TraveLodge. 2803 E. Valencia Rd., 85706; 294–2500. Cable TV. Heated pool. Spa. Airport transportation.

Tucson Airport Howard Johnson's. 1025 E. Benson Hwy, 85713; 623–7792. Airport service. Family plan. Courtyard. Saunas. Guest laundry. Pets allowed.

Wayward Winds Lodge. 707 W. Miracle Mile, 85705; 791–7526. Kitchenettes. Shuffleboard courts. Pool.

Inexpensive

Copper Cactus Inn. 225 W. Drachman, 85705; 622–7411. Kitchenettes. Pool. Pets allowed.

Desert Inn. Adjacent to I-10, at Congress St. exit, 85745; 624–8151. Cable TV. Heated pool. 24-hour coffee shop.

Franciscan Inn. 1165 N. Stone Ave., 85705; 622–7763. Clean rooms. Pool. Pets allowed.

Lamp Post Motel and Apartments. 5451 E. 30th St., 85711; 790–6021. Kitchenettes. Pool. Available on day, week, or month basis.

Lazy 8 Motel. 314 E. Benson Hwy., 85743; 622–3336. Pool.

Motel 6. 1031 E. Benson Hwy, 85713; 628–1264. Clean rooms.

Regal 8 Inn. 1222 S. Freeway, 85705; 624–2516. Close to shopping and golf course. Pool. Handicapped facilities.

Super Eight Motel. 4950 S. Outlet Center Dr., 85714; 746–0030. 121 units. Pool. Restaurant.

Tucson Inn Motor Hotel. 127 W. Drachman, 85705; 624–8531. Clean rooms.

Vista Del Sol Motel. 1458 W. Miracle Mile, 85705; 293–9270. Near shopping, restaurants.

HOW TO GET AROUND. By taxi. Some taxi companies in the Tucson area: *The Arizona Stagecoach* (airport shuttle), 889–9681; *Allstate Cab Company,* 881–2227; *Yellow Cab,* 624-6611; *Checker Cab,* 623–1133.

By bus. *Sun Tran* operates a citywide bus service from 6 A.M. to 7 P.M., with a few buses running till 9 P.M. The fare is 60¢, exact change required, and passes are available to seniors and students. Call 792–9222 for information; a map is available from Sun Tran, 4220 S. Park, Tucson, 85714.

By car. The best, most flexible way to get around southeastern Arizona. The nearest rental agencies are in Tucson. Toll-free numbers: *Hertz,* 800–654–3131; *Avis,* 800–331–1212. There are also several national and local agencies whose rates may be more competitive.

Tucson is a relatively easy town in which to find your way around. The streets are set up in a grid system running north–south and east–west, with few winding streets or confusing intersections. Some of the main east–west arteries running off the freeway (I-10) are Ina, Orange Grove, Prince, Grant, Speedway, 6th Street and Broadway. North-south arteries include Thornydale, Shannon, Oracle Road, Stone, Kino, Country Club, Alvernon, Swan, Craycroft, Wilmot, and Kolb.

As a city without a freeway system (Interstate 10 swings through the west and south parts of town), most driving is stop-and-go all day downtown and on main arteries during rush hours (7 to 9 A.M. and 4 to 6 P.M.). But a traffic jam in Tucson is mild in comparison with other cities. The outlying areas of the city are easy to get around in and make for delightful scenic drives. The foothills areas north and east of town are prime examples.

Parking is ample in all but the downtown and university areas. Most malls and businesses have parking. Downtown and the university have parking meters, but spaces are usually at a premium and restricted times are enforced.

TOURIST INFORMATION. There are *Arizona Tourist Information Centers* in Tucson (watch for the blue-and-white signs along I-10). These centers are brochure heaven, with information on every part of the state. The centers are also staffed with knowledgeable, helpful employees to answer your questions. For more information, contact the *Arizona Office of Tourism,* 1480 E. Bethany Home Rd., Phoenix 85014, 542–3618; or the *Metropolitan Tucson Convention and Visitors Bureau,* 130 S. Scott Ave., Tucson 85701; 624–1889.

RECOMMENDED READING. Would you like to know a little more about this city during your visit? Here are some books that are interesting and readable to add to your collection.

The Land of Journey's Ending. Mary Austin. University of Arizona Press. 45 pp. First published in 1924, Austin's perspective on the Southwest is still a vibrant work. The region provided a perfect backdrop for her interests, including history, anthropology, art, and folklore.

Father Eusebio Francisco Kino and His Missions of the Pimeria Alta. Book One: *The Side Altars,* 1982; Book Two: *The Main Altars,* 1983. Book Three: *Facing the Missions,* 1983. Southwest Mission Research Center, available from Cabat Studio, 627 N. Fourth Ave., Tucson 85705. $5 each, plus $1.50 mailing; set of three, $17.50 plus $1.50 mailing. Tucson artist Ernie Cabat provides a different look at the Kino Mission through his impressionist paintings executed between 1975 and 1983. The brief text was written by Jesuit historian Charles Polzer.

Life on the Tanque Verde, Book One: *The History.* 1983. 32 pp. $5.95. More paintings by Cabat and a text written by Charlotte M. Cardon, Tucson archaeologist and journalist on the historic Tanque Verde Ranch area.

Arizona Adventure: Action-Packed True Tales of Early Arizona. Marshall Trimble. Golden West Publishers, 4113 N. Longview Ave., Phoenix 85014. 1982. 160 pp. $5. Packed into one volume are stories of people and places, from Coronado and Anza to Buckey O'Neill and Tom Horn; from Tombstone and Pleasant Valley to Flagstaff and Prescott. The text is accompanied by small black-and-white photos of most of the people mentioned, as well as maps, a selective bibliography, and an index.

Indian Baskets of the Southwest. Clara Lee Tanner. University of Arizona Press. 256 pp. $40.95. Discover the world of weaving as practiced by the Hopis, Pimas, Papagoes, Yumans, Navajos, Utes and Paiutes, and Chemehuevis. More than 400 illustrations.

Pioneer Heritage, C. L. Sonnichsen, Arizona Historical Society, Tucson 1984. $15. An interesting look into those pioneers who settled in Arizona.

Early Arizona: Prehistory to Civil War. Jay J. Wagoner. University of Arizona Press, Tucson, 1975.

SEASONAL EVENTS. The Tucson area offers an uncommonly rich and diverse schedule of events throughout the year—far too many to list here. Only the major sporting events, fairs, fiestas, and public celebrations are included. For a more complete listing with specific dates and times, contact the Metropolitan Tucson Convention and Visitors Bureau, 130 S. Scott Ave., Tuscon 85701; 624–1889. Also provided are local numbers of the events headquarters, which can be called for specific information.

January. *The American Hot Rod Association Winter Nationals* is held at the Tucson Dragway. 885–1291.

Southern Arizona Square and Round Dance Festival is a four-day gathering at the Tucson Community Center for square and round dance enthusiasts from across the state. 791–4101.

Sun Country Circuit Quarterhorse Show is one of the largest quarterhorse shows in the country, featuring halter, Western pleasure, and roping. The show is held at the Pima County Fairgrounds. 624–1013.

February. *Tucson Gem and Mineral Show* at the Tucson Community Center features some of the world's finest gems and minerals. It is the largest show of its kind in the world, attracting thousands of enthusiasts. 791–4101.

Tucson Winter Classic Horse Show and Michelob Grand Prix World Cup at the Pima County Fairgrounds is a competition of more than 500 horses for $100,000 in prize money. 624–1013.

La Fiesta De Los Vaqueros is the biggest mid-winter rodeo in America. And the world's largest nonmechanized parade begins the four-day event held at the Tucson Rodeo Grounds. 792–2283.

March. *The Annual Southern Arizona Livestock Show and Sale* is one of the largest exhibitions in the Southwest, with hundreds of head of cattle exhibited at the Pima County Fairgrounds. 624–1013.

Circle K LPGA Tuscon Open. The finest women golfers in the world compete in this tournament held at Randolph Golf Course. 296–3555.

Taste of Tucson is a culinary festival spotlighting local restaurants. It is usually held in March or April at the Tucson Community Center. 882–3507.

Mt. Lemmon Ski Carnival, at Ski Valley, features costumes, contests, and races on skis. 576–1321.

Annual Wa:k Pow Wow Conference, adjacent to San Xavier Mission. Modern and traditional intertribal singing and dancing is performed by many Southwestern tribes. 622–6911.

April. *The Pima County Fair* is held at the Pima County Fairgrounds, with ten-days of rides, games, exhibits, and other entertainment. 624–1013.

International Mariachi Conference, held at the Tucson Community Center, is a four-day cultural, educational, and entertainment experience for mariachi musicians and those who enjoy mariachi music. 791–4101.

May. *Cinco De Mayo* is a Mexican holiday commemorating Mexico's independence. The four-day fiesta is held at Kennedy Park. 791–4873.

Southern Arizona Arabian Horse Jubilee is held at the Pima County Fairgrounds. 624–1013.

June. *Tucson Summer Arts Festival* is a celebration of arts and culture, held through mid-August, at the University of Arizona. 624–1889.

July. *Fourth of July Celebration* is a down-home celebration featuring traditional fireworks, parades, and picnics. 791–4873.

August. *La Fiesta De San Augustín* is a Mexican celebration honoring St. Augustine. The fiesta is held at the Arizona Heritage Center. 628–5774.

September. *Loggers Jubilee* is held at Mt. Lemmon Ski Valley and is a weekend full of various lumberjack competitions. It is usually held the third week in September. 576–1321.

Labor Day Golf Tournament, held in Douglas, is the oldest invitational golf tournament in Arizona. 364–3722

Mexican Independence Day is celebrated with a traditional fiesta at Kennedy Park. 620–1077.

October. *Tucson Meet Yourself* is held at El Presidio Park to celebrate the richness and diversity of Tucson's various ethnic cultures. Ethnic traditions, food, dance, and crafts are featured. 621–3392.

Northern Telecom Tucson Open hosts top PGA golfers at The Tournament Players Club at StarPass. 792–4501.

Oktoberfest is held the first two weeks of the month at Mt. Lemmon Ski Valley. It features German food, display booths, and arts and crafts. 576–1321.

Blues Festival, at Reid Park, features popular and regional blues musicians. 791–4079.

November. *Michelob Golden Eagle/Continental Rugby Classic,* at Reid Park, is a three-day tournament consisting of 72 matches. 327–7948.

Indian Arts and Crafts Show and Sale, at the Tucson Community Center. 791–4101.

December. *Territorial Holidays,* the annual exhibit at the Fremont House Museum, is a Victorian holiday setting complete with antique toys and ornaments inside the museum. 622–0956.

El Nacimiento, a dazzling rendition of the Mexican nativity scene, incorporates more than 100 figurines. Held at Casa Cordova. 624–2333.

TOURS. With so much to see in and around Tucson, it may be a good idea to sketch out a rough outline of what you want to see in a day and allot enough time to enjoy thoroughly the historical richness Tucson has to offer.

First is **Sabino Canyon,** located in the Santa Catalina Mountains. The canyon is an oasis of contradictions. It offers visitors such opposites as cacti and trees, desert sand and flowing water. You can also enjoy the abundant wildlife living in the canyon and surrounding mountains.

A good way to see the canyon is a ride on the open-air *shuttle bus.* You can get off at any of the designated stops and have a picnic, enjoy a hike, or marvel at the view. Tickets for the bus are purchased at the Visitor Center, which also has National Forest Service naturalists on hand to give you information on the canyon.

A favorite visitor tour is one that takes the inquisitive through the **heart of Tucson.** The *self-guided walking tour* encompasses the area within and immediately surrounding the Presidio of San Augustin del Tucson and pauses at all periods of Tucson history, from a prehistoric Indian dwelling to the most modern of art galleries.

Visit the John C. Fremont House, "Casa del Gobernador," built by a family in the 1850s, which later became the residence of the fifth territorial governor, or glance at the rustic 182 N. Court residence, which was deeded to Soledad Jacome in 1874. The two front rooms constitute the original adobe, built between 1862 and 1875, with saguaro rib ceilings and corner fireplaces.

It is a humbling yet thrilling experience to think that padres, Indians, soldiers, and Mexican colonials have all walked these same roads and by-ways. Along the way, a foot-weary modern-day adventurer can rest at park benches, restaurants, and grassy knolls. A tour pamphlet can be had by calling or writing to the *Metropolitan Tucson Convention and Visitors Bureau,* 130 S. Scott Ave., Tucson 85701, 624–1889.

If you'd rather leave the driving to someone else, Tucson has several tour companies that let you see the country from different points of view.

Gray Line Bus Tours offers a variety of day tours as well as seasonal overnight excursions. 622–8811.

Mountain View Transportation arranges half-day excursions in open-air jeeps. 622–4488.

How about a little high that's not harmful to the body? Try *Fox Balloon Adventures.* It is hot-air ballooning at its best. Tours are given seven days a week. 886–9191.

Wild Horizons organizes nature and photography safaris guided by pros. No strenuous hiking involved. 622–0672.

Sandpainter Guided Tours offer expeditions into Tucson's Sonoran Desert and historic districts. 323–9290.

PARKS. Tucson is surrounded by four mountain ranges—the Santa Catalinas on the north, the Rincons on the east, the Santa Ritas on the south, and the Tucson Mountains on the west.

Besides the beautiful vistas and clean air, the **Santa Catalinas,** located in the Coronado National Forest, offer a variety of activities throughout the year. *Mount Lemmon* is the Catalinas highest peak—9,157 feet high—almost 7,000 feet off the desert floor. As you climb, you pass through five life zones. These zones become evident as the vegetation changes from desert shrub and cactus at the base to pinon and fir at the top (this same change of flora would be evident if you were driving from Mexico to the Canadian border).

Mt. Lemmon boasts *Mt. Lemmon Ski Valley* —the southernmost ski area on the North American continent. A ski lift at the 8,200-foot elevation can take you to the 9,100-foot elevation for a breathtaking view of the San Pedro Valley. Temperatures up here are usually 30 degrees cooler than in Tucson.

If you forgot your skis, there is a rental shop and retail shop with many skiers' accessories available.

And if you're not too sure those little slats of wood can carry you down the slopes, the ski school has a competent staff of patient instructors. Mt. Lemmon's many slopes range from beginner to expert in level of difficulty, and from a couple of hundred yards to three-quarters of a mile in length.

There is also *Bear Canyon Recreation Area* in the Catalinas. A wonderful sight awaits you after about a two-mile hike past the recreation area— *Seven Falls,* one of the most often visited places in the "backcountry."

The **Rincon Mountains** offer the visitor a most extraordinary sight— *Colossal Cave.* It is the largest dry cave in the world, formed from limestone millions of years ago by the action of seeping water. It is unknown how far into the mountain the cave goes. The cave maintains a constant temperature of 72 degrees. There are guided tours into the cave's chambers and passageways.

It seems that birds of a feather flock together. Especially in the **Santa Rita Mountains' Madera Canyon.** Bird-watchers from around the world flock to this canyon, which is home to more than 200 species of birds, including some seen nowhere else in the United States.

Madera Canyon is a shady, secluded canyon. Its cool temperatures also make it a great hiking and picnicking area during the summer.

To the west is **Sentinel Peak Park,** This mountain peak has long been a lookout point for generations of the area's inhabitants. From here, Indians used to watch for flash floods or enemies approaching their village. Spanish missionaries later posted guards there to warn villagers of Apache raids. Today the peak is called A Peak, so named because of the large letter A that is whitewashed yearly by the University of Arizona freshman class.

Saguaro National Monument. The saguaro cactus grows only in two states in the country, and the Saguaro National Monument is a preserve for some of the largest and oldest stands. There are hiking trails and picnic sites in the monument.

The Arizona state flower, the saguaro blossom, is in bloom in May and June, and the profusion of flowers is a sight to see.

The older, larger saguaros grow in the eastern part of the monument, while the western unit is more densely populated by these southwestern symbols of beauty. Also in this area is *Wasson Peak,* towering 4,687 feet above the desert floor. A trail begins in *King Canyon* and climbs to the top. The trail is not suggested for those unused to strenuous exercise.

Tohono Chul Park. Ina Rd., west of Oracle Rd. Tohono Chul is a privately owned, nonprofit island of desert beauty. The park, in the center of Tucson, has 250 species of arid land plants, many varieties of wild birds, native fish, a desert tortoise, and nature trails, demonstration gardens, and a weather station.

ZOOS. Arizona-Sonora Desert Museum. Just 14 miles west of Tucson in Tucson Mountain Park is the Arizona-Sonora Desert Museum. The museum features live exhibits of animals, plants, and fish indigenous to the Sonoran Desert. It is rated among the top seven zoos of its kind in the world.

While touring the zoo, it may be difficult to tell which animals are part of the zoo collection and which are wild, because many small desert creatures live wild on the museum grounds and the museum keeps as few animals in cages as necessary. Most live in re-created natural-looking habitats.

But more exciting is the latest addition to the 12-acre facility—the *Steven H. Congdon Earth Sciences Center.* The center allows visitors to enter "real" limestone caves to see nature at work deep below the earth. Another section of the Earth Sciences Center consists of two rooms of exhibits showing how the Sonoran Desert was formed, taking the viewer back billions of years in geologic time.

The museum hosts a number of programs, including several for the blind and handicapped. There are exhibits for children, and a special tortoise enclosure lets visitors touch and hold the mild desert tortoise. Other exhibits include a walk-in aviary, desert garden, and underwater viewing of otters and beavers. Tour the museum as early in the day as possible.

The animals will be more active, and during the summer months, it will be much cooler. Open 8:30 to 5 daily; 7:30 to 6 June to September. Admission charge.

Reid Park Zoo. E. 22nd and Randolph Way. The zoo features everything from a recreated African veldt and Asian grassland to the Australian outback. Each exhibit is marked with a textbook definition of the animal as well as its habits and characteristics. Open 8 to 4 daily; weekends and holidays 8 to 6 from Memorial Day through Labor Day. Open 9:30 to 5 after Labor Day until Memorial Day. Closed Christmas. Admission charge.

GARDENS. Tucson Botanical Gardens. 2150 N. Alvernon Way. The five acres of gardens feature southwestern buildings landscaped with roses, herbs, iris, and native southwestern crops.

A greenhouse on the site contains plants of coffee, tea, macadamia nuts, and even pineapple and banana. Guided tours are offered on weekend afternoons. And throughout the year, classes and workshops are held for children and adults. Open 9 to 4 weekdays; 10 to 4 Saturdays; noon to 4 Sundays in the winter; open 9 to 4 weekdays in the summer. Closed holidays. Admission is charged.

CHILDREN'S ACTIVITIES. Besides introducing your child to the history of Tucson through its many museums (see Museums, following), consider miniature golfing, swimming, horseback riding (for a list of stables, see Participant Sports), renting a bicycle from one of several bike shops in town, flying a kite at Udall or Kennedy Parks, or even backpacking.

Golf 'N Stuff, 6503 E. Tanque Verde Rd., has every conceivable attraction, from miniature golf and an arcade to bumper boats and batting cages.

The *Tucson Children's Museum,* 300 E. University, is a health, science, and culture museum for children. Hands-on exhibits, as well as special traveling exhibitions, are featured.

Old Tucson, 201 S. Kinney Rd., 12 miles west of town, is a western fantasy land where visitors can ride stagecoaches, watch cowboy "shoot-outs" on Main Street, and tour sets where famous Westerns have been filmed. Other entertainment includes museums, medicine shows, and musical reviews.

PARTICIPANT SPORTS. World-renowned golf courses, championship tennis courts, horseback riding, greyhound racing, swimming, racquetball, hot-air ballooning, hiking, and skiing are just a few of the recreational sports Tucson has to offer.

Golf, one of Tucson's primary visitor attractions, is also a favorite pastime for residents. Following is a list of some of the more challenging courses. The Metropolitan Tucson Convention and Visitors Bureau, 130 S. Scott Ave., Tucson 85701, 624–1889, would be happy to send you a brochure on all the golf and tennis courts available in the Tucson area.

Tucson Country Club. 2950 Camino Principal. Par 72, 6,818 yards. This private course offers 18 holes and has a 71.3 championship rating.

Cliff Valley. 5910 N. Oracle Rd. Par 54, 2,233 yards. This public course offers 18 holes.

Fred Enke Municipal Golf Course. 8251 E. Irvington. Par 72, 6,809 yards. This public course offers 18 holes and a 72.7 championship rating.

49-ers Country Club. 12000 E. Tanque Verde Rd. 72 par, 6,680 yards. This private course has 18 holes and a 68.0 championship rating.

Silverbell Golf Course. 3600 N. Silverbell Rd. Par 72, 6,264 yards. This public course offers 18 holes and a championship rating of 71.6.

Tennis. If you'd rather swing a racquet, Tucson has 12 public tennis courts, 12 private courts, and 12 public school courts. Here are some:

Randolph Tennis Center. 100 S. Randolph Way, has 24 courts with 11 lighted. The cost is minimal.

University of Arizona Tennis Courts. Campbell & 4th St. (men's). Campbell & 2nd St. (women's). There are 14 courts altogether, with six lighted. Reservations are accepted until 11 A.M.

Or try your luck at one of the city parks. The courts are well maintained, and some are lighted. *Jacobs Park,* 1010 W. Lind Rd., has two lighted courts. And *Stefan Gollob Park,* 401 S. Prudence Rd., has four lighted courts.

And don't forget, Tucson is the headquarters for the **U.S. Handball Association.** *Handball Magazine* is published here, and Tucson Athletic Club boasts among its members the second- and third-ranked players in the country. If you're interested in playing, call 881–0140 for more information.

Horseback riding. A historic way to see the town is on the back of a reliable steed. But if you forget your horse, fear not—Tucson has a number of stables, including *Pusch Ridge Stables,* 11220 N. Oracle, offers trail rides, hay rides, pack trips, and breakfast and moonlight rides into the Santa Catalina Wilderness.

Tucson Mountain Stables. 6501 W. Ina Rd. Tucson Mountain provides guided rides into the Tucson Mountains and Saguaro National Monument.

Skiing. *Mount Lemmon Ski Valley* is just 35 miles northeast of Tucson. Slopes are open daily, 11 A.M. to 5 P.M., weather permitting.

Other activities to consider include **roller skating, bowling, snow tubing** during the winter, **ice skating,** and, of course, **swimming.** There are 15 city-operated pools located in the city parks. Or make use of the pool at your lodging.

SPECTATOR SPORTS. There is something for everyone in Tucson. **January** leads off with the *American Hot Rod Association Winter Nationals,* held at the Tucson Dragway.

During the **winter season** *University of Arizona (UA) Hockey* is held at the Community Center Arena. Or watch the *UA Basketball team* shoot the hoop under the direction of Coach Lute Olson. Also during the winter, the *Tucson Metro Soccer League* and the *Southern Arizona Soccer League* are active. Their games can be seen most Sundays at Reid, Jacobs, and Udall parks.

The *Cleveland Indians* come to Tucson in **March** for their spring training season at Hi Corbett Field. After the Indians leave, the *Toros* come to town.

Also in March, the *Circle K LPGA Tucson Open* is held at the Randolph Golf Course.

Or watch the *Cigna Michael Landon Celebrity Tennis Classic* in **April** at the Randolph Tennis Center.

Because of the summer heat, spectator sports dwindle. But as any desert inhabitant knows, the nights are much more bearable, so come and enjoy the cool nights and watch the *TCC Twilight Criterium Series,* a six-week series of bike racing held just west of the community center.

During the **fall,** the *El Presidio Criterium,* a bike race similar to the summer series, is held in the city streets of the historic El Presidio district.

In **October,** the *Northern Telecom Tucson Open* features top PGA golfers at The Tournament Players Club at StarPass.

HISTORIC SITES. Mission San Xavier del Bac. See *Southern and Southeastern Arizona.* **Fremont House,** 151 S. Granada Ave., is the restored home of Governor John C. Fremont, the Arizona Territory's most famous military governor. The house was built in 1856.

Fort Lowell Park and Museum, Craycroft Rd. and Fort Lowell Rd., is the original cavalry post established to protect early pioneers from hostile Apaches, from 1873 to 1891. You can still see the ruins of the original adobe hospital and several shells of barracks buildings.

The museum itself is a reconstruction of the commanding officer's quarters, furnished in the mode of 1885. The halls of the museum contain a display of military uniforms and equipment, maps, photos, and documents.

Edward Nye Fish House, North Main and Alameda, is now part of the Tucson Museum of Art complex, which comprises the northern portion of the Presidio. Fish established a merchandising business in Tucson in the 1860s.

El Tiradito (also known as the "Wishing Shrine"), Granada and Simpson, is listed in the National Register of Historic Places. Legend tells that a young herder who was killed in a lovers' triangle is buried on the spot. Because the ground was unconsecrated, pious townspeople lit candles and prayed for the young man. Today many people continue to burn candles here in the belief that their offerings will make their wishes come true.

Montijo House, Cushing and Church, was built during the Civil War and was remodeled in the 1890s for that prominent ranching family. The house was restored in 1974.

The Pit House Site, near Church in the El Presidio district, was discovered in 1954 when University of Arizona archaeologists were given a limited amount of time to dig for the northeast corner of the Presidio Wall. Eighteen inches below the old wall was discovered a hard-packed floor and remnants of a Hohokam Indian hut occupied between A.D. 700 and 900.

MUSEUMS. Tucson is rich and alive with the heritage of her first people. The ancient Indians, Spanish missionaries and conquistadores, and later the European pioneers helped mold the place that would, nearly 150 years later, house approximately 700,000 residents. This rich cultural heritage is brought into today's perspective thanks to Tucson's many museums and galleries.

Arizona Heritage Center, 949 E. 2nd St., has constantly changing exhibits recounting Arizona's history, beginning with the Indians and the arrival of the Spanish, through the territorial years. The center makes history come alive as you look into rooms that are furnished to look as they would have at the turn of the century.

Or walk through the largest indoor mining exhibit in the United States. There is an 85-foot replica of a copper mine, complete with track, an ore bucket, a miner's cabin, ore-stamping equipment, and an assay office.

Also of interest are antique cars, a stagecoach, and a fire engine. This museum houses the largest collection of artifacts in Arizona, with more than 30,000 relics in clothing, textiles, weapons, and folk art.

The center also is headquarters for the Arizona Historical Society, which, when founded in 1884, was called the Society of Arizona Pioneers. It's the state's oldest cultural institution and still one of the more vigorous. Open 10 to 4 Mondays through Saturdays; open noon to 4 Sundays. Closed major state and national holidays. Admission is free.

Flandrau Planetarium. University Blvd. and Cherry Ave. There are more telescopes and celestial observatories concentrated within a 50-mile radius of Tucson than anywhere else on earth. The planetarium, opened in 1975, was named for writer Grace H. Flandrau and was built with an eventual investment of $2.4 million. The planetarium offers dramatic and educational hour-long theater performances on astronomy and space exploration.

On many nights a volunteer is at the 16-inch telescope to assist visitors. You never know who the volunteer may be on a given night, but you may be lucky enough to get Erwin A. Whitaker, the man who made it possible for astronauts to bring back moon rocks. Open 10 to 5 Mondays through Fridays; 1 to 5 weekends. Also open 7 to 9 P.M. Tuesday through Saturdays. Free admission to exhibit halls; admission charge for theater shows.

Arizona State Museum. University of Arizona campus. Pottery, artifacts, and details about the daily routine of food gathering, trading, and commerce of prehistoric and modern Indians of Arizona are what the museum is all about. The Hohokam, Anasazi, and Mogollon tribes are featured. The museum also has a new exhibit called "In the Shelter of Caves." Other temporary displays have an international range of topics. Open 9 to 5 Mondays through Saturdays; 2 to 5 Sundays. Closed July 4, Labor Day, Thanksgiving, Christmas, and New Year's days. Free admission.

Pima Air Museum. Wilmot Rd. exit off I-10. With a collection of over 130 military and civilian aircraft, the museum offers a large sampling of the history of American aviation. Exhibits include a full-scale model of the Wright brothers' 1903 Wright Flyer and a mock-up of the world's fastest aircraft, the X-15. Open 9 to 5 daily (no admittance after 4 P.M.). Closed Christmas Day. Admission charge.

National Optical Astronomy Observatories (Kitt Peak National Observatory). Fifty-six miles southwest of Tucson, on State Route 86. Kitt Peak is the world's largest astronomical facility. For tour information, call 620-5350. The Visitor Center and three telescopes—a solar, 2.1, and 4 meter—are open to the public. Open 10 to 4 daily. Closed December 24 and 25. Admission is free.

Tucson Museum of Art. 140 N. Main Ave. Contemporary and historical art exhibits. Within the museum is the Plaza of the Pioneers sculpture courtyard. Open 10 to 5 Tuesdays through Saturdays; 1 to 5 Sundays; closed Mondays. Admission charge.

Center for Creative Photography. Olive Rd., University of Arizona campus. The center houses the life works of such acclaimed photographers as Ansel Adams, W. Eugene Smith, and Edward Weston. The center not only has prints but also negatives, contact sheets, experiments with different media, and various business correspondence of its photographers.

Devoted to "research, appreciation, and preservation," the center preserves the work of over 1500 photographers, with collections estimated at $30 million. Open 9 to 5 Mondays through Fridays; open noon to 5 Sundays. Closed Saturdays and major holidays. Free admission.

La Casa Cordova. 173 N. Meyer Ave. Another step back into history, the house is one of Tucson's oldest buildings. The adobe dwelling, restored by the Junior League of Tucson as a Mexican Heritage Museum, consists of five rooms of dirt floors and ceilings made of pine beams and saguaro ribs.

Inside the house are display cases filled with historical and cultural objects, Mexican folk art, and photographs. Open 10 to 5 Tuesdays through Saturdays and 1 to 5 on Sundays. Guided tours are provided Tuesdays through Fridays on request. Admission is free.

Tucson Children's Museum, 300 E. University is a health and science education center. The museum features participatory exhibits that help visitors learn about the human body. Open 10 to 5 Tuesdays through Saturdays; 1 to 5 Sundays. Admission charge.

Christine's Doll Museum. 4940 E. Speedway. The museum houses a collection of more than 4,000 antique and contemporary dolls. The collection includes Shirley Temple, Mutt and Jeff, and Kewpies. Most of the assemblage consists of French bisque, German bisque, and Poutys and Googly-Eyes.

The museum also has an assortment of cornhusk, cork, apple, and pressed paper dolls. Open 10 to 5:30 Mondays through Saturdays; closed Sundays. Admission is charged. Appointments suggested.

Old West Wax Museum, 205 S. Kinney Rd. Lifelike wax sculptures made by Josephine Tussaud. The sculptures include the likenesses of such actors as John Wayne and Jimmy Stewart. There are also reenactments of Old West scenes. Open 9 to 5:30 daily. Admission charge.

Mineral Museum. University of Arizona campus. Exhibits display a variety of minerals native to Arizona as well as fine gemstones and fossils. Open 8 to 12 Mondays through Fridays. Free admission.

University Museum of Art. University of Arizona campus. The museum presents several special exhibits throughout the academic year in addition to its permanent collections, which span the Middle Ages through the twentieth century. Open 9 to 5 Mondays through Saturdays; 12 to 5 Sundays in winter, 10 to 3:30 Mondays through Saturdays; 12 to 4 Sundays during the summer. Closed July 4, Thanksgiving, Christmas and New Year's days. Admission is free.

Western Postal History Museum. 920 N. First Ave. Founded in 1960, the main display is an early 1900s mahogany wrap-around post office counter from Arizona's territorial days.

The museum also offers a changing stamp display of nineteenth- and twentieth-century cover collections of Arizona, New Mexico, and California and houses one of the country's largest philatelic reference libraries. Open 8 to 12 Mondays through Fridays.

World of Miniatures. 4825 N. Sabino Canyon Rd. The museum houses 450,000 individual hand-carved miniatures. Using a scale of ⅜ inch = 1 foot, the collection includes an American Indian display that took three years to complete and an Americana display that is a replica of an 1890s town. All the carvings were created by Messrs. Jean LeRoy and Rudy Castilla. Open 11:30 A.M. to 10 P.M. daily. Free admission.

The Old Pueblo Museum at Foothills Center. Ina Rd. and La Cholla Blvd. Housed inside a shopping mall, this museum features a representative archeological dig, a gem and mineral exhibit, and changing cultural exhibits. Open 10 to 9 Mondays through Fridays; 10 to 6 Saturdays; 10 to 5 Sundays. Free admission.

INDUSTRIAL TOURS. R. W. Webb Winery. 13605 E. Benson Hwy., Vail 85641. Webb is the state's largest and oldest commercial winery. Tours and tastings from 10 to 5 Mondays through Saturdays; 12 to 5 Sundays. Admission is redeemable with purchase.

Tucson Citizen. 4850 S. Park Ave., 573–4560. The *Citizen* is an afternoon newspaper circulated Monday through Saturday.

MUSIC. Tucson Symphony Orchestra, 443 S. Stone Ave., 882–8585. The Tucson Symphony is southern Arizona's primary orchestra, under the direction of Robert Bernhardt. The symphony presents pops and classics, from early October through mid-May.

Tucson Boys Chorus. Founded in 1939, the chorus is under the direction of Dr. Julian M. Ackerley. The musical repertoire moves from Western folk songs to Broadway show tunes to the traditional boys choir classics. For information on performance dates, write or call Tucson Arizona Boys Chorus, Box 12034, Tucson 85732, 296–6277.

Southern Arizona Light Opera Company. Tucson Community Center Music Hall; 323–7888. Amateurs and semi-professionals offer light opera with the support of a full orchestra. The season runs from September through May.

Arizona Opera Company, 3501 N. Mountain Ave., 293–4336. Arizona's only resident opera company presents four professional productions annually, including such classics as *Madame Butterfly, La Boheme,* and *Barber of Seville.* The season lasts from October through March.

STAGE AND REVUES. The Arizona Ballet produces three ballets per season, including the *Nutcracker Suite* during the Christmas holidays. It is Arizona's only semi-professional resident classical ballet troupe. They perform at the Tucson Community Center Music Hall from October through April.

The Arizona Theatre Company performs November through mid-May at the Leo Rich Theatre. Founded in 1967, the company stages productions ranging from Broadway hits to classical theatre. The company has achieved national recognition from the Ford Foundation, the White House Committee on the Arts, and the National Endowment for the Arts.

Seasonal auditions are held in major U.S. cities. Entertainment includes comedy, drama, and musicals. Advance reservations are advised but not required. Tickets are discounted for students, the military, and senior citizens.

Ballet Folklorico Mexicano, Inc., performs colorful, traditional folk ballet.

Gaslight Theatre, 7000 E. Tanque Verde Rd., presents musical comedy-melodramas Wednesday through Sunday evenings. Matinee once a month. Tickets run about $10.

Invisible Theatre. Now a decade old, this experimental theater produces six plays a year from September through June at 1400 N. First Ave.

Orts Theatre of Dance, Inc., a contemporary modern dance troupe, adapts their style to a variety of spaces around Tucson.

Teatro del Sol presents original productions with a Chicano perspective, in both Spanish and English.

University of Arizona Repertory Theatre emphasizes the modern classics in both musicals and dramas at the University Theatre during the summer.

The University Theatre provides professional productions by the University of Arizona Department of Drama. Productions include plays by such authors as George Bernard Shaw, Jean Anouilh, and Shakespeare. The season is September through April at the University Theatre.

GALLERIES. If historical objects don't interest you, Tucson has a bevy of galleries featuring many art forms.

Gallery in the Sun, 6300 N. Swan Rd. The gallery was built by Ted De Grazia and contains the largest collection of his art. Because there is such a large collection of work, the gallery features several rooms containing permanent and rotating exhibits. Tours are available. Open 10 to 4 daily. Closed major holidays.

America West, 363 S. Meyer, has a collection of primitive and modern art, American Indian, as well as pre-Columbian and oriental art.

El Presidio Gallery, 201 N. Court Ave., features a collection of traditional and contemporary Southwestern art.

Etherton Gallery, 424 E. 6th St., specializes in vintage and contemporary photography, painting, sculpture, and mixed media.

Old Town Artisans, 186 N. Meyer, is an adobe restoration that fills an entire block in Tucson's El Presidio neighborhood, where a Spanish fort once protected early settlers. The block houses the works of 150 local American Indian and Latin folk artists.

Sanders Galleries, 6420 N. Campbell Ave., offers one of the larger selections of traditional Western and contemporary Southwestern art in the West.

SHOPPING. Tucson is a shopper's gold mine. Whether it's relics of the Old West, American Indian jewelry, Mexican artwork, or Western riding gear, Tucson stores have it all.

In addition to a large number of specialty shops and shopping centers, Tucson has four major shopping malls. **El Con Mall,** 3601 E. Broadway Blvd; **Park Mall,** 5870 E. Broadway Blvd; two are northside malls: **Tucson Mall** at 4500 N. Oracle Rd. and **Foothills Mall** at 7401 N. La Cholla Blvd.

Major stores in Tucson are **Broadway Southwest** and **Goldwater's.** Some popular specialty stores include **Summit Hut,** with three locations, Tucson's source for backpacking and hiking equipment; also provides maps, books, trail guides, and advice.

United Nations Center, 2911 E. Grant Rd. The center is a nonprofit corporation that sells imports to fund UNICEF and educational programs.

Kaibab Shop, 2841 N. Campbell Ave. Kaibab has been in business for more than 35 years, catering to those who appreciate distinctive Southwestern clothing, gifts, jewelry, furniture, and moccasins.

DINING OUT. Through the years, Tucson has become known as the Mexican Food Capital of the World. That's not hard to understand when you realize that the Mexican influence is as close as the border—only 60 miles away. It is no wonder that Tucson offers delicious authentic Mexican dishes on one hand plus a bevy of dishes from German, Greek, Oriental, Polynesian, Indonesian, Mediterranean, and French cuisines.

Restaurant price categories are as follows: *Deluxe,* $20 and up; *Expensive,* $15 to $20; *Moderate,* $8 to $15; and *Inexpensive,* under $8. These prices are for salad or soup, entree, and beverage. Not included are alcoholic drinks, tax, and tips. For a more complete explanation of restaurant categories, refer to Facts at Your Fingertips.

American

Deluxe

Baron's Restaurant. 2401 S. Wilmot Rd., 747–3503. Top-quality food in an authentic early Tucson atmosphere.

The Tack Room. 2800 Sabino Canyon Rd., 722–2800. Tucson's only five-star restaurant. The restaurant is housed in an old adobe house. The continental cuisine is expertly served.

Expensive

Las Campañas de las Catalinas. 6440 N. Campbell Ave., 299–1771. Set in mountain foothills. Menu offers such American favorites as prime rib, leg of lamb, Alaskan salmon, and homemade rolls. Also, complimentary fruit and cheese plate.

Houlihan's. 410 N. Wilmot Rd., 886–8885. Steaks and seafood. Disc jockey and dancing nightly.

Jerome's. 6958 E. Tanque Verde Rd., 721–0311. The regional American cooking is creative. The house specialties include Creole and Cajun dishes.

Keaton's Restaurant, Grill and Bar. 7401 N. La Cholla, 297–1999. Fresh seafood and oak-broiled chops and ribs. Oyster bar.

Moderate

The Cushing Street Bar and Restaurant. 343 S. Meyer, 622–7984. In a downtown historic district, patio dining and live music.

The Eclectic Café. 7053 E. Tanque Verde Rd., 885–2842. A little something for everyone. Menu consists of soups, quiches, Mexican food, omelets, and crepes.

Lunt Avenue Marble Club. 60 N. Alvernon Way, 326–4536. An old-time favorite serving imaginative dishes.

Inexpensive

The Good Earth Restaurant and Bakery. 6366 E. Broadway, 745–6600. Key word is *nourishing.* Menu features a large variety of beef, chicken, and seafood entrees. Soups, salads are always good. Bread, rolls, and pastries baked on the premises daily.

Millie's West Pancake Haus. 6530 E. Tanque Verde Rd., 298–4250. A variety of pancakes made from Millie's own recipes are served in quaint surroundings. Menu includes blintzes, Belgian waffles, and omelets.

American/Continental

Expensive

The Arizona Inn. 2200 E. Elm St., 325–1541. The elegant dining room is an Arizona favorite. Menu is American and continental.

Moderate

Cafe Terra Cotta. 4310 N. Campbell Ave., 577–8100. Casual Southwest dining in a contemporary Arizona setting. Menu includes black-bean chili, pizzas from a wood-burning oven, and goat cheese with red pepper.

American/Western

Expensive

Hidden Valley Inn Restaurant. 4825 N. Sabino Canyon Rd., 299–4941. True to the name, this 1880s atmosphere goes well with the mesquite-broiled steaks, prime rib, and seafood. Live music and dancing nightly.

Silver Saddle Steak House. I-10 and 4th Ave., 622–6253. Specializing in open pit mesquite-broiled steak, chicken, and ribs. Prime rib is served Thursdays through Sundays.

Moderate

Ft. Lowell Depot Restaurant. 3501 E. Ft. Lowell Rd., 795–8110. Fine Western cuisine, featuring prime rib, steaks, and char-broiled seafood. Live country music Tuesdays through Saturdays.

Li'l Abner's Steakhouse. 8500 N. Silverbell Rd., 744–2800. Mesquite-broiled steak and chicken in historic old tavern. Live music on weekends.

Pinnacle Peak. 6541 East Tanque Verde, 296–0911. Located in restored Savoy Opera House, the restaurant features steaks in an Old West atmosphere.

Continental

Deluxe

Charles Restaurant. 6400 E. El Dorado, 296–7173. Elegant surroundings in a converted mansion. Continental specialties include Dover sole and beef Wellington. Some dishes are prepared tableside.

Janos. 150 N. Main, 884-9426. Nouvelle cuisine and fine wines. Housed in an old home listed in the National Historic Register.

Palomino. 2959 N. Swan, 325–0413. Continental cuisine with special dinners offered weekly.

Expensive

The Olive Tree. 7000 E. Tanque Verde Rd., 298–1845. Features Greek and continental cuisine prepared from family recipes. Selections include fresh lamb, moussaka and dolmades.

Westward Look Resort. 245 E. Ina Rd., 297–1151. Very popular. The continental dishes are prepared by a superb chef.

Moderate

Café Magritte. 254 E. Congress St., 884–8004. Innovative meals in a stylish downtown eatery.

French

Deluxe

Penelope's. 3619 E. Speedway, 325–5080. Country French cuisine. Menu changes weekly. Reservations are required.

Le Rendezvous. 3844 E. Fort Lowell, 323–7373. Beautiful graphics. Some consider this the best French cuisine in Tucson. Excellent wine cellar. Good service.

Expensive

Daniel's Restaurant. 2930 N. Swan Rd., in Plaza Palomino, 742–3200. Regional French and classic Italian cuisine.

Italian

Deluxe

Scordato's. 4405 W. Speedway, 624–8946. Delicious Italian food. A large selection of regional Italian dishes, including veal, steak, chicken, and pasta. Huge wine selection.

Expensive

Capriccio Ristorante. 4825 N. First Ave., 887–2333. Sophisticated Italian specialties include veal, fresh seafood, and pasta.

Moderate

Larocca's. 5689 N. Swan Rd., 299–4301. Low fat, preservative-free Italian favorites baked in a stone oven.

Mama Louisa's. 2041 S. Craycroft Rd., 790–4702; and 2960 N. Campbell Ave., 795–1779. Homemade pasta; local favorites.

Mama's Pizza. 831 N. Park, 882–3993. Setting is plain, but they serve excellent pizza, homemade cheesecake, and submarine sandwiches.

Inexpensive

Corleone's. 1035 E. Mabel, 792–4128. The Italian menu offers shrimp and scallop scampi. Daily specials.

Mexican

Expensive

Carlos Murphy's. 419 W. Congress, 628–1956. Located in a former historic railroad depot, this restaurant offers delicious Mexican food and some American entrees. Also 21 flavors of margaritas.

El Charro Restaurant. 311 N. Court Ave., 622–5465. Tucson's oldest Mexican restaurant, family-run since 1922 in historic downtown home.

Moderate

El Adobe Mexican Restaurant. 40 W. Broadway, 791–7458. Dine in adobe-walled surroundings or on the patio of one of Tucson's most popular Mexican restaurants. California wines and Mexican beers.

El Parador. *Moderate.* 2744 E. Broadway, 881–2808. Many green plants make up a lush atmosphere. Serving fine Sonoran Mexican food since 1946. Flamenco and classical music Wednesday through Sunday evenings.

Inexpensive

Gordo's Mexicateria. 6940 E. Broadway, 886–5386. All-you-can-eat Mexican buffet. Margaritas, beer.

Lerua's Fine Mexican Food. 2005 E. Broadway, 624–0322. Serving some of the tastiest salsa in Tucson since 1922. Also known for its green corn tamales. Items are available for shipping. Service is deli-style.

La Parrilla Suiza. 5602 E. Speedway, 747–4838. Authentic Mexico City cuisine—the corn tortillas are homemade. Menu also offers char-broiled meats, fresh ingredients, and original recipes.

Middle Eastern

Moderate

The Sheik Café. 6350 E. Broadway, 790–5481. Lebanese and Syrian foods are the specialties here. Lamb, beef, and chicken dishes are served. Belly dancing on weekend nights.

Inexpensive

Marathon Gyros. 1134 E. 6th St., 623–1020. Greek and Middle Eastern cuisine, including gyros and souvlakis. Daily specials.

Oriental

Moderate

Japanese Kitchen International, Inc. 8424 Old Spanish Trail, 886–4131. Traditional Japanese interior. All food prepared at tableside. Menu consists of steak, seafood, and chicken dishes. Sunday sushi.

Lotus Garden Chinese Restaurant. 5975 E. Speedway Blvd., 298–3351. Cuisine from Szechuan and Canton provinces. Outdoor patio, full bar.

Szechuan Omei. 2601 E. Speedway, 325–7204. Szechuan and Hunan cooking are featured, with lunch and dinner specials.

Vietnamese

Inexpensive

Three Sisters. 2226 N. Stone, 628–1094. Vietnamese cuisine. Lunch buffet, and a seafood dish that contains 25 different ingredients.

NIGHTLIFE. Bobby McGee's Restaurant, 6464 E. Tanque Verde Rd., 886–5551. This fun-time restaurant/nightclub offers music and dancing every night of the week.

Cactus Club. Westin La Paloma, 3800 E. Sunrise Dr., 742–6000. A high-energy lounge featuring disc jockey, dancing and videos.

CCC Chuckwagon Suppers. 8900 W. Bopp Rd., 883–2333. Hearty suppers and stage show. Reservations advised.

Gaslight Theater. 7000 E. Tanque Verde Rd., 886–9428. A dinner theatre that features comedy and drama for the whole family.

Houlihan's Old Place. 410 N. Wilmot Rd., 886–8885. There is dancing nightly from 8 P.M. to 1 A.M. Nice cozy atmosphere of an English pub.

The Last Territory. 10000 N. Oracle Rd., 742–7000. In the Sheraton El Conquistador Resort. Live country-western music and dancing Tuesday through Saturday nights.

SOUTHERN AND
SOUTHEASTERN ARIZONA

Excursions Out of Tucson

Using Tucson as a starting point, there are several possible tours of the southern areas of Arizona. One takes you directly south along Interstate 19 to Nogales and the Mexican border. Another is guided by routes 10 and 19, which serve the southeastern corner of the state, including the Coronado National Monument and the towns of Bisbee and Douglas. Traveling north of Tucson on Interstate 10 brings you to the old city of Casa Grande (also a good starting point for a visit to Yuma or a tour of southwestern Arizona, covered in the next chapter). And one final tour goes farther along Interstate 10, westward through 125 miles of untraveled desert to the famed rock hounders' town of Quartzsite and the California border.

Exploring South of Tucson

From Tucson southward, you have a choice of two loop trips on Interstate 10 through scenic country steeped in history.

One excursion takes you south on Interstate 19 along an ancient route that during the Apache wars came to be known as Tubac, Tumacacori, to Hell because it was the site of numerous ambushes and massacres. Graves once could be seen along the entire trail.

Interstate 19 bypasses San Xavier del Bac, an 18th-century mission, and takes you through the attractive retirement community of Green Valley: Madera Canyon bird sanctuary; a Spanish fort at Tubac, and a mission at Tumacacori; Pena Blanca Lake; the twin border cities of both Nogaleses; then north through rolling grasslands and the communities of Patagonia and Sonoita.

The second takes you south from Interstate 10 on U.S. 90 to Fort Huachuca, Sierra Vista, Coronado National Monument; Tombstone, Bisbee, Douglas, Cochise Stronghold, Chiricahua National Monument, and Fort Bowie.

Let's be off on the first loop.

San Xavier del Bac

Just south of Tucson on I-19 is a turnoff to the right that takes you to San Xavier del Bac, the "White Dove of the Desert." This beautiful old mission is an architectural classic. Be sure to take enough film for your camera.

The mission originally was established some two miles west of this site in 1692, by Father Eusebio Francisco Kino, the Jesuit missionary-explorer, but later it was destroyed by the Apaches. The present building was brought to near-completion in 1797 by the Franciscan Order.

Inside the church are a main altar, two side altars, and a little room where baptisms are held, as well as a gift shop.

The architecture is a blend of Moorish, Byzantine, and Indian/Mexican. Its great dome over the main altar once was a bright gold gilt that has faded, and almost all the interior is decorated either with paintings or statues.

A recorded lecture is played about every 20 minutes over a speaker system. The mission is open daily, except Christmas day, from 9 to 5.

Green Valley

Back on I-19, Green Valley, an exclusive retirement community, is situated on the left against a backdrop of the Santa Rita Mountains. Green Valley carries out the Spanish influence of southern Arizona with its architectural design and tile roofs.

Coronado National Forest

Some 10 miles farther south, also on the left, is Madera Canyon, a beautiful area of the Coronado National Forest in the Santa Rita Mountains. This spot is high on the list for bird-watchers, who say more than 200 species can be found in this lovely wooded area. *Madera* is the Spanish word for "wood," and much of the wood for early Tucson buildings came from here.

Tubac

Tubac is a former Spanish *presidio* (fort) built in 1752 after some Indian tribes rebelled against the Spaniards and began to harass them and the peaceful Pima and Papago Indians. Later, it fell into disuse and then was revived just before the Civil War, when silver was discovered in the area.

It went into decline several more times, but now seems to be enjoying a more permanent reincarnation as a historical monument cum arts and crafts center.

Tumacacori

Three miles farther south is another Spanish mission, Tumacacori, founded in 1691 by Padre Kino, a Jesuit, but constructed mostly by Franciscans. This once-beautiful building still has some of its original arches and copings, but vandals took their toll. It is now a National Monument.

About 10 miles past Mission Tumacacori is a turnoff to the right on Arizona 289 that takes you to Pena Blanca (White Rock) Lake, a good little fishin' hole about a mile long in a mountain setting. They take trout, bass, bluegill, and crappies out of here, the compleat anglers say.

Ambos Nogales

Out on the road again (I-19), you are headed for Ambos Nogales ("both Nogaleses"), the twin cities on the border of Mexico. The towns derived their names from two walnut trees growing on opposite sides of the fence along the international boundary, set in a mountain pass at about 4,000 feet altitude.

The altitude makes for a delightful summertime climate and gentle winters. The cities also get more rainfall in summer because of the altitude and their location in the path of storms coming out of the Gulf of California.

Nogales, Arizona, has a population of around 18,000, but its twin, Nogales, Sonora, in Mexico, has upward of 180,000 residents. Both are distribution centers for vegetables and farm machinery as well as being important tourist stops. Walk across the border. Leave your car on the American side, or purchase Mexican automobile insurance.

Nogales, Sonora, is a piece of Mexico right out of the interior. It has blocks of shops and alleys of hole-in-the-wall booths where Mexican clothing, leather work, and silver jewelry are sold—sometimes aggressively—by sidewalk merchants. Dickering will get you nowhere in the stores, but it is a must when dealing with the street vendors or those in the little alleys. Often you can get good deals on leather purses, for example, by haggling over the price. Everybody speaks English—mixed with Spanish—and commonly called Spanglish.

You can bring back $400 worth of merchandise duty-free, and one liter of liquor. Border guards will ask you where you were born and if you are a citizen. Among the interesting places to eat in Nogales, Sonora, is La Caverna, an old Spanish prison.

Patagonia

North out of Nogales, take State Route 82 to the northeast of I-19. This takes you to some pretty rolling grasslands into the town of Patagonia. The town gets its name from the Patagonia in South America, another area of pretty rolling hills. The movie *Oklahoma* was filmed in this area, because it was supposed to look more like Oklahoma than Oklahoma.

One of the most interesting attractions in Patagonia is the Museum of the Horse. Here you'll see just about everything in the world related to

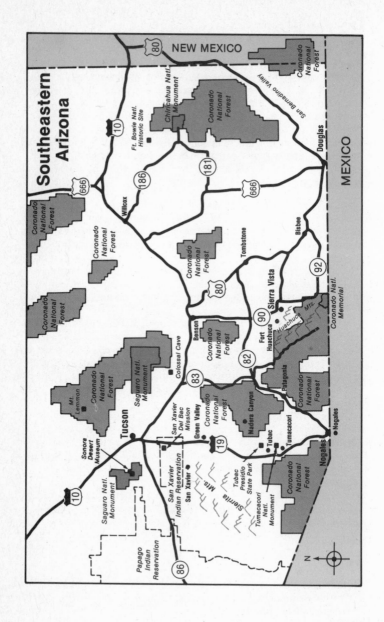

equines. There are saddles and bridles, harnesses, horseshoes, stirrups, martingales. These items come from everywhere and go back to Greco-Roman times. Included in the collection is the velvet saddle given to President Franklin D. Roosevelt by the bey of Tunis.

Just west of Patagonia is the Patagonia–Sonoita Creek Sanctuary, where cold-weather birds drop in on their way north in the spring and back in the fall on the way south.

North about 10 miles, State Route 82 meets State Route 83. Take Route 83 north to I-10 and back to Tucson.

Touring the Southeast Corner

Our next tour travels south of Benson (on I-10) along State Route 90–92. Past the Whetstone Mountains on your right, our first destination is some 30 miles distant: Fort Huachuca, one of a chain of forts established during the Indian wars.

Fort Huachuca

Fort Huachuca is the oldest continually active military installation in the United States. There is an excellent museum, and admission is free. Ramsey Canyon, about six miles down the road, is well known in birding circles as a major site for hummingbirds.

Sierra Vista, another Arizona community that is experiencing explosive growth, is located at a bend in the road south of the fort.

Coronado National Memorial

Another 15 miles or so south, where State Route 92 turns east, is a turn-off to the right to Coronado National Memorial. Some say this is near the spot where, in 1540, Franciso Vásquez de Coronado and his conquistadores first set food in what is now Arizona. Backroads in this area take you into some of the oldest gold camps in the Southwest.

Tombstone

Back to State Route 92 again, head north through Sierra Vista to State Route 82 and across to U.S. Route 80. Turn right and you're on the way to Tombstone, "The Town Too Tough To Die."

Here you'll find the original town, a compact little enclave, much as it was 100 years ago when Wyatt Earp, his brothers, and Doc Holliday bent the elbow at the Crystal Palace Saloon. There's the Bird Cage Theater, too, and Boothill Cemetery and the Tombstone Epitaph. Start your tour with a 30-minute film, *Historama,* right next to the OK Corral.

Bisbee

Our next stop on the tour is Bisbee, reached by continuing down State Route 80, through Mule Pass Tunnel, and down a long hill.

Bisbee, whose mines closed only a few years ago, is making a comeback as a retirement community and an arts-and-crafts center. Attractions here include the quaintness of the winding streets and the Victorian architecture; Brewery Gulch and the old Copper Queen Hotel. The old Queen has been almost restored to its one-time splendor.

The Queen can boast that Teddy Roosevelt and General John J. Pershing slept here. In its heyday, it was considered one of the finest hostelries between El Paso and Los Angeles.

You can tour the Lavender Pit, an out-in-the-open mine, by bus, and the underground Copper Queen by narrow-gauge rail. At the underground mine, you will be outfitted with a hard hat, slicker, and lamp. It's a constant 54 degrees in there. Both mines have an admission charge.

Douglas

Douglas is another mining/smelting town, 24 miles east on U.S. Route 80. Douglas once got a hail of bullets from across the border when Pancho Villa laid seige to Agua Prieta, Douglas's neighbor on the Mexican side. The historic old Gadsden Hotel is a point of interest in Douglas, and you can shop in Agua Prieta for bargains in coffee, fabrics, liquor, and vanilla.

Chiricahua National Monument

Take U.S. Route 666 north out of Douglas to State Route 181 (about 30 miles) and follow it to Chiricahua National Monument. Here, on paved loop roads, you can tour the Wonderland of Rocks, with evidence of volcanic eruptions and erosion on all sides. There are many strange formations with names like Punch and Judy, the Sea Captain, and Organ Pipe.

For a fee, you can drive through the monument some six miles to Massai Point. There you have long views into Sulphur Springs Valley on the west and San Simon Valley on the east. There's a geology exhibit building, and good hiking trails nearby.

This 17-square-mile monument was the mountain home of Cochise and Geronimo, the most famous of the Apache chiefs. Cochise had another camp at a spot now called Cochise Stronghold, west of the Chiricahuas, on the east face of the Dragoon Mountains.

To get there, go back out on the road you took to the monument, then take a dirt road off U.S. 666 about 10 miles northwest of the intersection with 181. Cochise is buried up there somewhere, but nobody knows the location of his grave. The stronghold is exactly as it was in Cochise's time, a rocky fortress with many places from which to look down on any approaching enemy.

Old Fort Bowie

There's one more exciting historic site to see dealing with the Indian wars. Go back on State Route 181 to the monument entrance, then take State Route 186 northwest to Old Fort Bowie, which once protected settlers and emigrants from the Apaches. A dirt road running in from State Route 186 leads 10 miles back to the fort grounds. From there, it's about a 1.5-mile walk to the ruins of the old buildings. A Park Service Ranger is on duty at this national historic site.

Back out on the highway, it's a little over 20 miles to Willcox (birthplace of movie cowboy Rex Allen) and Interstate 10, and another 80 miles back to Tucson.

Northwest of Tucson

Traveling north out of Tucson on Interstate 10, you lose about 1,000 feet in altitude by the time you reach Picacho, a picturesque outcrop whose name means "peaked" in Spanish. (That is *peaked* meaning "pointy," not "poorly.")

Picacho

Picacho was the site of the only Civil War battle in Arizona. It happened when a patrol of Rebels stationed at Tucson, then a Confederate stronghold, ran into a small advance force of Yankees coming east from California. The Union forces suffered two casualties—a dead lieutenant and a wounded enlisted man—but the Rebel group fled back to Tucson. When they got back to camp, they found the rest of the Confederate force getting ready to withdraw entirely from Arizona. They were faced by the column coming in from California and another Yankee force in New Mexico, which had sent the Rebels skeedadling after a sizable battle there.

Casa Grande

On up I-10 about 10 miles or so is a turnoff to State Route 87 that takes you another 18 miles to the Casa Grande Ruins National Monument. It was discovered in 1694 by Padre Kino, who founded San Xavier del Bac southwest of Tucson.

Casa Grande, meaning "big house" in Spanish, was built by the Hohokams, the vanished people, about A.D. 1350 and abandoned a hundred or so years later. Anthropologists are undecided about the purpose of the structure. Some think it was a fortress, others think it was a lookout point.

Lately, scientists have wondered if it wasn't used for astronomical observation. The walls have holes in them that line up perfectly with the sun at the spring and fall equinoxes, and with movements of the stars.

There is an admission fee and an interesting lecture tour as well as a self-guiding trail. (Practical Information for Casa Grande is included in the *Western Arizona* chapter.)

Take State Route 287 west out of Coolidge, make a slight jog to the right, and turn left on State Route 387, which takes you back to I-10.

An Excursion to the West

West out of Phoenix on I-10, you skirt Litchfield Park, a fine resort community founded early in the century and named for Paul Litchfield, president of the Goodyear Tire and Rubber Company. Litchfield pioneered experimentation here with long staple cotton, and the company has a proving ground for Goodyear implement tires.

Litchfield also was the location of a naval air training station that saw thousands of servicemen come and go during World war II and several decades afterward. Goodyear Aircraft Company also has a plant south of here, at the town of Goodyear.

After Litchfield comes Perryville, home of a medium-security state prison, and then Buckeye, a farming community settled by residents of Ohio, the Buckeye State.

Off to the left after Buckeye is Palo Verde Nuclear Plant, the largest of its type in the United States. Palo Verde cost $9.3 billion.

From here on, you are in desert country, with mountains to your right and left to punctuate the scenery. On the right, beyond Tonopah, are the Harquahalas, scene of a huge gold strike in the last century. There's also the ragtag remnants of a town and an old observatory on the top of Harquahala Peak.

On the left of the highway looms the Eagle Tail Mountains, in prehistoric times the site of innumerable Indian encampments. All that remains to tell the tale today is a canyon filled with petroglyphs, symbols pecked into rock.

Quartzsite

As you come down a gentle slope into Quartzsite, in the cool season you'll see an ocean of mobile homes and RVs of almost every size and description. The attraction? The annual Quartzsite Pow-wow!

Every winter the population of Quartzsite swells to more than 100,000 as rock hounds congregate at this huge gem show to sell and trade their wares and socialize. The jewelry for sale here is the highest quality you can find in this kind of personal ornamentation.

Near Quartzsite is a graveyard where one of the most interesting Arizona pioneers is buried. He was Haji Ali, a Syrian camel driver, who was part of an experiment by the U.S. Army to establish a Camel Corps for use as military supply carriers in the desert Southwest.

Haji Ali, along with other drivers, was imported to teach troopers how to handle the strange-looking mounts. The experiment began in 1857 and was abandoned when the Civil War broke out.

American cavalrymen hated the dromedaries, and the feeling was mutual. Many of the beasts ran off and proliferated in the wild, because they were bred for this kind of terrain. Sightings of camels were reported for the next 40 years.

Haji Ali, whose name was corrupted to Hi Jolly, stayed on in Arizona and became a prospector. He died in 1902.

On to Ehrenburg, and the Colorado River border with California.

PRACTICAL INFORMATION FOR SOUTHERN AND SOUTHEASTERN ARIZONA

HOW TO GET THERE. By air. Tucson is served by most major airlines, and from there you can choose from a variety of surface transportation.

By bus. *Greyhound-Trailways* serves Tucson, Huachuca City, Fort Huachuca, Sierra Vista, Bisbee, Douglas, Bowie, Willcox, and Benson. Contact your local Greyhound-Trailways office, or call toll-free, 800-531-5332, for reservations and information.

By train. *Amtrak* serves Benson and Tucson. For information and reservations, call Amtrak's toll-free number, 800-USA-RAIL.

By car. The best, most flexible way to get around southeastern Arizona. The nearest rental agencies are in Tucson. Toll-free numbers: *Hertz,* 800–654–3131; *Avis,* 800–331–1212.

HOTELS AND MOTELS. Hotel rates are based on double occupancy, European plan, and categories are determined by price: *Deluxe,* $65 and over; *Expensive,* $50 to $65; *Moderate,* $35 to $50; and *Inexpensive,* less than $35.

Willcox

Expensive

Best Western Plaza Inn. 1100 W. Rex Allen Dr., 85643; 384–3556. Lounge, TV, pool, pets allowed, dining room.

Douglas

Moderate

The Gadsden Hotel. 1046 G Ave., 85607; 364–4481. National historic site. TV, coffee shop, dining room, cocktails, golf.

Bisbee

Expensive

Bisbee Grand Hotel. 45 OK St., 85063; 432–5131. Filled with antiques and art. Lounge, bar, complimentary Continental breakfast, champagne in evening. Shared bathrooms.
Copper Queen Hotel. 11 Howell Ave., 85603; 432–2216. TV, restaurant, bar, pool. Historic landmark.

Moderate

El Rancho Hometel. 1102 Hwy. 92, 85603; 432–5969. Kitchenettes.
The Jonquil. 317 Tombstone Canyon, 85603; 432–7371. TV, private sunning area, very clean rooms.

Nogales

Deluxe

Rio Rico Resort. 1550 Camino a la Posada, 85621; 281–1901. Heated pool, dining room, lounge, golf course, tennis, horseback riding.

Moderate

Americana Motor Hotel. 850 Grand Ave., 85621; 287–7211. Cocktails, dining room, heated pool.
El Dorado. 1001 Grand Ave., 85621; 287–4611. Color TV, heated pool, pets allowed, dining room, cocktails, coffee shop.

Inexpensive

Best Western Siesta Motel. 910 Grand Ave., 85621; 287–4671. Air-conditioning, TV, movies, heated pool.

Sierra Vista

Moderate

Best Western Thunder Mountain Inn. 1631 State Hwy. 92, 85635; 458–7900. TV, pool, coffee shop, cocktails, dining room, Jacuzzi.

InnSuites. 391 E. Fry Blvd., 85635; 459–4221. Cable TV, pool, Jacuzzi, restaurant, lounge.

Tombstone

Moderate

Best Western Lookout Lodge. U.S. Hwy. 80 West, 85638; 457-2223. TV, pool.

CAMPING. The country off I-10 and I-19 ranges from low hot desert to rolling grasslands to soaring pine covered sky-island mountains. Camping spots abound.

Bonita Canyon. Thirty-six miles southeast of Willcox via State Route 186 and 181 within the Chiricahua National Monument. Open year-round, 14-day limit, fee, water, restrooms, RVs and tents allowed, visitor center.

Cochise Stronghold. Thirty-five miles southwest of Willcox on State Route 666 and Forest Service Highway 584. Open year-round, 14-day limit April through October; fee, water, restrooms, RVs and tents allowed.

Patagonia Lake State Park. Twelve miles east of Nogales on State Route 82. Open year-round, 15-day limit, fee, water, restrooms, RVs and tents allowed, waste disposal, boat ramp, and fishing.

Camp Rucker. Twenty-seven miles east of Elfrida. Open year-round, 14-day limit, fee, water, restrooms, RVs and tents allowed, fishing, nature trails.

Rustler Park. Sixteen miles northwest of Portal. Open April through November, 14-day limit, fee, water, restrooms, RVs and tents allowed.

TOURIST INFORMATION. The Arizona Tourist Information Center in Tucson (watch for the blue-and-white signs along I–10) is brochure heaven, with information on all parts of the state. The center is staffed by knowledgeable, helpful employees to answer your questions. For more information, contact the *Arizona Office of Tourism,* 1480 E. Bethany Home Rd., Phoenix 85014, 542–3618.

For information on specific areas within southeastern Arizona, contact the chambers of commerce for each town. Among the larger ones are: *Willcox Chamber of Commerce,* 1500 N. Circle I Rd., Willcox 85643; *Bisbee Chamber of Commerce,* 7 Naco Rd., Bisbee 85603; *Nogales/Santa Cruz County Chamber of Commerce,* Kino Park, Nogales 85621.

SEASONAL EVENTS. February. *The Tubac Festival,* featuring a juried art show and arts-and-crafts festival.

April. Bisbee, *La Vuelta de Bisbee,* largest bicycle race in the state, drawing many top racers from all over the country for this season opener.

October. *Tombstone Helldorado Days,* where Tombstonians relive the gory days of Wyatt Earp and the shootout at the OK Corral.

PARKS, MONUMENTS, AND HISTORIC SITES. Mission San Xavier del Bac. Nine miles southwest of Tucson, this is the most ornate example of Spanish mission architecture in the United States. Father Francisco Eusebio Kino first visited the site in 1692. Eight years later, Kino laid the foundations of the first church, about two miles north of the site of the present mission. The present mission was built during the administration of Father Juán Bautista Velderrain, from 1783 to 1797.

Coronado National Forest, 300 W. Congress St., Tucson 85701, 629–6483. The Coronado National Forest oversees nearly 2 million acres of forestland in southern Arizona and New Mexico. Unlike the broad interconnected swaths of forests in the rest of the state, the Coronado is comprised of "sky islands," isolated mountain ranges that jut up dramatically 5,000 to 7,000 feet above the surrounding desert floor. Radical climatic changes occur when ascending these mountains, traversing several life zones from Sonoran Desert to alpine conditions within a short distance. Therefore the Coronado is an extremely varied area for campers, hikers, and nature lovers.

Willcox Playa, southeast of the junction of I-10 and U.S. 666, southwest of Willcox. Huge, usually dry lake bed that, during rainy season, becomes a vast shallow breeding pond for freshwater shrimp. When the Playa has water in it, great flocks of various types of bird life can be found there.

Chiricahua National Monument, Dos Cabezas Star Route 181, Box 6500, Willcox 85643. Located 38 miles south of Willcox on State Route 186. Bizarre volcanic rock formations created millions of years ago have been eroded into intriguing shapes. The area also was one of the homes of the Chiricahua Apache Indians. Camping, hiking, car tours, and interpretive exhibits. Campfire programs are conducted April through mid-September. Fee, $3 per car.

Fort Bowie National Historic Site, Box 158, Bowie 85605. No direct route to the ruins of the fort. It can be reached by a 1.5-mile hiking trail that begins midway in Apache Pass. Reach the trailhead via a graded road 12 miles south of Bowie off I-10. Fort Bowie was the center of military activity during the battles with Geronimo and his Apaches. The site features walking tours, exhibits, wildflower and wildlife watching, and mountain climbing. No admission fee.

Coronado National Memorial, Rural Route 2, Box 126, Hereford 85615. Located 5 miles in on Montezuma Canyon Road off State Route 92, 25 miles west of Bisbee. Where Francisco Vásquez de Coronado, the first European to explore the Southwest, entered what is today the United States in 1540. The site features interpretive talks and exhibits, self-guided walks, hiking, climbing, horseback riding. No admission fee.

Tombstone, located 51 miles southeast of I-10 on U.S. Route 80. Touted as "the town too tough to die," Tombstone, site of the shootout at the OK Corral (Wyatt Earp, his brothers, and Doc Holliday versus the Clantons and McLowrys) survives today, appearing very much as it did in the late 1800s. Weekends feature reenactments of shootouts by the locals.

Ramsey Canyon, located in the Huachuca Mountains about 30 miles south of Benson off I-10. Ramsey Canyon is a wildlife sanctuary owned by The Nature Conservancy. A great number of rare hummingbirds visit the canyon at various times of year. Even without the birds, the riparian area is a jewel of a scenic area for nature lovers. Lodging is very limited and so is parking, so it is best to check in advance if much time is going to be spent here. For information and reservations, contact The Arizona Nature Conservancy in Tucson at 378–2785.

Tumacacori National Monument, Box 67, Tumacacori 85640. Located 45 miles south of Tucson on I-19, Tumacacori is one in a chain of missions built through northern Mexico and the American Southwest by the intrepid Father Eusebio Francisco Kino in the late 1600s. The monument features interpretive exhibits, self-guiding walks, living history exhibits. Admission fee, $3 per car.

Tubac Presidio State Historic Park, located on I-19, 40 miles south of Tucson. Once a Spanish fort, Tubac now showcases the contributions of Indians, Spaniards, Mexicans, and Anglos to Arizona's development. Interpretive exhibits and a closeup look at the historic structures provide new appreciation for this oldest community in Arizona established by people of European descent. Admission fee, $1 per adult.

PARTICIPANT SPORTS. Fishing. There are a number of small man-made impoundments along I-10 and I-19 stocked mostly with warm-water species. Bring equipment or purchase needs at sporting goods stores in Tucson. For information on lakes, licensing, and where the fish are biting, contact the *Arizona Game and Fish Department,* Region V, 555 N. Greasewood Rd., Tucson 85745; 628–5376.

Hunting. Duck, goose, dove, deer, javelina, mountain lion, and rabbits are some of the species that can be hunted in southern Arizona. For information and licenses, contact the *Arizona Game and Fish Department* at the address just given.

Golf. There's great golf to be found in southeastern Arizona. Among the better courses are *Rio Rico Resort and Country Club,* Nogales, 281–8567; *Pueblo Del Sol Golf Course,* Sierra Vista, 378–6444; *Tubac Valley Country Club,* Tubac, 398–2021; *Willcox Municipal Golf Course,* Willcox, 384–3814.

Hiking. Hundreds of miles of hiking trails await you in the Coronado National Forest and Arizona State Parks. For information, contact the *Coronado National Forest,* 300 W. Congress St., Tucson 85701, 629–6483; and *Arizona State Parks,* 800 W. Washington, Phoenix 85007, 542–4174.

MUSEUMS. Bisbee Mining and Historical Museum, 5 Copper Queen Plaza, Bisbee 85603. In the downtown historic district. Open 10 to 4 Mondays through Saturdays, 1 to 4 Sundays, closed Christmas Day. Admission fee $2 for adults. Simulated mine tunnel, mining equipment, plus ore samples and memorabilia of early mining days when Bisbee boomed. Research library and photo archives available by appointment.

Fort Huachuca Historical Museum, located at Boyd and Grierson at the mouth of Huachuca Canyon. Open 9 to 4 weekdays, 1 to 4 Saturdays and Sundays, closed federal holidays. Free admission. The museum is part of Fort Huachuca's "Old Post," built in 1892. Exhibits focus on the contributions of the Army in shaping the American Southwest. Displays include military uniforms, helmets, miniature wagons. Fully furnished period rooms show what life was like in the early years of the fort.

Amerind Foundation Museum, Box 248, Dragoon 85609. Open 10 to 4 Wednesdays to Sundays, closed Mondays and Tuesdays. Admission: $3 adults; $2 seniors and ages 12 to 18. Archeological and ethnographic exhibits of Indian cultures. Paintings and sculpture by Indian and other American artists. Also a museum shop and picnic area.

Back Streets of Tombstone Mining and Mineral Museum, on the corner of 5th and Toughnut Sts., Tombstone. Open 10 to 4; closed Wednesdays. Free admission. Combination museum and rocksmith shop filled with mining equipment and artifacts—lamps, scales, lunch buckets, crucibles, etc. The museum also features a tour of the Goodenough Silver Mine, directly below the museum.

Rose Tree Inn Museum, 4th and Toughnut Sts., Tombstone. Open 9 to 5 daily except Christmas Day. Admission, over 14, $1. The world's largest rose tree, plus a museum of furnishings and clothing dedicated to the town's pioneer families. Books and souvenirs in the gift shop.

Silver Nugget Museum, 6th and Allen Sts., Tombstone. Open 8:30 to 6; closed Sundays. Admission $1; under 12, free. Tombstone memorabilia, including Wyatt Earp's guns, historic photographs by C. S. Fly, opium pipes, masks, dolls, powder horns, leg irons, and more.

Tombstone Courthouse State Historic Park, 3rd and Toughnut sts. Open 8 to 5 daily except Christmas. Admission $1 for persons 18 and over. A gallows, invitation to a hanging, historic photographs, articles from an 1881 edition of the Tombstone *Epitaph,* Wyatt Earp's razor, a re-creation of an assay shop, and more take visitors back to the days when Tombstone boomed.

Museum of the Horse, Inc., 350 McKeown Ave., Patagonia. Located on State Route 82 between Sonoita and Nogales. Open 9 to 5 daily, closed Thanksgiving and Christmas days. Admission: adults, $2; children 6 to 11, 50¢. This six-room museum is filled with more than 50 horse-drawn vehicles and everything imaginable relating to the horse from all over the world.

Tubac Center for the Arts, corner of Plaza Rd. and Calle Baca in Tubac. Open 10 to 4:30 Tuesdays through Saturdays; 1 to 4:30 Sundays; closed Mondays. Donation requested. Primarily a showcase for artists, with changing exhibits monthly.

Pimeria Alta Historical Society Museum, 223 Grand Ave., Nogales. Open 9 to 5 Mondays through Fridays; 10 to 4 Saturdays; 1 to 4 Sundays; closed most holidays. Donation requested. Artifacts and memorabilia of southern Arizona and northern Mexico help explain the mixed cultures of the borderlands. Guided tours arranged. Research library on premises.

SHOPPING. Bisbee's downtown is experiencing a rebirth and has some charming shops, boutiques, jewelry stores, and art galleries.

For a unique shopping experience, try Nogales, Sonora, Mexico, right across the border from Nogales, Arizona. The downtown district features street after street of small shops selling jewelry, liquor, clothing, trinkets, ceramics, ironwork, woodcarving, fine leather goods, and much more, all at prices usually less than you'd find north of the border. Don't be afraid to haggle a little over the price of items; that's part of the fun. But there are some stores where prices are fixed, so don't be offended if the salespeople won't lower them for you. Also it is best to leave your car on the U.S. side of the border and walk across. That way you avoid the traffic hassles and the added expense of buying Mexican insurance.

DINING OUT. The price classifications of the following restaurants from Deluxe to Inexpensive are based on the cost of an average three course dinner for one person for food alone; beverages, tax, and gratuity add more: *Deluxe,* more than $20; *Expensive,* $16 to $20; *Moderate,* $10 to $16; and *Inexpensive,* under $10. Sales tax is 5 percent.

Bisbee

Copper Queen Hotel. *Moderate.* 11 Howell Avenue, 432–2216. A wide range of menu items: chicken, duck, veal, seafood, and beef.

Courtyard. *Inexpensive.* 202 Tombstone Canyon, 432–7304. Steaks, seafood, beef, veal, homemade soups and desserts served either indoors or outdoors in historic downtown Bisbee.

Golden China. *Inexpensive.* 15 Brewery Ave., 432–5888. Chinese cuisine. Lunch buffet Mondays through Fridays.

Shepherd's Inn. *Inexpensive.* 677 Main St., 432–2996. Homemade soups, quiche, fruit and cheese platters.

Tombstone

Lucky Cuss Restaurant. *Moderate.* 414 Allen St., 457–3561. The mesquite-barbecued ribs reputedly are world-famous. Also served are homemade soups and chili, ice cold beer and cocktails.

The Outback Supper Club and Antique Emporium. *Moderate.* Highway 80 between Tombstone and Bisbee, 432–2333. Seafood, prime beef, and European specialties plus a good wine list and cocktails, with a terrific view of the Mule Mountains. Also, antiques may be purchased there.

Wagon Wheel. *Moderate.* 401 E. Fremont, 457–3656. An 1880s-style bar and restaurant serving steaks, chicken, and seafood in the heart of historic Tombstone.

Adobe Lodge Restaurant. *Inexpensive.* 5th and Fremont, 457–2241. American and Italian food, also a complete salad bar.

Sierra Vista

Thunder Mountain Inn. *Moderate.* 1631 State Hwy. 92, 458–7900. Prime rib and seafood are great, plus the lounge has live entertainment nightly.

Douglas

Dawson Tavern and Steakhouse. *Moderate.* 1929 A Ave., 364–5322. Mesquite-broiled steak and seafood served in a casual atmosphere.

WESTERN ARIZONA

Casa Grande to Yuma

Just south of Casa Grande, Interstate 8 begins its almost 200-mile journey to Yuma and the California border.

In the last century, this was the Gila Trail, part of the emigrant route from the East. It was stalked by gold seekers in the 1840s and later, and stagecoach travelers who, for a fee enormous for the time, had also to fight off Indians, help push when the stage got stuck, and hope their stomachs would last the trip, due to the poor food at stage stops. The route crossed the dry "40-mile Desert" between Maricopa Wells and the Bend of the Gila, which eventually became Gila Bend, Arizona. From here the track continued west through rough country until the Colorado River was reached, then breached at Yuma Crossing, from which developed the present-day city of Yuma.

In the seventeenth century, Padre Kino founded a Maricopa Indian ranching operation near Gila Bend, raising two crops per year using irrigation. Now the area is watered with storage from Gillespie Dam.

Organ Pipe Cactus National Monument

At Gila Bend, turn off Interstate 8 to the left on State Route 85 for a trip to a desert wonderland called Organ Pipe Cactus National Monument. It's a 150-mile round-trip, so be sure to check tires and water containers before you leave.

Follow Route 85 to the mining town of Ajo, then on to the crossroad settlement of Why, Arizona.

Continue south on State Route 85. (State Route 86, which junctions here, leads directly through the Papago Indian Reservation, where shopping for baskets at trading posts becomes an art form in itself. State 86 ends at Tucson.) South from Why to the monument headquarters is less than an hour's drive. Two easy-to-negotiate loop trails through the monument let you explore at your leisure, among some of the more curious and rare fauna on earth. Here too is Quitobaquito (Little Spring), an oasis in this desert clime.

Return to I-8 via the route taken to the monument.

Painted Rocks State Park

About 15 miles past Gila Bend is a turnoff to Painted Rocks State Park, an acre of rocks 40 to 50 feet in height and covered with ancient pictographs. Anthropologists believe the park was once a boundary marker between the lands of Maricopa and Yuma Indians.

Ghost Towns and Farmlands

Back on I-8, at Sentinal, a road to the right leads to Agua Caliente (Hot Water), a hot spring and once a popular resort, now a ghost town. North from here, the U.S. Army operated a desert training camp during World War II.

Back on I-8 and continuing to the west, the communities of Dateland, Tacna, Roll, and Wellton are farming centers. From the road, you can see the neat rows of date-bearing palms that give Dateland its name.

On the approach to Yuma, you go up and over a stretch of the Gila Mountains, giving you a panoramic view of where you've been and where you're going.

The Kofa Mountains

About 35 miles to the north along U.S. Route 95 are the Kofa Mountains, a national wildlife refuge. Kofa is a contraction of "King of Arizona," a rich gold mine no longer operating.

If you are in this area during the cool season of the year, take a tour of the Kofas via the dirt road that leaves the highway at Stone Cabin. You may get to see bighorn sheep in their natural habitat. Farther north is another turnoff to the right. This takes you to Palm Canyon, about nine miles to the east. This is one of the few places in Arizona where you'll find native palm trees.

Also along U.S. Route 95, see Imperial Dam and Martinez Lake, great for fishing, boating, and river touring.

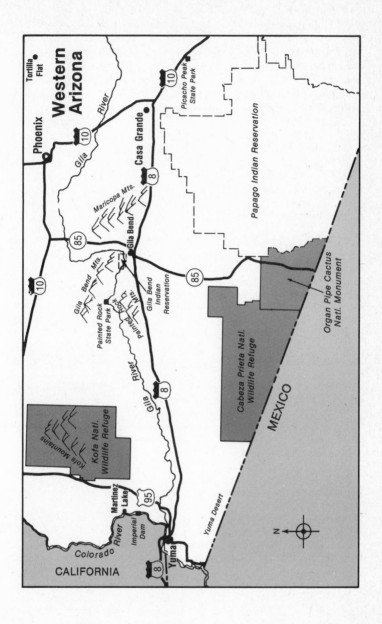

PRACTICAL INFORMATION FOR
CASA GRANDE AND INTERSTATE 8

HOW TO GET THERE AND AROUND. By bus. Casa Grande and Gila Bend are served by *Greyhound-Trailways.*

By car. Interstate 8 is an excellent four-lane highway across some vast desert stretches. Be sure to carry plenty of water for you and your car. At various times of the year, blowing dust can obscure visibility to zero. If you are caught in one of these storms, pull off the road as far as possible and turn off your lights. Dust storms usually don't last long, and you should be able to resume your travels within 30 minutes to an hour. The nearest rental agencies are in Phoenix, Tucson, and Yuma. Toll-free numbers are *Hertz,* (800) 654–3131; and *Avis,* (800) 331–1212.

HOTELS AND MOTELS. A number of good hotels are available in the Casa Grande/Gila Bend area. Expect to pay an average of between $25 and $50 per night, double occupancy. Rates vary with the season, and you can expect a drop of from $5 to $15 from June to October. All hotels listed accept MasterCard and Visa, most accept American Express, some accept Carte Blanche.

The pricing classifications are: *Deluxe,* over $70; *Expensive,* $40 to $69; *Moderate,* $25 to $39; and *Inexpensive,* under $25.

Casa Grande

Francisco Grande Resort. *Deluxe.* Box 326, 85222; 836–6444. Located 4.5 miles West of Casa Grande on State Route 84. Carriage Investment reopened this resort on the site of the old Francisco Grande. Tennis courts, 18-hole championship golf course, heated pools, cocktails, dining, entertainment.

Sandman Inn. *Expensive.* Off I-10 south of Casa Grande, 85222; 836–5000. Pool, cable TV, dining room.

Boots and Saddle Motel. *Moderate.* 509 W. Second St., 85222; 836–8249. TV, air-conditioning, pool.

Gila Bend

Best Western Space Age Lodge and Restaurant. *Expensive.* 401 E. Pima, 85337; 683–2273. Air-conditioning, color TV, heated pool, spa, coffee shop.

CAMPING. The country along I-8 is warm, sunny desert from November through early May. In summer, warm and sunny turns blazing hot. So winter is the only time to camp in the area, and a number of delightful desert campsites abound. Camping fees are usually $5 per day.

Painted Rocks State Park Historic Unit and Lake Unit. Fifteen miles west of Gila Bend and 12 miles north on Painted Rocks Road. Open year-round, fee, water, restrooms, RVs and tents allowed, waste disposal, boat launch, fishing.

Picacho Peak State Park. Forty miles north of Tucson on Interstate 10. Open year-round, fee, water, restrooms, RVs and tents allowed.

Organ Pipe Cactus National Monument. Thirty-five miles south of Ajo on State Route 85. Open year-round, fee, water, restrooms, RVs and tents allowed, waste disposal.

TOURIST INFORMATION. For information on the Casa Grande Area, contact the *Casa Grande Chamber of Commerce,* 575 N. Marshall St., Casa Grande 85222; or the *Pinal County Visitor and Tourist Center,* 912 Pinal, Florence 85232. For information on Gila Bend, contact the *Gila Bend Tourist Information* Center, 644 W. Pima St., Gila Bend 85337.

SEASONAL EVENTS. Winter: *O'odam Tash* at Casa Grande. Huge gathering of Indians from all over North America. The event includes parades, native dances, costumes, food, all-Indian rodeo, and more.

PARTICIPATION SPORTS. Hiking. Tramping through the warm desert in the winter is a delightful pastime. *Picacho Peak* and *Painted Rocks* state parks have marked trails to the more scenic areas.

Golf. Golf courses in the Casa Grande area are: *Casa Grande Golf Course,* in Casa Grande, 836–9216; *Francisco Grande Golf Course,* in Casa Grande, 836–6444; *Gila River Golf Club,* in Florence, 868–5301; *Hohokam Country Club,* in Coolidge, 723–7192.

Tennis. *Francisco Grande Resort* has fine courts (see listing under "Hotels and Motels"), and several of the cities have municipal courts. (Contact the chambers of commerce listed under Tourist Information.)

Hunting. Quail, dove, javelina, and other desert species are hunted in the open country off I-8. For information and licenses, contact the *Arizona Game and Fish Department,* 2222 W. Greenway Rd., Phoenix, 942–3000.

PARKS AND MONUMENTS. Casa Grande Ruins National Monument. Box 518, Coolidge 85228. Located 1 mile north of Coolidge on State Route 87. Massive four-story building constructed of adobe by the vanished Hohokam Indians of central Arizona. Thought to have been an ancient astronomical observatory. Interpretive talks and exhibits, walking tours. Fee, $1 per adult. Museum located at visitor center open 7 A.M. to 6 P.M. daily.

Organ Pipe Cactus National Monument. Route 1, Box 100, Ajo 85321. The park entrance is 14 miles southeast of Ajo on State Route 85-86. Sonoran Desert plants and animals found nowhere else in the United States are protected here. Also traces of historic trails. Activities include interpretive walks and talks, scenic drives, hiking, photography, wildlife watching, camping, picnicking, backcountry hiking with permits. No interpretive programs May through October. This is low desert country, with extremely high summer temperatures and little water. Be sure car and tires are in good shape and carry at least an extra gallon of water for you and your car. Stay on roads and graded turnoffs. Fee, $3 per vehicle.

Picacho Peak State Park. Forty miles north of Tucson on I-10. A landmark for early Arizona travelers, Picacho Peak was also the site of Arizona's only serious Civil War battle. Today it is a favorite area for desert nature study and hiking. In spring, following a wet winter, poppies positively carpet the base of the mountain. Fee, $3 per vehicle.

Painted Rocks State Park. Fifteen miles west of Gila Bend and 12 miles north of I-8 on Painted Rock Road. Two units provide a variety of activities in this desert park. One unit features an outstanding group of petroglyphs (carvings in rocks) made by early Arizona Indians near the historic Gila Trail, pioneer route across the Southwest to California. The other unit includes a lake below Painted Rocks Dam with water recreation, picnicking, and camping. Fee, $3 per vehicle.

Gila River Indian Crafts Center and Heritage Park. Twenty-six miles south of Phoenix, half a mile west of I-10 on Casa Blanca Road (Exit 175). In season, stroll through 2,000 years of history while touring authentic replicas of Indian villages from the Hohokam culture through such modern tribes as the Papago, Pima, Apache, and Maricopa. Story boards along the way fill in the facts about each tribe. Also there's a museum, gift shop, and dining room open year-round.

McFarland Historic State Park. Corner of Main St. and Ruggles Ave., Florence. Open 8 to 5 Thursdays through Mondays. Admission: adults, $1; 17 and under, free. This adobe building served as the Pinal County courthouse and county hospital. The museum now includes a courtroom from the early twentieth century and a sheriff's office and jail from the 1880s.

DINING OUT. Good restaurants on I-8 are clustered around the east end. The Casa Grande area and Gila Bend have the most and best, with mostly roadside cafés scattered along the rest of the route.

Price classifications of the following restaurants from Deluxe to Inexpensive are based on the cost of an average three course dinner for one person for food alone; beverages, tax, and gratuity adds more: *Deluxe,* more than $20; *Expensive,* $16 to $20; *Moderate,* $10 to $16; *Inexpensive,* under $10. Sales tax is 5 percent.

The Property. *Moderate.* On the Gila Bend Highway near Thornton Rd., 836–1101. American-style steaks, sandwiches, specialty items in a comfortable setting. Cocktails. Where the locals go for entertainment and dancing on weekends. Lunch, Mondays to Fridays; dinner Mondays to Saturdays.

Sandman Inn. *Moderate.* Off I-10 south of Casa Grande, 836–5000. American, Friday-night fish and chicken specials, nightly dinner specials. Lunch and dinner daily.

Iron Skillet Restaurant. *Inexpensive.* I–10 at Sunland Gin Road, Casa Grande, 836–3983. Warm, friendly atmosphere. Good home cooking 24 hours a day, every day. Nine "all-you-can-eat" dinners. Extensive menu, delicious pies.

YUMA

With air-conditioned cars, motels, bars, and shops, Yuma is a far cry from what it was even 30 years ago. For most then, it meant a gas and food stop on the way to the cool California coast.

Yuma's summertime temperature routinely goes up to 118 degrees and the locals have one answer when asked what they do when the mercury climbs that high: "We just let it get hot."

Yuma has been a crossing point on the Colorado River for centuries. Before the Spaniards arrived in 1540, Quechan Indians had been swimming the river, transporting goods in floating baskets they pushed as they swam.

The Spaniards rigged crude rafts to ferry their goods across, and the Indians followed their example. The Quechans made other major changes in their life-style, including wearing clothing and improving the construction of their houses. However, the Spanish did not attempt to colonize the Indians until 1697, when Spaniards sought a land route to Baja California missions.

It was Father Eusebio Francisco Kino, a Jesuit priest, who discovered that California was not an island after all, and a land route was established. The Spaniards and later explorers followed the Gila River to its confluence with the Colorado when they crossed Arizona to California. In 1776, as the Spaniards were establishing a mission in San Francisco, another was being founded at what is now Yuma.

After 1800, American mountain men, including James Ohio Pattie, came to the Yuma crossing after following the Gila River. Pattie, the first mountain man to write and publish an account of his adventures in the Southwest, was trapping beaver, which were in plentiful supply. Their pelts were in great demand for making hats for the military at that time.

These frontiersmen, who encountered terrible hardships, including starvation, dehydration, and attacks by wild animals and hostile Indians, nevertheless blazed a trail for others to follow. Their efforts gave the United States Army a vantage point in the war with Mexico.

After the Mexican war, the United States came into possession of the huge tract of land that today we call the Southwest—Colorado, Texas, New Mexico, Arizona, Nevada, and California. In 1846, Colonel Stephen Watts Kearney and a hundred soldiers marched west from Santa Fe to San Diego to occupy the newly acquired territory. Following were Colonel Philip St. George Cooke and the Mormon Battalion.

It was Louis J. F. Jaeger, however, an entrepreneurial Pennsylvanian, who established the first commercial ferry service at Yuma Crossing and made himself a bundle of cash. In one year, nearly 60,000 emigrants used the ferry. Because of the growing traffic along Cooke's Wagon Road, as it had come to be called, military protection was provided.

Further improvements to the quality of life came with the introduction of steamboats, flat-bottom craft that brought supplies to the crossing from ocean going vessels anchored at the mouth of the Colorado River. In a short time, the boats were challenging the river's current as far north as Callville, now lost beneath the cold blue waters of Lake Mead. Wagon routes then were established, on which mule trains hauled freight to the mines, military posts, and tiny communities deep in the interior. As a result of Yuma Crossing and the steamboat era, and unlike any other section of the United States, Arizona developed from west to east instead of the other way around.

In June, 1877, the Southern Pacific completed a railroad line from San Diego to Yuma, crossing the Colorado River and ringing the death knell for steamboating. Yuma then became a major shipping point. In 1883, the rail line extended across the extreme southern United States to New Orleans.

The original town site of what is now Yuma was laid out in 1854, and the settlement was called Colorado City. Later it was known as Arizona City and still later as Yuma. The little community grew, despite being known as the hottest place in the world; "so hot in the summertime that wings melt off mosquitoes and flies die in the excessive heat of the scorching sun. . . . "

Nevertheless, the community prospered, and in 1876, the Yuma Territorial Prison was established as a federal penal institution to serve the Southwest. The prison had quarters for both men and women, and even though it was considered a hellhole, it was a progressive institution. Inmates learned job skills and had a library and school.

Convicts were used to recondition city streets, construct buildings, and rebuild the town levee. They also quarried granite. The prison was moved to Florence in 1909, and the old territorial lockup became a tourist attraction.

In the same year, 1909, Laguna Dam was built, establishing a reservoir for a stable irrigation system. Yuma was on its way to becoming a growing center for vegetables and citrus as well as a tourist attraction. Another thing people were discovering about Yuma was that winters were delightful there.

Yuma has since grown into one of the state's outstanding cities. It is the hub of a large and rapidly expanding agricultural region, made fertile by Colorado River water. It also is a prime vacation base for Colorado River recreation, rock hunting, and even journeys to Mexico. Without irrigation, the land is among the most arid in Arizona, often receiving less than three inches of rain annually. Westward, in California, sand dunes are so desertlike that Hollywood movie companies use them instead of the Sahara. Yet the mountain-ringed Yuma area is more green than brown, thanks to water, and this apparently sterile land has actually been made very fertile.

Today Yuma's 80,000 population swells to something like 120,000 in winter. The estimated 40,000 winter visitors come mostly in recreational vehicles ranging from humble little trailers to motor homes costing up to $400,000. They're responding to what Yumans have been boasting for years—that it gets 93 percent of the possible 4400 hours of sunlight each year.

The winter people obviously like the climate, the friendly Yuman spirit, and the lack of congestion. The low crime rate is another attraction.

Today Yuma concentrates on the recreational-vehicle trade and has many large parks with not only the basic hookups but social centers, laundry facilities, and crafts shops where woodworkers and other craftspeople can do their thing.

The city fathers are also looking into improving the cultural climate with a performing arts center. At present, there is the annual Garces Celebration of the Arts, a spring festival that includes everything from theater and ballet to a walking tour of historic places on the riverfront.

Other Yuma attractions include The Century House, a branch of the Arizona Historical Society. The nineteenth-century home once belonged to a pioneer merchant. There are gardens and an aviary. The Territorial Prison State Park lies on a knoll above the Colorado River. St. Thomas

Mission and the Quechan Indian Museum are interesting sites. The latter marks the site of Old Fort Yuma across the river in California. The mission has roots deep in the eighteenth century.

The Customhouse is a riverfront adobe structure that served as a quartermaster depot in the 1850s and later became headquarters for the U.S. Customs Service.

Lute's Casino, billed as Arizona's oldest poolhall, is actually a showcase for old movie posters, quaint signs, and big pictures of movie stars.

Yuma also is home to a U.S. Marine Corps Air Base.

PRACTICAL INFORMATION FOR YUMA

HOW TO GET THERE. By air. Yuma is served by *America West* and *Skywest* from Phoenix and from Palm Springs, Los Angeles, and El Centro, California. For reservations, contact your local travel agent.

By bus. *Greyhound-Trailways* serves Yuma. For information and reservations, call toll-free 800–531–5332.

By train. *Amtrak* serves Yuma. For information and reservations, call Amtrak toll-free at 800–872–7245.

HOTELS AND MOTELS. Hotel and motel rates are based on double occupancy, European plan, and categories are determined by price: *Deluxe,* $70 and over; *Expensive,* $55 to $70; *Moderate,* $40 to $55; *Inexpensive,* under $40.

Expensive

Best Western Chilton Inn. 300 E. 32nd St., 85364; 344–1050. TV, pool, pets allowed, coffee shop, cocktails.

Best Western Yuma InnSuites. 1450 Castle Dome Ave., 85364; 783–8341. TV, coffee shop, pool, Jacuzzi, tennis courts, guest laundry facilities, pets allowed, kitchenettes, complimentary continental breakfast and cocktails.

Stardust Resort Motor Inn. 2350 4th Ave., 85364; 783–8861. Suites, air-conditioning, color TV, heated pool, therapy pool, putting green, guest laundry, pets allowed, dining rooms, tennis and raquetball courts, cocktails, exercise rooms, transportation to airport.

Moderate

Ramada Inn. 3181 S. 4th Ave. at 32nd St., 85364; 344–1420. Heated pool, air-conditioning, TV, movies, spa, pets allowed.

Royal Motor Inn. 2941 S. 4th Ave., 85364; 344–0550. TV, heated pool, Jacuzzi, pets allowed, coffee shop, sauna, air-conditioning.

TraveLodge-Yuma Airport. 711 E. 32nd St., 85364; 726–4721. TV, pool, air-conditioning, restaurant.

Yuma Cabana Motor Hotel. 2151 4th Ave., 85364; 783–8311. TV, heated pool, kitchens, suites, air-conditioning.

Inexpensive

Sixpence Inn. 1445 E. 16th St. (I–8 and Hwy. 95), 85364; 782–9521. TV, air-conditioning, heated pool.

HOW TO GET AROUND. By car is really the only way. There are *Hertz* and *Avis* rental agencies in Yuma. Toll-free numbers are Hertz, (800) 654–3131; Avis, (800) 331–1212.

RECREATIONAL VEHICLE PARKS. Winters are terrific on the desert shores of the Colorado River near Yuma. And a great comfortable way to enjoy a stay there is in your own recreational vehicle. The Yuma area features a number of fine RV parks, some quite luxurious, featuring clubhouses, exercise facilities, and organized activities. Some of the more popular RV parks are:

Bonita Mesa RV Park, 9400 N. Frontage Rd. Paved streets, telephone-mail room, laundry, showers, pool, Jacuzzi, cable TV to each space.

Spring Garden RV Park, 3550 W. 8th St. Adults only, open year-round, therapy pool, planned recreation.

Sun Vista RV Resort, 7201 E. Hwy. 80. Adults only; recreation hall, pool, Jacuzzi, dining and golf nearby.

TOURIST INFORMATION. A *Tourist Information Center* is located near downtown Yuma off I-8. Watch for the blue-and-white sign on the highway. These centers are a brochure bonanza, with information on the Yuma area plus many other parts of the state. The centers are staffed with friendly, knowledgeable people, ready to help you enjoy your stay in Yuma. For more information, contact the Arizona Office of Tourism, 1480 E. Bethany Home Rd., Phoenix 85014, 542–3618.

Other sources of information include: the *Yuma County Chamber of Commerce,* 377 Main St., Yuma 85364; *Yuma Visitor Bureau,* 1440 Desert Hills Dr., Yuma 85364.

SEASONAL EVENTS. January. *Gem and Mineral Show; Southwest Seniors Golf Tournament.*

February. *Silver Spur Rodeo and parade.*

March. *Square Dance Festival.*

April. *Yuma County Fair; Military Appreciation Day.*

October. *Bathtub Races at Martinez Lake.*

November. *Greyhound Dog Racing.*

HISTORIC SITES AND MUSEUMS. U.S. Army Quartermaster Depot. 2nd Avenue behind City Hall, 180 1st St. Open 8 A.M. to 5 P.M. Thursdays through Mondays; closed Tuesdays and Wednesdays. Admission $2; under 17, free. Probably the oldest American-built structure in Yuma. During the 1870s, it was used as a major supply center for troops engaged in Arizona's Indian wars. It was later used by the customs service until 1955.

Century House Museum. 240 S. Madison. Open 10 to 4 Tuesdays through Saturdays; Sundays, noon to 4, October through April. Free admission. Once the home of Yuma pioneer E. F. Sanguinetti, the museum now exhibits artifacts, photographs, and furnishings of Arizona's territorial period. Gardens, aviaries, historic library, and gift shop.

Quechan Indian Museum. Located across the Colorado River near the Territorial Prison. Open 8 to 12 and 1 to 5 Mondays through Fridays. Closed holidays. Admission 50¢. Fort Yuma is one of the older military posts associated with Arizona Territory. It protected settlers and secured the Yuma Crossing. The building now houses the headquarters for the Quechan Indian Tribe. The museum features tribal artifacts.

Yuma Territorial Prison State Park. Located at Giss Parkway and Prison Hill Road. Open 8 to 5 daily; closed Christmas Day. Admission $2; under 17, free. Between 1876 and 1909, this hulking adobe penitentiary held some of the West's most desperate and dangerous criminals. Literature, movies, and television have ensured Yuma Prison's fame as the hellhole of the Southwest. Cells, main gate, and the guard tower remain as grim reminders of frontier justice. The museum exhibits document the history of the prison.

Yuma Art Center. 281 Gila St. Open 10 to 5 Tuesdays through Saturdays; 1 to 5 Sundays, September through June 15. Admission $1; under 12, 50¢. Located in the spacious and historic restored Southern Pacific Railroad Depot, the Yuma Art Center presents a 10-month season of changing exhibits featuring contemporary Arizona artists. The Western Galleries offer a selection of paintings, prints, bronzes, and American Indian arts from private collections, other museums, and Arizona galleries. Art by Yuma artists as well as contemporary artists throughout the state is for sale.

Yuma City-County Library. 350 Third Ave. Open 9 A.M. to 9 P.M. Mondays through Thursdays, 9 A.M. to 5 P.M. Fridays and Saturdays. Admission is free. This 1920s vintage library features the usual library fare plus such special features as a large Arizona history collection and regularly changing programs and art exhibits.

PARTICIPANT SPORTS. Golf. *Desert Hills Golf Course,* 344–4653; *Arroyo Dunes Golf Course,* 726–5622; *Mesa Del Sol Golf Club,* 342–1283.

Tennis. There are several public tennis courts in Yuma. For information, contact *Yuma Department of Parks and Recreation,* 783–1271. Private clubs include *Mesa Del Sol,* 342–1283; and *Yuma Racquet Club,* 726–8386.

Fishing. The Colorado River flows right through Yuma, and Martinez Lake is just a few miles north of town. For information and fishing licenses, contact the *Arizona Game and Fish Department,* 3005 S. Pacific Ave., Yuma, 344–3436.

Hunting. Deer, antelope, javelina, rabbit, and other species can be hunted in western Arizona. For information and licenses, contact the *Arizona Game and Fish Department* at the address above.

Boating and waterskiing. *Martinez Lake Resort* north of Yuma rents boats and skis; 783–9589.

SPECTATOR SPORTS. Yuma is the spring training home for the *San Diego Padres* baseball team each February and March. For ticket information and game schedules, telephone 782–2567.

SHOPPING. Yuma has a variety of shops throughout downtown; in *Southgate Mall,* 3020 S. 4th Ave., which features a J.C. Penney; and at *Foothill Plaza Shopping Center,* 11242 Foothill Blvd.

DINING OUT. Price classifications of Yuma restaurants from Deluxe to Inexpensive are based on the cost of an average three course dinner for one person for food alone; beverages, tax, and gratuity adds more. *Deluxe,* more than $20; *Expensive,* $16 to $20; *Moderate,* $10 to $16; *Inexpensive,* under $10. Sales tax is 5 percent.

American

Inexpensive

Bobby's Restaurant. 2951 S. 4th Ave., 344–0033. Famous for their steaks.

Chester's Chuck Wagon. 2256 S. 4th Ave., 782–4152. Char-broiled steaks, roast beef, seafood, chicken.

Garden Cafe and Spice Company. 250 Madison, 783–1491. Housed inside the Historical Society. Sandwiches, salads, and muffins, served in a casual atmosphere. Sunday brunch.

Moderate

Hensley's Beef, Beans & Beer. 2855 S. 4th Ave., 344–1345. Custom-cut beef, steak and lobster, ham, chicken, halibut in a steakhouse atmosphere.

Hungry Hunter. 2355 S. 4th Ave., 782–3637. A varied menu in a cozy setting. Good beef, seafood, soups and salads, plus pasta dishes. Live entertainment in the lounge.

Martinez Lake Restaurant and Cantina. Off U.S. 95 on the shore of Martinez Lake, 783–9589. Fine dining, cocktails, dancing overlooking Martinez Lake. Also sunset dinner cruises available.

Chinese

Moderate

Imperial China. 195 S. 4th Ave., 783–4306. Authentic Szechuan- and Cantonese-style lunch and dinner. Separate rooms for nonsmokers.

Mandarin Palace. 350 E. 32nd St., 344–2805. Mandarin and Szechuan cuisine, cocktails, breakfast and lunch specials daily.

Mexican

Inexpensive

Chretin's. 485 15th Ave., 782–1291. A Yuma institution since 1946. Great Mexican food and margaritas.

El Charro. 601 8th St., 783–9790. Another old-timer. Good Mexican fare in a family-owned establishment.

NORTH-CENTRAL ARIZONA

Prescott and Red Rock Country

We refer to north-central Arizona as the area north of Phoenix and al-most to Flagstaff, which is served by Interstate 17 and includes the city of Prescott. An excursion to the Prescott area is packed with scenic side trips off I-17, such as the ghost town of Jerome, the artistic and retirement community of Sedona in the heart of Red Rock Country (known for red-dish brown and grayish white rock formations that rise above pine and oak forests), the Montezuma Castle and Fort Verde monuments, and the historic mining town of Wickenburg.

Exploring North of Phoenix

Traveling north out of the great Phoenix complex on I-17 delivers you into beautiful desert country, with a view of mountains and a quick glance at the Central Arizona Project Canal which delivers Colorado River water to the thirsty land. At the Carefree Highway turnoff, you have three travel choices: continue on I-17 north; visit Carefree and Cave Creek; or trek to the left to world-class Black Canyon Shooting Range (open to the public Wednesdays through Sundays); and Lake Pleasant, a big blue-water play-ground for swimming, fishing, and boating.

Continuing on I-17 north, a host of adventures awaits you. Immediately beyond the Carefree exit is a turnoff to the Pioneer Arizona Museum. This is a faithful replica of a pioneer village from the last century, complete with docents and volunteers in costume, who will show you what baking, weaving, and blacksmithing were like in those days of yesteryear.

Rock Springs and Black Canyon City

North on I-17 again, you realize you're gradually gaining altitude. But then you drop down again at Rock Springs and Black Canyon City. That marvelous mountain on your left filling the skyline is the Bradshaw range. It's crowned with tall timber and old mine sites.

The old-time store, ice cream parlor, restaurant, bar, and hotel at Rock Springs date back to a time early in the century when it was a trading post for miners and ranchers. The food is good, the pies are legendary, and the old store is high in nostalgia appeal.

Climbing up out of Black Canyon, still heading north, you'll glimpse a turnoff to Horsethief Basin, Bumble Bee, Cleator, and Crown King. The latter three are the remains of once colorful old mining camps. It's a Forest Service dirt road and sometimes pretty rough. To Crown King it's a switchback to the top of the mountain. Horsethief Basin is a popular mountain recreation area, with campgrounds, cabins and a store—a fun stop for your own high-country adventure. As you start up the grade out of Black Canyon on I-17, you may want to turn off your automobile air-conditioning, particularly if you're pulling a heavy load in warm weather. Overheating could become a problem.

At the top of the hill, the road levels for a short distance. Just ahead is Sunset Point, a fine rest stop with a terrific view over one of Bradshaw Mountain's big canyons. If you look closely, you'll be able to make out the old stagecoach road corkscrewing through the brush. It goes up the mountain and on to Prescott. Sunset's generous parking lot is even large enough for huge motor homes.

Bloody Basin

Just before Cordes Junction, the next turnoff, is a sign that says Bloody Basin. Out on the desert to the east was the site of a bloody battle between cavalry forces and Indians. Today the route is a four-wheel-drive trail to the Verde River.

Your next multiple choice turnoff is at Cordes Junction, where there is a garage, a large fast-food restaurant, and a service station. On the the right of the junction is Arcosanti, a visionary architect's city of the future. Still under construction, it looks out over endless miles of open rangeland. The architect is Paolo Soleri, who trained under the late Frank Lloyd Wright. Arcosanti is open to the public (admission is charged).

Exploring Around Prescott

Left at Cordes Junction, on State Route 69, starts you on a sightseeing adventure that loops through Mayer, Dewey, Prescott, the famous almost–ghost town of Jerome, Sedona–Oak Creek Canyon, and back to I-17. (Or, after Prescott, drive south on U.S. Route 89 on a loop through beautiful forest and mountain country, cattle range, and the communities of Yarnell, Congress Junction, Wickenburg, and back to Phoenix.)

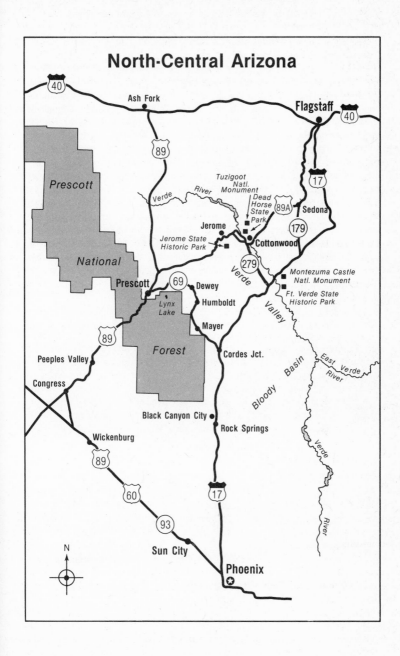

North-Central Arizona

Mayer

Mayer is about 10 miles west on State Route 69 from Cordes Junction. Take the turnoff to the left and visit the old downtown section (including the once-upon-a-time hotel that looks like it belongs in a Western movie set). The town was once a supply center for prospectors and miners. Back on State Route 69, that tall smokestack on the east side of the road is all that remains of a once busy smelter that operated back in the heyday of mining in this area. You'll catch a glimpse of mine tailings off to the left as we continue toward the quaint little mining town called Humboldt.

Most of the areas around Humboldt, Mayer, and Prescott are pockmarked with old mine shafts. Some were fabulously rich, too. Even today amateur weekend prospectors still find gold dust and an occasional nugget in the creeks and streams near these settlements.

At Dewey, you can detour 100 yards north on Route 169 to Young's Farm Store, a country grocery overflowing with home-baked goods, fresh produce, organic poultry raised on the premises, and locally made crafts. Area schoolchildren come here on field trips to learn about farm life. Back on State Route 69, Prescott Valley is the next stop, a community that sprang to life some 20 years ago. It's a retirement haven, but there also are people living there who commute to Prescott jobs.

Lynx Lake

Approximately three miles beyond Prescott Valley is a turnoff to the left marked Lynx Lake. It's about three more miles via hardtop road through the woods to the lake entrance. There's a store-restaurant and an overlook. Boats are for rent, and you can fish—if you have an Arizona license. It's perfect for picnics or just strolling among the pines. Back out to the hardtop, and State Route 69, from here it's just up the hill and around the bend to Prescott, the mile-high city and Arizona's first capital. It's notorious for looking just like everyone's home town.

Downtown Prescott

Gurley Street takes you into the heart of the city, where the first striking sight is the courthouse and plaza, complete with an equestrian statue of William "Buckey" O'Neill, a hell-for-leather former sheriff, territorial legislator, journalist, and Rough Rider with Teddy Roosevelt. Buckey died in his late thirties near San Juan Hill, believing that no Spanish bullet would every strike him down.

At Montezuma Street, just across the grassy plaza, is another historic area called, quaintly, "Whiskey Row." The Palace is a beautiful reminder of bygone days, complete with mahogany bar and backbar shipped to Prescott via sailing vessel around Cape Horn and then overland by mule-drawn freight wagon.

The Down East–Yankee influence of Prescott's founders is evident in the many old Victorian structures around town. Some of the finest in America are on Pleasant Street.

The plaza, with its big shade trees, is an inviting place in summer, the scene of community activities ranging from huge arts and crafts fairs to square dances on Saturday nights. Once, back in territorial days, a fire ignited Whiskey Row. Unfrazzled, the enterprising barkeepers simply moved their bottled goods across the street to the square and quickly went back to pouring drinks for thirsty customers.

Farther up Gurley Street is the Sharlot Hall Museum filled with antiques from Prescott's—and the territory's—colorful past. Arizona's first governor's mansion, a log house, is here too, as is the Bashford house, another restored territorial home, now a museum and arts and crafts boutique. The museum commemorates Sharlot Hall, Arizona's poet laureate and fighter for statehood.

Prescott's delightful summer weather makes the town a popular haven for desert dwellers and visitors from around the world. Even though temperatures may occasionally climb into the 90s on a summer day, nights remain cool enough for a blanket at this mile-high city in the pines.

Prescott has boomed in the last 10 years and spread out, with much to see and do. Aside from golf, fishing, arts, crafts, outings to explore the countryside, square dancing, ballet and musical concerts, and horse racing, you can drive out north to Granite Mountain on pleasant weekends and watch mountain climbers at work scaling the high cliff.

Prescott is home to Embry–Riddle Aeronautical University, where future airline pilots, engineers, and others are trained; Yavapai Community College, which offers liberal arts studies and special courses designed for Senior Citizens; and the U.S. Veterans Administration Hospital, at historic old Fort Whipple on Route 89, the Ash Fork highway, northeast of town. Here, too, are the Yavapai Indian Reservation, the Smoki Museum, and much more.

Should you plan your Prescott trip around the Fourth of July, make sure you make reservations far in advance. At this time of year, at the height of the season, Prescott literally explodes with crowds who come to see the nation's oldest world champion rodeo (Payson, beneath the Mogollon Rim, also claims the oldest rodeo) and participate in the galaxy of special events surrounding Prescott Pioneer Days.

Jerome

Jerome is the almost-ghost town on the slope of Cleopatra Hill. Pick up U.S. Route 89, the Ash Fork highway mentioned previously—it's the road that went off to the right as you entered town. Just ahead is a junction with Route 89A. This is the road to Jerome. The town is about 35 miles ahead. Be prepared for some mountain driving, steep grades, and curves. It's a good road, though, with lots of scenery.

Travelers find Jerome a fascinating place. Locals have gently restored many of the interesting old houses that perch precariously on the side of the hill, looking out over hazy miles of rolling country to the faroff heights of the Mogollon Rim.

Jerome, in its boom days, had a population of 15,000. Then, in 1951, the mine closed, and the people disapeared quickly. The town was named for Eugene Jerome, New York financier and grandfather of Sir Winston Churchill.

Nostalgia buffs always enjoy the genuine old-time atmosphere that envelops the town, once home to rough, rowdy miners from all over the world who over the years tore out of the mountain millions of dollars worth of raw copper, gold, and silver.

There were luminaries here, too, like Pancho Villa, who hauled water up to Jerome with a pack train, back in the days before a town water system was functioning.

Take time to see the Jerome State Historic Park, once the mansion of mine owner James S. "Rawhide Jimmy" Douglas, and the Mine Museum. The streets here are very narrow. You may find it best just to get out of your car and walk around a bit. As a matter of fact, we recommend it. There are crafts shops and restaurants. And if you enjoy backcountry travel and are equipped for it, ask locally about driving the Perkinsville Road. It's a full day's journey through country time forgot.

Exploring Red Rock Country

Stay on Route 89A as you leave Jerome. It takes you through Cottonwood, a growing little town on the Verde River, and your next stop: Sedona and Oak Creek Canyon, in the heart of Red Rock Country.

Sedona

Sedona began life as a little country settlement named after Sedona Schnebly, wife of a pioneer settler. For many years a quiet artists colony, it recently bloomed into an exclusive resort and retirement community. Its famous Red Rocks are described in Zane Grey's *Call of the Canyon* and are the subject of innumerable paintings and photographs. Art galleries and fine restaurants abound throughout Sedona; Tlaquepaque is a tastefully designed shopping village straight out of Old Mexico that offers a fine selection of both.

In the center of town you'll notice several jeep tour companies with their colorful vehicles parked along the main street. They are an exciting way to explore the surrounding country, showing you Indian ruins and spectacular scenery that's not accessible to ordinary cars. You'll also see the Sedona Trolley making its one-hour scenic loop around town and partway up Oak Creek Canyon; the driver provides fascinating narration, and you can either ride the whole loop as a guided tour or get on and off at various stops.

Oak Creek Canyon

Oak Creek Canyon is the mother lode of this beautiful area, and its awesome scenery includes huge monoliths, bright colors, stunning trees. Stop and take a hike, or bathe in the cool mountain waters of Oak Creek.

Leaving Sedona, you can go on to Flagstaff and the San Francisco Peaks by continuing up through Oak Creek Canyon, a scenic drive on paved road that winds up the canyonside. Or take Route 179 back to I-17, which delivers you to Flagstaff on a superhighway winding gently through high country.

Tuzigoot National Monument

To reach Tuzigoot National Monument, back track on Route 89A. Tuzigoot is a pueblo of a hundred or so rooms, built by a highly civilized people called Sinagua in the 13th century. Thrusting skyward atop a high hill, the structure commands a 360-degree view of the Verde Valley. There is a trail walk and a fine museum.

After your tour, you can leave Tuzigoot via Route 89A, continue southeast to Cottonwood, then turn right on State Route 279 and continue on to I-17.

Montezuma Castle and Fort Verde

I-17 at this point offers visitors two more major attractions: Montezuma Castle and Fort Verde.

Montezuma Castle National Monument is one of the Southwest's more incredible prehistoric cliff dwellings. (By the way, Montezuma, the Aztec emperor, had nothing at all to do with the castle.) The 20-room, five-story structure is perched in a recess high on a cliff face. There is a museum, a paved walk, and talks by park rangers.

Nearby is Montezuma Well, another prehistoric development worth seeing, a deep limestone pool that supplied water to the inhabitants of the Castle.

South of Montezuma Castle is the quaint little town of Camp Verde, in the heart of the well-watered Verde Valley. During the Indian wars of the late 19th century, an important cavalry post was here. Today it is the 10-acre Fort Verde State Historic Park. The museum contains relics of the period. Officers' homes also can be toured.

Touring Southwest of Prescott

As mentioned earlier, there's another loop trip available from Prescott to the south through Wickenburg and eventually back to Phoenix. Follow Montezuma Street (Whiskey Row, in Prescott) to U.S. Route 89 and Peeples Valley.

This wide-open range country derives its name from A.H. Peeples, a pioneer who found thousands of dollars worth of gold nuggets in Antelope Creek near here.

Peeples Valley is a beautiful farming and ranching area today, with lush fields of hay watered with runoff from the mountains. A beautiful scenic drive.

You emerge from big tree country at Yarnell. Then it's downhill, back once again to the desert, through an area rich in gold-mining lore and legend.

As you approach Wickenburg, you will pass turnoffs to some of the most famous (and infamous) ghost towns in the west. Stanton and Weaver were run by lawless gangs in the 1890s, while Octave shipped more than 8 million dollars in gold from 1863 to the end of World War II. The dirt roads to the old town ruins can be pretty rough. The tailings dump of the old Congress Mine is still visible from the present town of Congress Junction.

At the junction with State Route 93, turn left (southeast). From here, it's about three miles to Wickenburg. Take in the terrific mountain views as you ride along, including Vulture Peak, where, in the last century, Henry Wickenburg, for whom the town was named, stumbled onto incredible wealth and opened the Vulture Mine, the richest gold strike in Arizona history. Henry died penniless but left a rich heritage of colorful folk tales that never will die.

Wickenburg

In Wickenburg, known as "The Dude Ranch Capital of the World," walk down Frontier Street, where you'll feel you've just stepped into the last century. Near the bridge over the Hassayampa River, look for the old Jail Tree, an ancient mesquite the marshal chained prisoners to because the town lacked a jail. At the Desert Caballeros Western Museum, conclude your tour with a close-up look at what mining in the Old Southwest once was all about.

Take U.S. Route 60-89 out of Wickenburg. Sun City is ahead.

Big and beautiful, Sun City, which in 1985, observed its twenty-fifth anniversary, was so successful that the developers, the Del E. Webb Company, built a companion community called Sun City West.

The two municipalities have a total of 58,000 residents, who participate in a full program of activities for retirees, ranging from sports to concerts and arts and crafts.

Another 15 miles ahead and you are once again back in Phoenix.

PRACTICAL INFORMATION FOR
NORTH-CENTRAL ARIZONA

HOW TO GET THERE. By air. Sedona and Cottonwood are served by *Air Sedona* from Phoenix and Scottsdale. *Golden Pacific Airlines* serves Prescott from Phoenix.

By bus. *Arizona Central Lines* serves Cordes Junction, Prescott, and Camp Verde in comfortable vans. *Sedona Transportation Company* serves Sedona, Camp Verde, and Cottonwood.

By train. *Amtrak* serves Phoenix and Flagstaff.

By car. The nearest rental agencies are in Phoenix. Toll-free numbers are: *Hertz,* 800–654–3131; *Avis,* 800–331–1212.

Running north and east through the heart of Arizona, the paved four-lane Interstate 17 travels from low Sonoran Desert to the high pine-clad mountains of Flagstaff in about three hours. State Routes 69, 279, 179, and U.S. 89A are all good paved two-lane roads.

HOTELS AND MOTELS. Hotel and motel rates are based on double occupancy with categories determined by price during high season (usually April through October): *Deluxe,* $85 and over; *Expensive,* $65–$85; *Moderate,* $45–$65; *Inexpensive,* less than $45. All hotels and motels listed accept MasterCard and Visa, many accept American Express, and some accept Diners Club.

Sedona and Verde Valley

L'Auberge de Sedona. *Deluxe.* 301 Little Lane (Box B), Sedona 86336; 282–1161, 800–272–6776. Country French Inn; rooms have fireplaces and canopy beds; private cottages available.

Poco Diablo Resort. *Deluxe.* On Hwy. 179 (Box 1709), Sedona, 86336; 282–7333. Villas and suites, each with fireplace, private spa, and wet bar. Golf, tennis, racquetball, restaurant.

Best Western Arroyo Roble Hotel. *Expensive.* 400 N. Hwy. 89A (Box NN), Sedona 86336; 282–4001. Color cable TV, pool, balconies.

Best Western Cottonwood Inn. *Expensive.* Junction Hwy. 89A and State Route 279 (Drawer 2039), Cottonwood, 86326; 634–5575. Restaurant, lounge, pool, Jacuzzi.

Bell Rock Inn. *Moderate.* 6246 Hwy. 179, Sedona, 86336; 282–4161. Pool, tennis courts, restaurant, lounge.

Red Rock Lodge. *Moderate.* Hwy. 89A in Oak Creek Canyon (Box 537), Sedona, 86336; 282–3591. Kitchenettes, fireplaces, Jacuzzi.

The View Motel. *Inexpensive.* 818 S. Hwy. 89A, Cottonwood, 86326; 634–7581. Barbecue, pool, spa, playground.

Prescott

Best Western Prescottonian. *Expensive.* 1317 E. Gurley St., 86301; 445–3096. Restaurant, lounge, color cable TV.

Hassayampa Inn. *Expensive.* 122 E. Gurley St., 86301; 778–9434. Beautifully restored Prescott landmark. Restaurant and lounge.

Hotel Vendome. *Moderate.* 230 S. Cortez, 86303; 776–0900. Historic restored 1917 hotel. TV, complimentary breakfast. Two-room suites available.

Prescott Pines Inn Bed & Breakfast. *Moderate.* 901 White Spar Rd., 86303; 445–7270. Country Victorian house with one- and two-bedroom units. Fireplaces, kitchens. Separate A-frame cabin for 8 available.

GUEST RANCHES. If it's a real Old West experience you're looking for, you can't do better than a stay at one of the world-famous guest ranches in the Wickenburg area. Horseback riding and desert cookouts are still as popular as they were forty years ago when "dude-ranching" first got started (and when one-third of the guest ranches in the West were in Wickenburg). Today you'll find swimming, tennis, golf, and gourmet meals in addition to the old favorites. Each ranch has its own unique character. The smaller ones accommodate as few as 20 guests, so advance reservations are essential. Most ranches are open for guests during the winter season only, approximately October to May. For a complete list of ranches write the *Wickenburg Chamber of Commerce,* Box CC, Wickenburg, 85358. Some of the best-known guest ranches are:

Flying E Guest Ranch. Box EEE, Wickenburg, 85358; 684–2690. Great riding trails; informal atmosphere, small and personable.

Kay El Bar Ranch. Box 2480, Wickenburg, 85358; 684–7593. Listed on the National Historic Register. Group and family units; pool; rustic charm.

Rancho de los Caballeros. Box 1148, Wickenburg, 85358; 684–5484. Elegant and spacious; 18-hole golf course; private airstrip.

Rancho Casitas. Box A-3, Wickenburg, 85358; 684–2628. One- and two-bedroom furnished "casitas"; kitchens, pool, breathtaking views.

Wickenburg Inn Tennis and Guest Ranch. Box P, Wickenburg, 85358; 684–7811. Luxury ranch with an emphasis on tennis; dining room open to the public.

CAMPING. There are a variety of camping opportunities along I-17, from warm, sunny desert for the winter to cool mountain lakes surrounded by pines in the summer. For camping in the red rocks near Sedona, contact *Coconino National Forest,* 2323 E. Greenlaw Ln., Flagstaff 86004, 527–7400. For camping information around Jerome and Prescott, contact the *Prescott National Forest,* 344 S. Cortez St., Prescott 86301, 445–1762. *The Arizona State Parks Department,* 800 W. Washington, Phoenix 85007, 542–4174, is another agency that supervises camping areas and historic parks off I-17. Fees are usually $6 to $8 per day. The better camping areas include:

Cave Springs. Twelve miles north of Sedona on U.S. 89A. Open May to September, seven-day limit, fee, water, restrooms, RVs and tents allowed, fishing.

Dead Horse Ranch State Park. Across the river from Cottonwood, enter on North 5th Street. Open year-round, 14-day limit, fee, water, restrooms, RVs and tents allowed, waste disposal, fishing.

Granite Basin. Eight miles northwest of Prescott via Iron Springs Road. Open year-round, 14-day limit, no fee, restrooms, boat ramp, fishing.

Lynx Lake. Eight miles southeast of Prescott via State Route 69, and Walker Road. Open May through October, fee, water, restrooms, RVs and tents allowed, boat ramp, fishing.

Pine Flat. Thirteen miles north of Sedona on U.S. 89A. Open May to September, seven-day limit, fee, water, restrooms, RVs and tents allowed, fishing.

TOURIST INFORMATION. For information on what's going on in Sedona–Oak Creek Canyon, contact the *Sedona–Oak Creek Chamber of Commerce,* Box 478, Sedona 86336. For the Verde Valley towns of Cottonwood, Clarkdale, and Camp Verde, contact the *Verde Valley Chamber of Commerce,* 1010 S. Main St., Cottonwood 86326. *The Prescott Chamber of Commerce* can be reached at Box 1147, Prescott 86302. The *Wickenburg Chamber of Commerce* publishes a particularly good guide to local attractions there. They can be reached at Box CC, Wickenburg, 85358.

SEASONAL EVENTS. February. *Wickenburg's Gold Rush Days.* Shootouts, gold panning, and rodeos. **May.** Prescott hosts the *George Phippen Memorial Western Art Show and Sale* on the Courthouse Plaza lawn.

June. *Sharlot Hall Museum Folk Art Fair* in Prescott draws a good number of craftspeople demonstrating nearly every type of folk art.

July. *Prescott Frontier Days Rodeo,* the world's oldest and one of the best. Don't miss the partying downtown on Whiskey Row. Also Prescott schedules a young but good *bluegrass festival* late in the month.

September. *Sculpture Show,* Sedona. This outdoor show in a park-like setting displays work by more than 100 artists.

MONUMENTS AND SCENIC ATTRACTIONS. Nearly 3 million acres of high forest, deep canyons, lakes, streams, and high desert await the visitor in two national forests off I-17. Hiking, good fishing, and many other recreational opportunities abound. For more information, contact the *Prescott National Forest,* 344 S. Cortez St., Prescott 86301; and the *Coconino National Forest,* 2323 E. Greenlaw Ln., Flagstaff 86004.

Tuzigoot National Monument, Box 68, Clarkdale 86324. The visitors center is two miles east of Clarkdale. This large Indian pueblo, occupied from around A.D. 1100 to 1450, was built and inhabited by the Sinagua culture. The monument offers interpretive exhibits in the museum, walking tours, and hiking. Fee, $3 per vehicle.

Montezuma Castle National Monument, Box 219, Camp Verde 86322. The visitor center is 2.5 miles off I-17, five miles north of Camp Verde. This five-story 20-room pueblo is one of the better-preserved cliff dwellings in the United States, surviving for more than 700 years. Montezuma Well, 10.5 miles north of the castle, is fed by a spring at the rate of 1.5 million gallons a day. Picnicking, photography, self-guided walking tours, exhibits, and a museum. Fee, $3 per vehicle.

Oak Creek Canyon cuts into the Mogollon Rim, creating a wonderland of red rock and lush green vegetation. One of the most beautiful scenic areas in the Southwest. Fourteen miles northwest of I-17 on State Route 179.

Jerome. Once a copper-mining boomtown, turned ghost town, turned art colony. It still exudes a turn-of-the-century ambience and charm. Also features stunning views of the Verde Valley and Red Rock Country. West of I-17, 17 miles on State Route 279, then U.S. 89A.

PARTICIPANT SPORTS. Golf. Several challenging, scenic golf courses lie within a short drive of I-17. Among them are: *Poco Diablo Resort* in Sedona, 282–7333; *Prescott Country Club,* east of Prescott on Highway 69, 772–8984.

Tennis. Prescott has several municipal courts, *Yavapai College,* and other school facilities. In Sedona, *Poco Diablo Resort* has fine tennis facilities, and so does the *Bell Rock Inn.*

Fishing. Oak Creek is stocked by the Game and Fish Department and so are many of the lakes in the Prescott Area. For information and licenses, contact the *Arizona Game and Fish Department,* Region II, 310 Lake Mary Rd., Flagstaff 86001, 774–5045.

Hunting. Deer, wild turkey, antelope, javelina, and mountain lion can be hunted in areas off I-17. For information and licenses, contact the Game and Fish department at the address just given.

Hiking. Hundreds of miles of hiking trails scribe the mountains and canyons of the Prescott and Coconino forests off I-17. For information, contact the *Coconino National Forest,* 2323 E. Greenlaw Ln., Flagstaff 86004, 527–7400; and the *Prescott National Forest,* 344 S. Cortez St., Prescott 86301, 445–1762. Two of the finest hiking areas are the West Fork of Oak Creek, in Oak Creek Canyon, and Sycamore Canyon Wilderness, northwest of Cottonwood.

SPECTATOR SPORTS. Prescott features *horse racing* at the Yavapai County Fairgrounds each summer. Also at the fairgrounds each Fourth of July weekend is the *Frontier Days Rodeo,* the world's oldest and one of the country's finest.

MUSEUMS AND HISTORIC SITES. Fort Verde State Historic Park, Box 397, Camp Verde 86322. From Main Street, turn north on Lane Street. Open 8 to 5 daily; closed Christmas. Admission charge: adults, $1; under 18, free. The original site of Fort Verde, used during the Apache

Indian wars of the 1880s. Museum emphasizes the miners, prospectors, settlers, and military who settled the area.

Jerome Historical Society Mine Museum, Box 156, Jerome 86331. Located on the corner of Main and Jerome streets in downtown Jerome. Open 9 to 4:30 daily. Closed Thanksgiving, Christmas, and New Year's days. Admission charge, 50¢ Combination gift shop and museum chronicling the copper mining history of the area.

Jerome State Historic Park, Box D, Jerome 86331. Located on Douglas Road off U.S. Route 89A east of Jerome. Open 8 to 5 daily. Admission charge: adults, $1; 17 and under, free. Originally the Douglas Mansion, home of the owner of Jerome's Little Daisy Mine, the museum holds exhibits and mining memorabilia.

Sharlot Hall Museum, 415 W. Gurley, Prescott. Open in winter from 10 to 4 Tuesdays through Saturdays, 1 to 5 Sundays; in summer, 10 to 5 Tuesdays through Saturdays, 1 to 5 Sundays. Closed Mondays. Donation requested. Named for Sharlot Hall, the first Arizona State Historian, this exquisite small museum features the restored first governor's mansion and other restored homes from territorial days, also artifacts from Indian cultures of the area, and Prescott memorabilia from the town's beginnings in the last century.

Phippen Museum of Western Art, Box 1642, Prescott 86301. Located on U.S. Route 89, six miles north of Prescott. Open 1 to 4, closed Tuesdays. Western art from the late Cowboy Artist George Phippen and a handful of top artists, including Vic Donahue, Ross Stephan, Russ Vickers, and Paul Calle.

Sedona Arts Center, Box 569, Sedona 86336. Located on U.S. Route 89A and Art Barn Road. Open 10:30 to 4:30 Tuesdays through Saturdays, 1:30 to 4:30 Sundays, closed Mondays. Free admission. Two fine art galleries, a stage, classrooms, and a consignment gift shop make up this charming center featuring major art exhibitions monthly.

Desert Caballeros Western Museum, 20 N. Frontier St., in Wickenburg. Open Mondays through Saturdays 10 A.M. to 4 P.M., Sundays 1 to 4 P.M. Dioramas illustrating history of cultural Arizona, artifacts from the late 1800s, a full Western art gallery, Indian art and artifacts. Fee, $2 for adults.

SHOPPING. Perhaps the most unique shopping in northern Arizona is *Tlaquepaque* in **Sedona.** This re-creation of a Mexican village features the finest in Southwestern boutique items, including jewelry, weavings, antiques, leather goods, plus exceptional restaurants. On the left side of State Route 179 as you enter Sedona from the south. The town of Sedona also glitters with boutiques and a number of fine art galleries.

Prescott has a number of interesting shops and boutiques surrounding the Courthouse Plaza and elsewhere in downtown Prescott. Also there are several shopping centers and malls. The more complete ones are: *Ponderosa Plaza,* 1316 Iron Springs Rd., which includes J. C. Penney, Sears, Super X, and B. Dalton Booksellers; and *Park Plaza,* 1519 W. Gurley St., which has a Fry's Food Store, a locally owned pharmacy, and two movie theaters.

DINING OUT. Travels along I-17 include many fine restaurants, especially in the Sedona/Verde Valley area and in Prescott.

The price classifications of the following restaurants, from Deluxe to Inexpensive, are based on the price of an average three-course dinner for one person for food alone; beverages, tax, and gratuity would be more. *Deluxe,* more than $20; *Expensive,* $16 to $20; *Moderate,* $10 to $16; *Inexpensive,* under $10. Sales tax is 5 percent.

Sedona/Verde Valley

L'Auberge de Sedona. *Deluxe.* 301 Little Lane, Sedona, 282–7131. Dining room of the resort hotel features French gourmet cuisine. A different 5-course menu every night.

Oak Creek Owl. *Expensive.* 329 State Route 179, Sedona, 282–3532. Gourmet cooking including steak, seafood, veal, and daily specials.

Oaxaca Restaurante and Cantina. *Moderate.* 231 U.S. Route 89A, Sedona, 282–4179. Impressive view of the red rocks of Oak Creek Canyon from this top-notch Mexican restaurant.

Shugrue's Restaurant Bakery & Bar. *Moderate.* On West U.S. Route 89A in Sedona, 282–2943. Wide variety of menu items from salads and sandwiches to vegetarian dishes to fresh seafood and steaks. Also fresh-baked items in the dining room or to take out.

Prescott

Murphy's. *Moderate.* 201 N. Cortez, 445–4044. Spacious cheerful atmosphere and mesquite charcoal broiled fresh seafood and steaks. Mezzanine for nonsmokers.

Peacock Room. *Moderate.* 122 E. Gurley, 778–9434. Dining room of landmark Hassayampa Inn offers seafood, beef, and fowl, as well as daily specials. Elegant Victorian atmosphere.

Prescott Mining Company. *Moderate.* 155 Plaza Dr., 445–1991. Beautiful rustic atmosphere overlooking a creek. Fresh seafood is the specialty, with chicken, beef, and various soups among the other favorites.

NORTHERN ARIZONA

New Mexico to the Colorado River

A vast, lovely, largely untouched area, the northern half of Arizona is perhaps the most exciting to explore. In addition to the Grand Canyon, there are the stunning and remote Mogollon Rim and White Mountain range in the east-central section; hundreds of square miles of Navajo and Hopi reservations and monuments filling the northeast corner of the state; and, to the west, bordering Nevada and California, Lake Mead and the Colorado River. We have approached a tour of northern Arizona from east to west—from New Mexico to the Colorado River—an expanse crossed by Interstate 40 and lined with extraordinary natural sights and historic towns, as well as the main city of the north, Flagstaff. The Practical Information that follows covers the area served by Interstate 40 but gives specific information for those visiting the Indianlands or the Mogollon Rim and White Mountains.

Indian Ruins

As you come into Arizona from the east on Interstate 40, the view remains wide and open for miles on end, with distant vistas of high mesas. But if you look closely, from time to time you might see roundish shaped structures here and there. These are Navajo hogans—log homes.

Between the towns of Lupton and Houck, archaeologists have excavated Pueblo and earlier ruins some 1,200 years old. These excavations were done by the Smithsonian Institution and other groups, and may be viewed by getting off the main highway.

Farther west, between Tuba City and Kayenta, the prehistoric cliff dwellings of Betatakin and Keet Seel can be reached via U.S. Route 160 and State Route 564, which leads into the Navajo National Monument.

The ruins of Betatakin are visible in the distance from the visitors center. The settlement was home to the Anasazi Indians about 700 years ago. Daily, from Memorial Day to Labor Day, rangers lead hikers on the strenuous climb to the ruins. Keet Seel, at eight miles from the visitors center, is even harder to reach. This cliff village, with more than 160 rooms, is the largest Indian ruin in Arizona.

To make reservations to hike or ride to the ruins, contact: Superintendent, Navajo National Monument, HC71, Box 3, Tonalea, AZ 86044; 672–2366.

Touring the Navajo Nation

For an exciting tour of the Navajo Reservation and a close look at the people—and some spectacular scenery—turn right on U.S. Route 191 from Interstate 40 at the town of Chambers. This takes you through an area of long views to Ganado, site of the famous Hubbell Trading Post, and beyond it Canyon de Chelly (pronounced dee-shay) National Monument.

Ganado and Canyon de Chelly National Monument

Now a national historical site, the trading post was established by John Lorenzo Hubbell in the 1870s. Hubbell, who became a valued friend of the Navajos while prospering from his trade with them, went on to set up 24 trading posts on the 25,000-square-mile reservation.

During a smallpox epidemic in 1886, Hubbell turned his home into a hospital to care for the Indians. He did not get the disease himself because he had had smallpox as a boy. The Indians, not understanding immunity, attributed his ability to fend off the disease to the powers of the Great Spirit.

Ganado also is the site of a Presbyterian mission dating back to the 1920s. Here the Navajos were educated at a church school operated in the white man's way. There also was the mission hospital, made famous by the late medical missionary Dr. Clarence G. Salsbury for turning out the first Indian registered nurses.

Just past Ganado, U.S. Route 191 resumes its northward course to Chinle, where a right turn takes you to Canyon de Chelly National Monument. It's probably one of the most photographed areas in the United States.

The main gorges—Canyon de Chelly, Canyon del Muerto, and Monument Canyon—slice into the high red plateau, cutting deeper as they radiate from the immediate Chinle area. Most of the tall walls are as straight and smooth as those in your own home; ancient pictographs decorate some of the cliffs. Within the canyons, gigantic stone formations like 832-foot-high Spider Rock (taller than some New York skyscrapers) rise above small streams, hogans, tilled fields, peach orchards, and grazing lands. Tucked into some of the thousand-foot cliffs are prehistoric dwellings such as 900-year-old White House, Standing Cow, and Antelope House ruins. In Mummy Cave, archaeologists have found evidence of human habitation from A.D. 348 to 1284, a period covering the four principal eras of prehistoric Indian culture. A rim drive affords views of the highlights from a distance; for intimate sightseeing, take one of the jeep trips from Thunderbird Lodge.

Painted Desert

Back on I-40 past Chambers, the landscape changes; you've entered the vast, strange, and beautiful Painted Desert.

The desert, which runs for some 300 miles along the north bank of the Little Colorado River, is the product of millennia of erosion by wind and rain. These forces have worn down the highly colored shales, sandstones, and marls to expose their awesome beauty. Sometimes, depending on weather conditions, the reflections of these colors carry into the air above the land.

Reds and yellows, which are dominant, come from the presence of limonite and hematite. There also is some gypsum present in the form of veins. The best times for the most dramatic colors are at dawn and sunset, when the oblique light causes the shadows to deepen and makes the smaller chasms glow bright red.

Petrified Forest National Park

Along I-40 is Petrified Forest National Park, which offers another glimpse into the mists of time. Here are the preserved-in-stone trees from a time when dinosaurs roamed the land millions of years ago.

Because the petrified wood is extremely hard and takes a high polish, the area once was mined. Carloads of rock were hauled away and sold to jewelers and curio shops. Finally, in 1906, an area of about 40 square miles was made a national monument and, in 1962, designated a national park.

Each year erosion brings new petrified trees to light that have remained hidden for millennia. Chief districts in the park are the Painted Desert, Blue Mesa, Jasper Forest, Crystal Forest, Long Logs, and Giant Logs. Of these, the area around Rainbow Forest Museum and the Jasper Forest section are the most highly colored. Other attractions include the ruins of ancient Indian villages; Newspaper Rock with numerous petroglyphs; 111-foot-high Agate Bridge, spanning a windswept arroyo; and the Rainbow Forest Museum, with its displays of polished petrified wood.

The scientific explanation for the Petrified Forest is that some 150 million years ago, the area was part of a large tree-covered valley that covered part of Texas, New Mexico, Utah, and northeastern Arizona. Trees similar to the Norfolk Island pine grew here in abundance along banks of streams that coursed through the valley.

Occasionally the streams rose to flood stage and carried in sediment from the nearby highlands, eventually covering the forest to a depth of 3,000 feet. It happened so quickly that the trees did not have time to decay. Water containing the sediments seeped into the trunks, replacing the water in the tree cells with stone. The mineral makeup of the petrified logs includes silica, iron oxide, manganese, aluminum, copper, lithium, and carbon.

Up until about 60 million years ago, the forest was under a shallow ocean, which dried when the bottom was pushed up to 5,000 feet above sea level, during the upthrusts that created the surrounding mountain ranges.

Tour the park; get out and hike the trails. There's also a museum as well as a restaurant and shops. It's unlawful to pick up petrified wood in the park. It's for sale at rock shops just beyond the gates.

Holbrook and the Hashknife Cowboys

Holbrook, some 20 miles west of the Painted Desert and Petrified Forest, is a little city that grew up from a wild cowtown of yesteryear. Named after the railroad civil engineer who began the first railroad bridge over the Little Colorado, the town at first was the capital of a cattle empire. A group of eastern financiers and attorneys formed a company to use the railroad right-of-way grants for grazing. At one time, they had about one million acres of land on which they had 33,000 longhorns that had been driven over from Texas.

The company was named the Aztec Land and Cattle Company and was the third largest ranch in the West. In Arizona, the company was known as the Hashknife Outfit because its brand suggested the shape of this cowboy cooking utensil.

The Hashknife cowboys were known as some of the most rugged and skillful in the West. As in many Arizona localities in territorial days, some of the cowboys were drifters with a price on their heads for such crimes as murder and robbery. Their antics, such as galloping into Holbrook on Saturday nights and shooting out the lights in the saloons and elsewhere, are the stuff of many legends.

Nowadays Holbrook functions as the seat of Navajo County and as a quiet trading center along the Santa Fe Railroad.

Touring Payson and the Mogollon Rim

For gorgeous country that some have likened to Switzerland or Bavaria, turn south from Holbrook on State Route 77. This loop, which will take all day to do justice, brings you back to I-40 at Winslow.

It's about 30 miles south to Snowflake through grazing country with a little scrub forest growth thrown in. Snowflake, incidentally, was named after two Mormon pioneer families, the Snows and the Flakes. Proceed south on State Route 77 through Taylor and Shumway to Show Low and out to State Route 260.

Show Low got its name when two partners, C. E. Cooley and Marion Clark, played a game of Seven-Up to see who would locate at the town site. Cooley needed one more point to win, and Clark, running his hands over the cards, said, "If you can show low, you win." Cooley laid his cards down and said, "Show low it is." Clark moved up the creek near Pinetop, and Cooley stayed to found Show Low.

By now you are in big tree country, which gets more so as you travel west along State Route 260. There are small lakes and springs, and the woods get deeper and deeper.

You go through little communities like Pinedale, Overgaard, Heber, and Forest Lakes, and suddenly there you are on the edge of the world, with

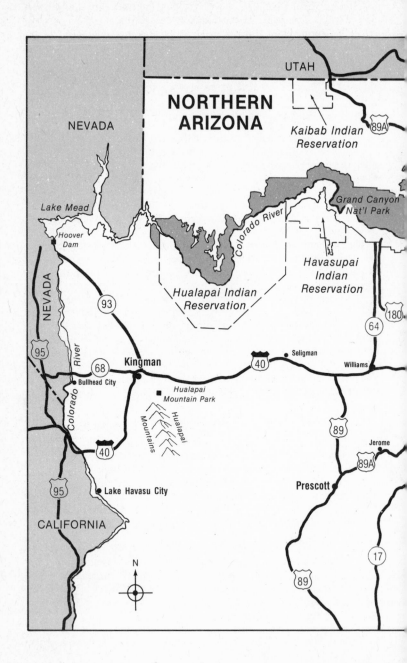

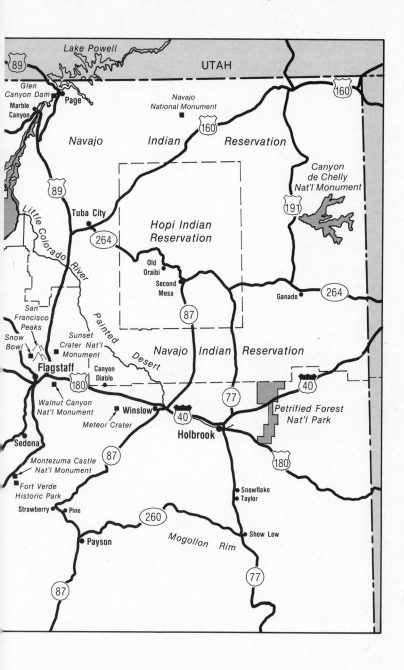

a carpet of trees stretching in all directions far below and as far as the eye can see. It's called the Mogollon Rim (pronounced *muggy-own*). There are overlooks along here that are really breathtaking.

Follow State Route 260 into Payson, a lumber-cattle-sportsman town, just below the rim. There are numerous accommodations, good restaurants, and arts-and-crafts shops.

This also is where Zane Grey came to write many of his books and do research for still others. Grey's cabin, now a museum near Payson, was lovingly restored by the late Bill Goettle, a Phoenix manufacturer. It is open to the public. Grey aficionados from all over the world have signed the register at the museum.

Take State Route 87 north out of Payson through gorgeous mountain scenery. Eleven miles later turn off to **Tonto Natural Bridge,** the largest natural travertine bridge in the world, rising 183 feet above the waters of Pine Creek. The bridge is privately owned; there is an admission fee.

The Mogollon Rim is a gigantic rock escarpment extending nearly 300 miles, all the way into New Mexico. Along the rim are the towns of Pine, settled about 100 years ago by the Mormons, and Strawberry, a summer retreat for Phoenix residents.

Winslow and Meteor Crater

Twenty miles or so west of Winslow—another division point on the Santa Fe Railroad—be ready to make a left turn to one of the curiosities of the scientific world: Meteor Crater.

This is where a huge meteor slammed into the earth at an angle from the north approximately 22,000 years ago. The crater is about one mile wide by some 600 feet deep, and is believed to have replaced about 6 million tons of rock and soil. Fragments of the meteor found in the area contain iron, nickel, and platinum and, occasionally, diamonds.

A little farther west on I-40 on the right is Canyon Diablo, a gorge about 225 feet deep and 500 feet wide. Besides being a scenic spot, it also is the site of an early Wild West town of the same name. In 1889 an Atlantic and Pacific train was held up here. The four bandits who pulled off the robbery were pursued 300 miles in two weeks before they were caught.

By now you should be seeing the majestic San Francisco Peaks to the west, which means Flagstaff is not far away. These mountains are the highest in Arizona—12,680 feet above sea level. They are always spectacular, but in winter they are snowcapped, which gives them a Christmas card quality.

Flagstaff, Queen City of the North

Flagstaff, the seat of government of Coconino County, developed from a railroad and sawmill town into a modern city that is a tourist mecca and a center of learning. It was named on Independence Day, 1876, when a centennial flag was flown from a pine chosen for its great height. The tree served as a guide for years afterward for wagon trains going to California.

This fast-growing city is still permeated with the clean smell of fresh-cut lumber, and long trains continue to chug through along Santa Fe Avenue, the main street. But a new look has come to the foot traffic along Flagstaff's main drag.

Instead of cowboys and Indians, loggers and sawmill workers, the pedestrians now are mostly students from Northern Arizona University (NAU) and tourists. NAU, formerly a small state teachers' college, literally blossomed once it was given university status, and expanded its curriculum in arts and sciences. Its forestry school is considered one of the finest in the nation. NAU now has nine colleges.

And with the improvement of the interstate highway system to the south, Flagstaff has become a summer capital and a favorite winter skiing area. The Snow Bowl, a short distance north and west of the city, attracts thousands of Arizonans each winter. (The chair lift also operates in the summer.)

All around Flagstaff, new residential developments have brought in both summer and year-round residents who enjoy the vigorous four-season climate and the spectacular scenery.

The summertime temperatures in Flagstaff range from the mid 70s to the low 80s during the day but can drop as low as 40 at night. Wintertime temperatures in the daylight hours stay in the mid-40s and drop into the teens at night. Flagstaff usually gets considerable snow in the winter.

Among its cultural, educational, and outdoor attractions are the Museum of Northern Arizona, the Flagstaff Symphony Orchestra, the Flagstaff Art Barn, Pioneers Historical Museum, the NAU art gallery, the Festival of the Arts, the Snow Bowl, a golf course, 12 tennis courts, an ice-skating rink, and a skeet and trap facility.

In addition, there is the Lowell Observatory, a world-famous space-watching facility. Scientists here discovered the planet Pluto in 1930 and have contributed much other important data on the solar system and its evolution. Tours are available.

Because of its 7,000-foot altitude and its clear air, Flagstaff has other research in astronomy going on in a research observatory at NAU. This program is sponsored by the U.S. Air Force.

Besides having its own scenic locations, Flagstaff also is a gateway to many other tourist attractions, such as Lake Powell; Monument Valley; Jerome, the famous near-ghost town; Walnut Canyon; and the Sedona–Oak Creek area.

Walnut Canyon and Sunset Crater

Walnut Canyon, seven miles east of Flagstaff on I-40, is a national monument where you can see the remains of some 300 Sinagua Indian cliff dwellings dating back to the thirteenth century. The Sinaguas built walls in limestone shelves in the canyon sides to create series of joined rooms. They were protected from the weather and their enemies by the overhanging rock. After nearly a century, the Sinaguas mysteriously disappeared. There is a trail from the visitor center that takes you right past some dwellings and gives you a good view of some others.

Sunset Crater and the Wupatki Indian ruins northeast of Flagstaff makes a good half-day tour. Take U.S. Route 89 to the loop road that brings you to Sunset Crater, a 1,000-foot-high volcanic cone that has been dormant since A.D. 1065. Here you can also get a good view of the Painted Desert and visit Indian ruins that show the influences of the Hohokam, Anasazi, and Coconino cultures.

Flagstaff to the San Francisco Peaks

For those who love forests, a tour of Hart Prairie takes you through high meadows with stands of aspen and Ponderosa pine. Take U.S. Route 180 north to Forest Road 151 on the right. This makes a 10-mile loop and returns you to 180.

Touring South of Flagstaff—Off the Beaten Path

Another scenic tour to the south of Flagstaff provides a view of many of the lakes and fishing holes in this region. This is an all-day tour.

Take I-17 toward Phoenix to the Sedona–Lake Mary Road exit to U.S. Route 89-A. Turn left on Lake Mary Road to Lower and Upper Lake Mary. You then follow Lake Mary Road to Ashurst Lake turnoff. Return to Lake Mary and proceed south to Mormon Lake, which runs along the road. Then continue south to Kinnickinick Lake turnoff.

Return and continue south on Lake Mary Road to Stoneman Lake turn-off on the right. Return to Lake Mary Road and turn right to Happy Jack, a former lumber camp. Continue south to State Route 87 at Clint's Well, turn left and go approximately three miles to Forest Road 751 and Blue Ridge Reservoir. Return to State Route 87 and turn right to Winslow, then left on I-40 to Flagstaff.

Flagstaff to the Snow Bowl

A nice 28-mile tour is the one called Top of the Peaks. This one takes you to the Fairfield Snowbowl, where there is skiing in winter and a chair lift ride, picnic facilities, snack shop, and beer and wine bar still operating in summer.

Take U.S. Route 180 north for seven miles and turn right at Snow Bowl Road. Proceed another seven miles to the lodge at the end of the road. You return to Flagstaff by the same route.

North of Flagstaff to Lake Powell

Another longer tour, probably a two-day jaunt, is to the Hopi Villages, Monument Valley, and Lake Powell in the extreme north end of the state.

Take State Route 89 north out of Flagstaff into the Navajo reservation, past Gray Mountain on the right and Cameron to the junction with State Route 160. To the left near the junction are the preserved tracks of dinosaurs that once roamed this terrain.

On Route 160, you bypass Tuba City, where there are trading posts, a shopping center, hospital, community center, and other facilities, and travel on through a land of soft brown and pink.

Hopiland

Motoring eastward on route 264, you meet the Hopi Mesas backward—that is, the Third Mesa is the first and First Mesa is third. First of the Hopi villages are Hotevilla and Bacobi on Third Mesa. These are very conservative communities. Most of the stone, mud-plastered homes are one story. The women here weave a twined type of basketry. Old Oraibi, at the other edge of the mesa, is more imposing despite being partially deserted. It claims to be the oldest continuously inhabited town in the country, dating back to about 1100. Some of the older structures, which are beginning to crumble with age, are terraced and rise to two and three stories. Check on arrival whether you may visit the village; policy changes. If it's all right, by all means do go. Between Oraibi and Shungopavi on Second Mesa, just off the north edge of the road, stands the workshop and showroom of Fred Kabotie and his Hopi Silversmith Guild. Kabotie, a noted artist, has revived interest in silver overlay work in many forms. Other types of Hopi crafts—basketry, pottery, Kachina dolls, and some leatherwork—also are on sale. Not far away is the Hopi Cultural Center, not to be missed, with a coffee shop and a good modern motel.

Principal Second Mesa villages are Shungopavi and Mishongnovi, both known for their pulsating ceremonials, including the famous Snake Dance, a religious rite. Dances are held throughout the year. Main handicraft items here are the excellently made coiled baskets and plaques in Kachina and geometric designs. As in other villages, kivas or underground ceremonial chambers are quite numerous. They also are off-limits to visitors. You can recognize the kivas by the long pole ladders sticking above the flat roofs.

For the most part, even in the more conservative villages, you'll find that the Hopi people are among the friendliest residents of Arizona. At times, they may seem shy or reserved, but an amiable approach is almost always reciprocated.

This is particularly true of the residents of First Mesa, where the schism between old and new is most apparent. From Polacca on the highway, a swing-back road up the rocky mesa goes in safe though often scary fashion to Hano. Park your car here and walk the rest of the way to the end of the mesa. Hano blends into Sichomovi so closely that they seem one long village of back-to-back, one-story homes. Pottery and Kachina dolls are for sale at some of the homes.

Continue on to the narrow saddle, about 10 feet wide and deeply rutted by wagons and trucks over the years. Just beyond, rising like a mystic, terraced Near Eastern village, is Walpi, where homes are often built into the mesa rock. Hopis have lived here for 300 years amid natural air-conditioning and tremendous views that include the San Francisco Peaks near Flagstaff. The path around the village often borders the sheer cliff, and retaining fences are reassuring. Kivas line sections of the precipice and are only an arm's length away.

At this point, you may want to remain overnight at the motel at the Hopi Cultural Center.

Your return on this tour is west to the junction of State Route 264 and U.S. Route 160 once again. Turn right to continue your journey to Navajo National Monument and Monument Valley.

Monument Valley

Back on U.S. 160, your next turnoff is about 15 miles ahead on the left, U.S. Route 163 to Kayenta, a small Indian settlement. Another 20 miles brings you into Monument Valley. These unique and colossal formations you may recall seeing in a number of classic Western movies, such as *Stagecoach* and *She Wore a Yellow Ribbon*. Park tours are available. Off

U.S. 163 on a side road, stop to visit Goulding's Lodge for lunch or dinner and perhaps an overnight stay.

Back on U.S. Route 160 is a turnoff to the right marked State Route 98. This will take you through the Kaibito Plateau along Antelope Creek to Page.

Page and Lake Powell

This newly built city, which came into being as the result of Glen Canyon Dam, has become one of the most important population centers in northern Arizona. It is 4.5 miles from the dam that backs up the Colorado River to make Lake Powell.

The lake is the second largest artificial impound in the United States. Lake Mead downriver on the west side of the state still is number one.

Wahweap Marina has just about everything a resort would need in the way of hotel space, restaurants, picnic areas, campgrounds, and marina facilities. The Canyon King, a diesel-powered paddle wheeler, takes visitors on tours daily. Or you can rent a houseboat and plan your own cruise.

There are half-day and all-day trips by large power boats that go up to Rainbow Bridge National Monument some 50 miles distant. These trips take you past a photographer's paradise of bays and fjords and red sandstone walls.

The lake is named for John Wesley Powell, a former Union Army major who lost an arm in the Civil War. Powell and a crew of men explored the Colorado River by boat from Green River, Wyoming, through the wild rapids of the Grand Canyon.

Heading back toward Flagstaff, you have a good view of the Vermilion Cliffs on your right, then later the Echo Cliffs on the left. Ahead also are the San Francisco Peaks, just north of Flagstaff.

Exploring West of Flagstaff and Williams

West out of Flagstaff are lush forested areas and miles of scenic backwood in and around the peaks. The beautifully forested terrain continues into Williams, about 40 miles west of Flagstaff. Originally a trading center for ranches in the area, Williams later developed into a lumber town after the railroad arrived in 1882. Nowadays its biggest economic base is the tourist industry. A recent changeover in the routing of I-40 has bypassed the old downtown, much to the irritation of business owners. However, if the planned revitalized rail service to the Grand Canyon occurs, it is expected to give tourists a reason for stopping rather than breezing on through.

The town and the mountain to the south of the highway are named for Bill Williams, a lean mountain man who was said to be the best guide in the West. Williams, who was a Baptist circuit rider as a young man, lived for 10 years with the Osage Indians as one of them. It was that experience that developed his skills as a pathfinder in the wilderness. Williams was killed by the Utes, with whom he had once lived and who had accepted him as a tribesman.

Ash Fork, the next city west of Williams, is a railhead for ranches in the area and a trading center. If you are interested in stalactites and stalagmites, ask about Cathedral Cave.

Seligman and Kingman

Seligman is another shipping and trading center on the Santa Fe line. It was here that old U.S. 66 took a turn to the northwest and still goes on to Kingman and beyond in a serpentine route.

Kingman brings you into high desert country where, it is estimated, it takes about 20 acres to support one cow. At least that is what ranchers used to tell the tax people down at the capital in Phoenix. But sparse as the vegetation is, the dry-looking mountains around here have yielded millions of dollars in gold. In fact, the region is pockmarked with ghost towns where miners once made it big and then went bust.

Four of those ghost towns preceded Kingman as the seat of government of Mohave County. But they all faded away, even though they had saloons, undertakers, and other amenities of civilization. One even had a red-light district.

Kingman began as a siding on the railroad and continued to grow. Presently the population followed, and an election was held in 1887 that gave the county seat to Kingman.

Another claim that Kingman has to fame is as the birthplace of Andy Devine, the rusty-voiced movie star who played a long list of supporting roles in Westerns. Proud Kingman citizens named a boulevard after him.

Now a major division point on the Santa Fe railroad, Kingman is something like Flagstaff in that it is the gateway to several scenic and interesting places.

Lake Mead

To the northwest 83 miles on U.S. Route 93 is Hoover Dam, one of the engineering marvels of the twentieth century, which impounds the water for Lake Mead and provides electric power for much of the Southwest. And in this desert country, Lake Mead with all its expanse of water is a marvel, too.

Lake Mead is 105 miles long and has a good selection of recreation sites that include lodging, restaurants, boat ramps, boat rentals, and campgrounds. You can drive on past Hoover Dam to Boulder Beach, or you can turn off U.S. Route 93 about 55 miles out of Kingman and go to Temple Bar, a resort for fishermen.

Hualapai Mountain Park

To the southeast of Kingman about 15 miles is Hualapai Mountain Park, where you leave high desert for pine country. This forested oasis in the desert rises to more than 8,000 feet in altitude and offers cabins, campgrounds, picnic sites, and a lodge with overnight accommodations and meals.

Bullhead City

About 30 miles west of Kingman on State Route 68 is Bullhead City on Lake Mohave. It's just across the Colorado River from Laughlin, Nevada, where gambling is available in plush casinos.

Bullhead City's fall and winter climate is delightful, and it's a relaxed place for good fishing and boating and backcountry touring. If you'd rather try your luck at games of chance, there is a free 24-hour ferry service across the river to Laughlin.

Lake Havasu City and London Bridge

About 40 miles south on I-40 from Kingman is the turnoff to State Route 95, which takes you another 20 miles south to Lake Havasu City and London Bridge. It arrived in pieces, which were put back together again. Now London Bridge is a wonderful tourist attraction, and Lake Havasu City, a relatively new community with a wealth of its own attractions, has become a mecca for winter visitors.

PRACTICAL INFORMATION FOR

NORTHERN ARIZONA

HOW TO GET TO AND AROUND NORTHERN ARIZONA. By air: *Air Sedona* (282–7935) serves Sedona. *Golden Pacific* (800–352–3281) serves **Sedona** and **Kingman.** *Havasu Airlines* (855–4945) serves **Bullhead City** and **Lake Havasu City.** *Skywest Airlines* (774–4830) serves **Flagstaff, Lake Powell,** and **Page.**

By train. *Amtrak* serves **Winslow, Flagstaff, Seligman,** and **Kingman.** For information and reservations, call Amtrak's toll-free number, (800) USA–RAIL.

By bus. *Greyhound-Trailways* has regular service to communities along Interstate 40, including **Houck, Holbrook, Winslow, Flagstaff, Williams, Ashfork, Seligman, Kingman, Bullhead City,** and **Page.** Contact your local *Greyhound-Trailways* office for reservations and information, or call toll-free 800–531–5332.

For custom bus or jeep tours, try: *Nava-Hopi Tours,* Box 339, Flagstaff 86002 (774–5003); *Seven Wonders Scenic Tours,* 4836 E. Half Moon Dr., Flagstaff 86004 (526–2501); or *Wild and Scenic Expeditions,* Box 460, Flagstaff 86002 (774–7343 or 800–231–1963).

Note: No airlines, trains, or buses serve the vast eastern segment of Arizona, which includes the Mogollon Rim, White Mountains, and Payson.

By car. The best way to see the areas served by I-40 is by car. The nearest rental agencies are in **Flagstaff.** Toll-free numbers are: *Hertz,* 800–654–3131; *Avis,* 800–331–2112.

By car is also really the only way to get around the **Indian reservations. Flagstaff** and **Page** have the nearest car rental agencies (telephone numbers above). Although they are not divided highways, good roads crisscross the reservations: U.S. Routes 89 and 160, north of Flagstaff; and U.S. Route 191; State Routes 77, 87, and 99 branching north off I-40, and State Route 264 cutting east and west through the heart of both reservations. Watch for farm animals and slow-moving vehicles both night and day. Stay on existing roadways. This is private land.

Mogollon Rim and the White Mountains. By car is the only way to get to this segment of Arizona. Nearest rental agencies are in the **Phoenix** metropolitan area. Most major chains, as well as smaller local agencies, provide service.

The most scenic route to the Mogollon Rim from Phoenix is State Route 87 northeast to Payson. From there you can explore northwest a short way to Strawberry and Pine, or begin a tour of the length of the rim east on State Route 260 toward the White Mountains.

From I-40, several routes connect this area with northern Arizona: U.S. Route 666 south from Sanders is a direct route to Springerville and on to the White Mountains; State Route 77 winds south from Holbrook directly to the White Mountains; and State Route 377 runs southwest to about the middle of the Mogollon Rim; State Route 87 southwest from Winslow puts you at the west end of the rim; and for a superbly scenic drive from Flagstaff, Forest Highway 3 cuts through gorgeous forest and intersects with State Route 87 north of Strawberry.

From southern Arizona, the White Mountains and the Mogollon Rim can be reached from Tucson by taking U.S. Route 89 north to State Route 77 through Globe, then on to near Seneca Lake, where the highway turns into U.S. Route 60. U.S. Route 60 runs to Show Low. From I-10 west of Tucson, take U.S. Route 666, the Coronado Trail, north to Safford, then U.S. Route 70 east to U.S. Route 666 and on to Alpine. Coming into Arizona from the east, take U.S. Route 70 from Lordsburg, New Mexico, northwest to Duncan, Arizona; then take State Route 75 to U.S. Route 666 and on to Alpine.

TIME. Unlike the rest of Arizona, which is always on *Mountain Standard Time,* the Navajo reservation is on *Mountain Daylight Time.*

IMPORTANT TELEPHONE NUMBERS. *Highway Patrol,* 526–1922; *Navajo Tribal Police,* 871–4191; *Hopi County Police,* 738–2234; *Navajo County Sheriff,* 289–4601 (Winslow), 524–3969 (Holbrook); *Coconino County Sheriff,* 774–4523 (Flagstaff, Page, and Sedona areas); *Mohave County Sheriff,* 757–0753 (northwestern Arizona); *Poison Control,* 800–326–0101. Local calls from pay phones cost 25¢.

HOTELS AND MOTELS. Because the type of accommodations available in the three major areas of northern Arizona—the cities and towns served by I-40, the Navajo and Hopi reservations, the Mogollon Rim, and White Mountains—vary a great deal, we have devised separate categories for each. For the cities and towns of northern Arizona, hotel and motel rates are based on double occupancy, and categories are *Deluxe,* $65 and over; *Expensive,* $50 to $65; *Moderate,* $35 to $50; *Inexpensive,* less than $35. All hotels and motels listed accept MasterCard and Visa, most accept American Express, and some accept Diners Club.

Holbrook

Best Western Arizonian. *Expensive.* 2508 E. Navajo Blvd., Holbrook 86025; 524–2611. Cable TV, pool; restaurant adjacent.

Best Western Adobe Inn. *Moderate.* 615 W. Hopi Dr., Holbrook 86025; 524–3948. Cable TV, pool; restaurant adjacent. Pets allowed.

Winslow

Best Western Town House. *Moderate.* One-half mile east of I-40, exit 252, Winslow 86047; 289–4611. Cable TV, pool, restaurant.

Freeway Inn. *Moderate.* Highway I-40 at Northpark Dr., Winslow 86047; 289–4687. Cable TV, pool, restaurant.

Flagstaff

Little America. *Deluxe.* 2515 E. Butler Ave., Flagstaff 86001; 779-2741. Color TV, pool, coffee shop, cocktails, gift shop, dining room, lounge, entertainment.

Holiday Inn. *Expensive.* 1000 W. Highway 66, Flagstaff 86001; 774–5221. Cable TV, pool, restaurant, pets allowed, handicapped facilities.

Comfort Inn. *Moderate.* 914 S. Milton Rd., Flagstaff 86001; 774–7326. Cable TV, pool; restaurant adjacent. Pets allowed.

Evergreen Inn. *Moderate.* 1008 E. Santa Fe, Flagstaff 86001; 774–7356. TV, pool, Jacuzzi, weight room.

Wonderland Motel. *Moderate.* 2000 E. Santa Fe, Flagstaff 86001; 779–6119. Cable TV, heated pool, air conditioning, kitchenettes.

Page

Wahweap Lodge. *Deluxe.* 4 miles north of Glen Canyon Dam, on Lake Powell, Box 1597, Page 86040; 645–2433. Marina, fishing, boat tours, pool, dining room, cocktails, entertainment. Pets allowed.

Holiday Inn. *Expensive.* 287 N. Lake Powell Blvd., Page 86040; 645-8851. Pool, dining room, cocktail lounge.

Lake Powell Motel. *Moderate.* Four miles north of Glen Canyon Dam on U.S. 89, 86040; 645–2477. View of lake, cable TV. Pets allowed.

Williams

Quality Inn Mountain Ranch Resort. *Expensive.* Deer Farm Rd., Williams 86046; 635–2693. Pool, tennis, dining room.

Williams Downtown TraveLodge. *Moderate.* 430 E. Bill Williams Ave., Williams 86046; 635–2651. Cable TV, pool, coffee shop opposite.

Ash Fork

Stage Coach Motel. *Inexpensive.* 823 Park Ave., Ash Fork 86320; 637–2278. Air-conditioning, color TV, pets allowed.

Kingman

Holiday Inn. *Expensive.* 3100 E. Andy Devine, Kingman 86401; 753–6262. TV, pool, restaurant, lounge, handicapped facilities, pets allowed, laundry.

Quality Inn. *Moderate.* 1400 E. Andy Devine Ave., Kingman 86401; 753–5531. Cable TV, pool, coffee shop, cocktails, exercise room, Jacuzzi, some kitchenettes.

Navajo and Hopi Reservations

Cities of any size are few and far between on the Navajo and Hopi reservations, and so are hotels. Most are clean and reasonable but usually not luxurious. Expect to pay between $30 and $50 per night for two. Rates noted are for in-season, double occupancy; they'll drop $5 to $15 in the off-season (winter). *Season* in northern Arizona is loosely defined as May through October. All properties listed accept MasterCard and Visa, and most also take American Express. Some take Diners Club and Carte Blanche as well. The following hotels and motels are all *Moderate*.

SECOND MESA. Hopi Cultural Center Motel. Box 67, Second Mesa 86043; 734–2401. In the heart of the Hopi reservation. Hopi museum, craft shops, restaurant.

GRAY MOUNTAIN. Best Western Gray Mountain Motel. Box 81, Gray Mountain 86020; 679–2214. At the western edge of the Navajo reservation near a trading post. TV, pool, restaurant opposite.

KAYENTA. Holiday Inn. U.S. 160 and 163, Box 307, Kayenta 86033; 697–3221. TV, pool, restaurant, coffee shop, handicapped facilities, pets allowed, laundry.

Wetherill Inn Motel. Box 175, Kayenta 86033; 697–3231. On U.S. 163, one mile north of junction with U.S. 160 near Monument Valley and Navajo National Monument. Air-conditioned, color TV, café.

WINDOW ROCK. Window Rock Motor Inn. Box 1687, Window Rock 86515; 871–4108. Center of Navajo Tribal Government and near Canyon de Chelly National Monument. TV, pool, pets allowed, coffee shop.

CHINLE. Thunderbird Lodge. at the entrance to Canyon de Chelly National Monument, Box 548, Chinle 86503; 674–5841. Color TV, restaurant, gift shop, Navajo rug room. Guided tours of Canyon de Chelly and Canyon del Muerto in open-air truck.

Mogollon Rim and White Mountains

The Mogollon Rim and White Mountains feature a number of accommodations ranging from inexpensive cabins in the woods to ski lodges and resorts.

In this area we define *Deluxe* as above $75 per night, double occupancy; *Expensive,* $50 to $74; *Moderate,* $30 to $49; *Inexpensive,* $29 and less.

All hotels and motels listed accept MasterCard and Visa. Most accept American Express and some accept Diners Club.

PAYSON. Swiss Village Lodge. *Deluxe.* 801 North Beeline Highway, Payson 85541; 474–3241. Pool, TV, coffee shop, cocktails, dining room.

Kohl's Ranch Resort. *Expensive.* East Highway 260, Payson 85541; 478–4211. Seventeen miles east of Payson on State Route 260. Units and cottages located on Tonto Creek. Air-conditioning, pool, sauna, fishing, hunting, horseback riding, dining room, cocktails.

Paysonglo Lodge. *Expensive.* 1005 S. Beeline Highway, Payson 85541; 474–2382. TV, pool, some fireplaces.

Charleston Motor Inn. *Moderate.* 302 S. Beeline Highway, Payson 85541; 474–2201. Cable TV, kitchenettes, some fireplaces.

Star Valley Motel. *Moderate.* Four miles east of Payson on State Route 260; H C Box 45A, Payson 85541; 474–5182. Cable, color TV.

SHOW LOW. Best Western Maxwell House. *Moderate.* Box 2437, Show Low 85901; 537–4356. Cable TV, pool, restaurant, lounge, coffee shop.

PINETOP. Murphy's Cabins. *Expensive.* Box 117, Pinetop 85935; 367–2332.

Whispering Pines Resort. *Expensive.* Box 1043, Pinetop 85935; 367–4386. Cable color TV, restaurant, cocktails.

Northwoods Resort. *Expensive.* Box 397, Pinetop 85935; 367–2966. TV, cottages, fireplaces, kitchens.

Bonanza Motel. *Moderate.* Box 358, State Route 260, Pinetop 85935; 367–4440. Cable color TV, pets allowed, kitchenettes.

Meadowview Lodge. *Moderate.* Box 325, Pinetop 85935; 367–4642. Full kitchens, color TV. Nearest lodging to Fred's Lake.

MCNARY. Sunrise Ski Resort. *Expensive.* Box 217, McNary 85930; 735–7676. Color TV, pool, Jacuzzis, sauna, restaurant, lounge.

GREER. Greer Mountain Resort. *Expensive.* Box 145, Greer 85927; 735–7560. Cable TV, RV park, one- and two-bedroom cabins, some fireplaces, restaurant with lounge, live music. Close to skiing and Greer Lake.

Molly Butler Lodge. *Moderate.* Box 139, Greer 85927; 735–7226. Cocktails, dining room, cabins.

CAMPING. Camping places abound in northern Arizona. The gorgeous scenery, from pine-covered mountains to rolling high desert to canyon lands, and a variety of other outdoor attractions, make for a terrific area to spend a day, a month, or a season. For wilderness camping in the **Coconino National Forest** surrounding Flagstaff, contact the forest offices at 2323 E. Greenlaw Ln., Flagstaff 86001; 527–7400. For camping west of Flagstaff, contact the **Kaibab National Forest,** 800 S. 6th Street, Williams 86046; 635–2633.

Fees for campsites generally range from $6 to $8 per night in U.S. Forest and National Park Service campgrounds. Privately managed campgrounds cost a little more. Following is a partial listing of campgrounds in the area.

Cholla Lake County Park. Two miles east of Joseph City, off I-40, Exit 277. Open year-round, 14-day limit, fee, restrooms, RVs and tents allowed, boat launching, fishing.

Fort Tuthill. Four miles from Flagstaff off U.S. Route 89A across from Flagstaff airport. Open May through September, fee, water, restrooms, RVs and tents allowed, raquetball.

Ashurst. Twenty-four miles southeast of Flagstaff on Forest Highway 3 and Forest Road 82E. Open from mid-May to mid-September, 14-day limit, fee, water, restrooms; RVs and tents allowed, boat launch, fishing.

Forked Pine. Twenty-four miles southeast of Flagstaff on Forest Highway 3 and Forest Road 82E. Open from mid-May to mid-September, 14-day limit, fee, water, restrooms; RVs and tents allowed, boat launch, fishing.

Kinnickinick. Thirty-three miles southeast of Flagstaff on Forest Service Road 3 and Forest Service Road 82. Open from mid-May to mid-September, 14-day limit, no fee, no water, restrooms; RVs and tents allowed, boat launch, fishing.

Wahweap. Seven miles northwest of Page in the Glen Can. Recreation Area. Open year-round, 14-day limit, fee, water, RVs and tents allowed, waste disposal, boat launch, fishing.

Wahweap Trailer Village. Seven miles northwest of Page in t. Canyon National Recreation Area. Open year-round, fee, water, rooms; RVs and trailers only, waste disposal, boat launch, fishing.

Lees Ferry. Five miles north of Marble Canyon off U.S. 89A. Op year-round, 14-day limit, fee, water, restroom; RVs and tents allowed, boat launch, fishing.

Kaibab Lake. Two miles north of I-40 on State Route 64. Open year-round, 14-day limit, no fee, water, restrooms; RVs and tents allowed, boat launch, fishing.

White Horse Lake. Eight miles south of Williams, then 11 miles east on Forest Service Road 110. Open mid-May through October, 14-day limit, fee, water, restrooms, RVs and tents allowed, boat launch, fishing.

Hualapai Mountain Park. Fourteen miles southeast of Kingman. Open year-round, 14-day limit, fee, water, restrooms, RVs and tents allowed.

Navajo and Hopi Reservations

It is best to camp only in designated camping areas on the reservations; there are several developed sites run by the tribes or the National Park Service. For information on wilderness camping on the **Navajo Reservation,** contact the *Navajo Tourism Office,* Visitor Services, Box 308, Window Rock 86515; 871–4941. For camping on the **Hopi Reservation,** contact *Hopi Tribal Council,* Box 123, Kyakotsmovi 86039; 734–2445. Fees are usually $2 to $6 per day.

Navajo National Monument. Twenty miles southwest of Kayenta on U.S. 160, then 10 miles northwest on State Route 564. Operated by the National Park Service, open May through October, seven-day limit, no fee, water, restrooms, RVs and tents allowed, waste disposal.

Monument Valley. Twenty-four miles north of Kayenta on U.S. 163, then four miles east. Operated by the Navajo Tribe. Open April through October, 14-day limit, fee, water, restrooms, RVs and tents allowed, waste disposal, laundromat, arts and crafts at visitor center.

Cottonwood. One mile east of Chinle in the Canyon de Chelly National Monument. Operated by the National Park Service. Open all year, 14-day limit, no fee, water, restrooms, RVs and tents allowed, waste disposal.

Wheatfields Lake. Forty-four miles northeast of Window Rock on Indian Route 12. Operated by the Navajo Tribe. Open year-round, 14-day limit, no fee, water, restrooms, RVs and tents allowed, waste disposal, ice fishing in winter.

Second Mesa. East of Cultural Center at Indian Highway 4 and State Route 264. Operated by the Hopi Tribe. Open year-round, no stay limit, no fee, water and restrooms available at the Cultural Center, RVs and tents allowed.

Keams Canyon. Across State Route 264 from the Keams Canyon Trading Post on the Hopi Reservation. Operated by the Hopi Tribe. Open year-round for day use only, fee, restrooms, trading post, picnic facilities, service station, restaurant.

Summit. Eight miles west of Window Rock on State Route 264 on the Navajo reservation. Operated by the Navajo Tribe, open year-round, 14-

...er, restrooms, RVs and tents allowed, primitive
...nicking.

day ogollon Rim and White Mountains

...on Rim and White Mountains provide tall-pine high-
...ing at its best. This land has plenty of water—streams, rivers,
...and many of the most beautiful areas are on U.S. Forest Ser-
...and open to the public. Literally thousands of developed and
...ped campsites range across this great green swath of Arizona.

...s Well. Fifteen miles south of Happy Jack on Forest Service High-
.... Open May through November, 14-day limit, no fee, restrooms,
...all RVs and tents allowed.

Kehl Springs. Twenty-six miles south of Happy Jack on State Route 87 and Forest Road 300. Open May through November, 14-day limit, no fee, restrooms, RVs and tents allowed.

Ponderosa. Thirteen miles northeast of Payson on State Route 260. Open mid-May through mid-September, 7-day limit, fee, water, restrooms, RVs and tents allowed, waste disposal.

Tonto Creek. Fifteen miles northeast of Payson on State Route 260. Open all year, fee, water; 7-day limit, restrooms, RVs and tents allowed, fishing.

Upper Tonto Creek. Fifteen miles northeast of Payson on State Route 260. Open May through September, 7-day limit, restrooms, RVs and tents, fishing.

Christopher Creek. Eighteen miles northeast of Payson on State Route 260. Open mid-May through mid-September, 7-day limit, fee, water, restrooms, RVs and tents allowed, fishing.

Chevelon Crossing. Eighteen miles northwest of Heber on State Route 260 and Forest Service Highway 504. Open May through September, 14-day limit, no fee, restrooms, tents only, fishing.

Aspen. Twenty-six miles southwest of Heber on State Route 260 and Forest Service Highway 300–105. Open May through September, 14-day limit, fee, water, restrooms, RVs and tents allowed, waste disposal, boat launch, fishing.

Canyon Point. Eighteen miles southwest of Heber on State Route 260. Open mid-May through September, 14-day limit, fee, water, restrooms, RVs and tents allowed, waste disposal.

Show Low Lake. Five and a half miles southeast on State Route 260, take the Show Low Lake Rd. Open May through September, 14-day limit, fee, water, restrooms, RVs and tents allowed, boat launch, fishing.

Lakeside. Half a mile north of Lakeside on State Route 260. Open late May through mid-September, 14-day limit, fee, water, restrooms, RVs and tents allowed.

Big Lake Recreation Area. Twenty miles southwest of Springerville on State Route 273. Open mid-May through September, 14-day limit, fee, water, restrooms, RVs and tents allowed, waste disposal, boat launch, fishing.

Hawley Lake-White Mountain Apache Indian Reservation. Eight miles south of State Route 260 on State Route 473. Open year-round, fee, water, restrooms, RVs and tents allowed, waste disposal, boat launch, fishing.

Winn. Seven miles southwest of Greer on State Route 273. Open mid-May through October, 14-day limit, fee, water, restrooms, RVs and tents allowed, boat launch, fishing.

Strayhorse. Twenty-six miles south of Alpine on U.S. Route 666. Open May through October, 14-day limit, water, restrooms, RVs and tents allowed.

KP Cienega. Twenty-three miles southwest of Alpine on U.S. Route 666. Open June through September, 14-day limit, water, restrooms, RVs and tents allowed.

RECREATIONAL VEHICLE PARKS. Painted Desert Inn and Campground, Box 400, Navajo 86509; 688–2971. **Big Tree,** 6500 N. U.S. 89 (Box 2816), Flagstaff 86003; 526–2583. **Black Bart's,** 2760 E. Butler, Flagstaff 86001; 774–1912. **Flagstaff KOA,** 5803 N. U.S. 89, Flagstaff 86001; 526–9926. **Circle Pines KOA,** 1000 Circle Pines Rd., Williams 86046; 635–4545. **Kingman KOA,** 3820 N. Roosevelt St., Kingman 86402; 757–4397. **Gordon Canyon RV Ranch,** Star Route 162B, Payson 85541; 478–4582.

TOURIST INFORMATION. *Arizona Tourist Information* centers are open in **Winslow, Page, Williams,** and **Kingman.** (Look for the blue-and-white signs along I-40 in Winslow, Williams, and Kingman, and along State Route 97 in Page.) These centers are brochure heaven, with nearly every attraction and area in the state represented. Experienced, knowledgeable staff are on duty to help you. For more information, contact the *Arizona Office of Tourism,* 1480 E. Bethany Home Rd., Phoenix 85014, 542–3618.

Navajo and Hopi Reservations. The tribal economies rely heavily on tourism dollars and the governments go out of their way to accommodate tourists. Contact the *Navajo Tourism Office,* Visitor Services, Box 308, Window Rock 86515; 871–4941. *Hopi Tribal Council,* Box 123, Kyakotsmovi 86039; 734–2441.

Mogollon Rim and White Mountains. For detailed information on the Mogollon Rim, the White Mountains, and the White Mountain Apache Indian and San Carlos Apache Indian reservations, contact *The White Mountain Chamber of Commerce,* Box 181, Springerville 85938; *The White Mountain Tourist Service,* Box 128, Pinetop 85935; *Greer Chamber of Commerce,* Box 54, Greer 86927; *Lakeside Chamber of Commerce,* Box 266, Pinetop 85935; *Payson Chamber of Commerce,* Drawer A. Payson 85547; *Pinetop Chamber of Commerce,* Box 266, Pinetop 85935; *Show Low Chamber of Commerce,* Box 1083, Show Low 85901; *Snowflake Chamber of Commerce,* Box 776, Snowflake 85937; *White Mountain Apache Tribe,* Box 700, Whiteriver 85941.

SEASONAL EVENTS. For a calendar of events for northern Arizona, contact the chambers of commerce in *Flagstaff,* 101 W. Santa Fe, Flagstaff 86001; 774–4505; in *Holbrook,* 324 Navajo Blvd., Holbrook 86025; 524–6558; in *Winslow,* Box 460, Winslow 86047; 289–2434; in *Page,* Box 727, Page 86040; 645–2741; in *Williams,* Box 235, Williams 86046; 635–2041; and in *Kingman,* Box 1150, Kingman 86402; 753–6106.

January. *Hopi Social Dances,* Hopi Reservation. Call 734–2441 for exact dates. *Hashknife Pony Express Ride,* in Holbrook. Navajo County

Sheriff's Posse carries the U.S. Mail from Holbrook to Scottsdale over the Mogollon Rim. Call 524–6558 for exact date.

February. *Arizona Statehood Day* is celebrated throughout the state on February 14. Call 542–3618 for information on local festivities.

March. *Snowbird Jamboree,* in Lake Havasu City. A celebration of the region's winter visitors. Call 855–4115 for details.

May. *Bill Williams Mountain Men Parade and Rodeo,* in Williams. The townspeople of Williams dress as mountain men and women and reenact events of the mid-1800s.

Northern Arizona Amateur Triathlon, in Winslow.

June. *Pine Country Rodeo,* weekend-long competition among some of the Southwest's best cowboys. In early June, at Fort Tuthill on U.S. Route 89 across from the Flagstaff airport.

July. *Festival of Native American Arts,* in Flagstaff. One of the finest collections of contemporary Southwest Indian art, jewelry, pottery, and weaving found anywhere.

Flagstaff Festival of the Arts, a month-long celebration of symphony, jazz, dance, opera, folk music, and more; centered around Northern Arizona University.

Loggers Festival, in Payson, draws men and women of the logging industry from all over the United States and Canada to test skill, strength, and determination against the trees and each other.

August. *Payson Rodeo.* "The World's Oldest Continuous Rodeo," featuring some of the nation's best cowboys. Contact the Payson Chamber of Commerce, Drawer A, Payson 85547, 474–4515.

Frontier Frenzy, Pinetop. Two-day re-creation of the Old West including shoot-outs, gunfights, and old-fashioned tent revivals. Call 367–4290 for details. *Arizona Cowpunchers' Reunion,* Williams. Open only to real working cowboys. Call 635–2041.

September. *Old-Time Fiddlers Arizona State Contest* in Payson is tops for country and bluegrass fans. Contact Payson Chamber of Commerce, above. *White Mountain Apache Rodeo and Fair,* Labor Day Weekend; contact White Mountain Apache Tribe, Box 700, Whiteriver 85941. *Andy Devine Days,* in Kingman, when the town celebrates its favorite son.

October. *London Bridge Days,* Lake Havasu City. Ten-day celebration includes parade, triathalon, kinetic sculpture races, and costume contests. Information at 855–4115.

November. *Havasu Classic Outboard World Championships.* Contestants drive several classes of racing boats for cash and trophies. Call 855–4115 for details.

December. *Festival of Lights,* Page. A parade of decorated boats on Lake Powell. Call 645–2741. *All-Indian Fair,* Navajo County. An international event featuring Indian dances, food, and crafts displays. Call 524–6558.

Summer and fall are important seasons on the **reservations,** with *All-Indian Rodeo Association rodeos* held in different towns virtually every weekend throughout the summer. *Spring and summer ceremonial dances* occur at some villages nearly every weekend on the Hopi Reservation. These are religious in nature, and cameras, tape recorders, and sketch pads are prohibited. Weather is hot and crowds are large. Food and lodging are at a premium, so either make reservations ahead of time or bring your own food and gear and camp out.

The Navajos hold their *fairs* at Window Rock in September and Tuba City in October. They are colorful events featuring agricultural products and native crafts.

FORESTS, PARKS, MONUMENTS, AND SCENIC ATTRAC-TIONS. Petrified Forest National Park, 86028 (602–524–6228). Enter from I-40, either at 19 or 26 miles east of Holbrook. The Petrified Forest includes a large portion of the Painted Desert, Indian ruins, and petroglyphs, as well as the famous trees that have been turned to multicolor stone. Paved trails, wilderness hiking. Interpretive hikes, talks, and films in summer are available at the Painted Desert Visitor Center. Fee, $5 per car.

Meteor Crater. Located 19 miles west of Winslow and six miles south of I-40. This natural National Landmark is the world's best-preserved meteor crater, formed when a meteoric mass traveling 33,000 miles per hour struck Earth, splashing nearly a half-billion tons of rock from the surface and destroying all life within 100 miles. The crater is 4,150 feet in diameter and 570 feet deep, and has been used for terrestrial and interplanetary research. Meteor Crater also features an astrogeological museum and the Astronaut Hall of Fame. Fee: adults, $6; seniors, $5; ages 12 to 17, $2; ages 6 to 12, $1. For seasonal hours, phone 774–8350.

Walnut Canyon National Monument. Route 1, Box 25, Flagstaff 86001. Enter from I-40, 12 miles east of Flagstaff. The monument features 800-year-old Sinagua Indian cliff dwellings set in a beautiful secluded canyon. Interpretive exhibits, hiking, and picnicking are available. Fee, $3 per car.

Grand Falls of the Little Colorado River. On Indian Highway 70, north of Winona. At spring runoff or after summer storms, the Little Colorado forms dramatic falls of muddy brown water. Often called the Chocolate Niagara. No fee.

Sunset Crater National Monument. Route 3, Box 149, Flagstaff 86001. Enter from U.S. Route 89, 15 miles north of Flagstaff, and go east on loop road connecting Sunset Crater with Wupatki National Monument. This volcanic cinder cone was formed by an eruption in A.D. 1064–65. The volcanic ash and cinders enriched the soil in the area, making it an agricultural paradise for the prehistoric cultures that settled here. Audiovisual and campfire programs are available in summer, and the area features hiking and picnicking. Fee, $3 per vehicle.

Wupatki National Monument. Tuba Star Route, Flagstaff 86001. The visitor center is on the loop road between Sunset Crater and Wupatki. Turn east off U.S. 89, 15 miles north of Flagstaff. These red sandstone ruins were built around A.D. 1065 by agricultural Pueblo Indians. The monument offers interpretive exhibits, hiking, walking, and auto tours. Fee, $3 per vehicle.

Coconino National Forest. 2323 E. Greenlaw Ln., Flagstaff 86004; and the **Kaibab National Forest,** 800 S. 6th St., Williams 86046; 527–7400. These Ponderosa pine national forests surround the Flagstaff area and feature great camping areas, sparkling lakes filled with a variety of fish, scenic hiking trails, and remote wilderness areas. Many Arizonans escape to these outdoor vacation paradises during the summer months, and in the winter, cross-country and downhill skiing delight visitors.

Glen Canyon National Recreation Area. Box 1507, Page 86040. North of Flagstaff 136 miles lies one of the Southwest's premier recreation areas,

Lake Powell. At 185 miles long and covering 250 square miles with brilliant blue water, Powell is truly one of the great lakes. Formed by the Glen Canyon Dam on the Colorado River above the Grand Canyon, Lake Powell fills the stunning sandstone canyon country, forming a scenic wonder often referred to as Monument Valley with water.

A complete resort at Wahweap provides everything necessary for a terrific stay, whether for a night, a week, or a month. Included are four marinas with houseboat and ski boat rentals; daily boat tours of the lake, including Rainbow Bridge National Monument, the beautiful sandstone arch rising 290 feet above the lake; and scenic airplane tours. Lake Powell has great fishing, miles of hiking trails in the rugged sandstone canyons on its shores, and some of the best waterskiing around.

Grand Canyon Caverns. Between Seligman and Kingman on Old Highway 66. Electrically lighted beautiful natural caverns 21 stories beneath the earth's surface. Guided tours, paved walkways. Admission: adults, $5.75; children ages 6 to 14, $3.75.

Hualapai Mountain Park. Fourteen miles southeast of Kingman. Cool mountain paradise in the middle of the desert. Camping, picnicking, and hiking.

Lake Mead National Recreation Area. 601 Nevada Highway, Boulder City, NV 89005. Fishing, swimming, boating, waterskiing, tours of Hoover Dam, horseback riding, diving, backcountry hiking, car tours, hunting, and camping are all available at Lakes Mead and Mohave. These two lakes that comprise the recreation area are not as scenic as Lake Powell, but they offer just as much recreational fun. Mead and Mohave both feature fine resorts and marinas plus houseboat, powerboat, and ski rental.

NAVAJO AND HOPI LANDS NATIONAL AND TRIBAL PARKS.

Fees where required for national and tribal parks are usually $3 per car. Camping fees range from $2 to $6 per day.

Four Corners Monument. The only place in the United States where the boundaries of four states meet. Camping, but no water.

Canyon de Chelly National Monument. Box 588, Chinle 86503; 674–5436. Beautiful sandstone canyon and Indian ruins. Facilities include a visitor center, camping, inner canyon travel by permission, ranger-conducted tours in summer, self-guided trail to archaeological sites open year-round, campfire programs in summer, interpretive talks. Concessionaire motel, cafeteria, jeep tours. Concession jeep tours are available from Thunderbird Lodge, Box 548, Chinle 86503. Hiking within the canyon requires a Park Service permit plus an authorized Navajo guide, except along the White House Ruin Trail. A $7.50 per hour fee for up to 15 people is paid directly to the guide. To drive on the canyon bottom, you must obtain a Park Service permit and be accompanied by a Navajo guide. Fee is $7.50 per hour for up to five vehicles. Four-wheel drive vehicles are mandatory. Horses can be rented by prior arrangement with the monument staff.

Three Turkey Ruins. Southeast of Chinle. One of the better-preserved archaeological sites in the Southwest. Overlook, camping, but no water. Hiking prohibited.

Hubbell Trading Post National Historic Site. Ganado 86505. One of the earlier trading posts on the Navajo reservation, with arts and crafts sales, rug weaving demonstrations, naturalist guided tours. No camping.

Kinlichee Ruins Navajo Tribal Park. West of Window Rock. Prehistoric archaeological site, now partially restored, featuring a self-guided tour and camping, but no water.

Bowl Canyon Recreation Area (Lake Asaayi). North of Window Rock. A small mountain lake with trout fishing and camping.

Window Rock–Tse Bonito Tribal Parks. Navajo Tribal Museum and Zoological Park, camping, site of the Navajo Nation Fair in September.

Little Colorado River Gorge Navajo Tribal Park. West of Cameron on State Route 64. Views of the 800-foot-deep Little Colorado River Gorge. Overlooks; camping, but no water.

Navajo National Monument. Tonalea 86044, 672–2366. Archaeological sites, visitor center, camping, rim walk, ranger-guided hike (strenuous 2.5 miles), concessionaire horse rentals.

Comb Ridge Natural Landmark. Northeast of Kayenta. A scenic geologic area on the southern edge of Mystery Valley, featuring Agathla Peak, a volcanic plug soaring hundreds of feet into the sky. No development.

Monument Valley Navajo Tribal Park. Box 93, Monument Valley, UT 84536. Beautiful valley with sandstone buttes and monuments. The site of many Western movies. Visitor center; 14-mile backcountry loop drive through the Valley of the Monuments; camping; jeep tours.

Note for Photographers: Permission must be asked and obtained before taking pictures of the Navajo people. A gratuity should be paid. A special permit is required for commercial photography.

NATIONAL FORESTS AND INDIAN RESERVATIONS. Most of the land along the Mogollon Rim and in the White Mountains National Forests and Indian Reservations is controlled by the U.S. Forest Service under the jurisdiction of three separate national forests. For maps and information on these forests, contact *Apache-Sitgreaves National Forest,* Box 640, Springerville 85938, 333–4301; *Coconino National Forest,* 2323 E. Greenlaw Lane, Flagstaff 86004, 527–7400; *Tonto National Forest,* Box 5348, Phoenix 85010, 225–5200; *White Mountain Apache Tribe,* Box 700, Whiteriver 85941, 338–4346.

PARTICIPANT SPORTS. Northern Arizona offers countless summer and winter options for all kinds of sports, from glorious downhill skiing to boating or fishing on one of many scenic lakes and, of course, endless hiking and horseback riding.

Skiing. The Flagstaff area serves as one of Arizona's winter playgrounds, featuring downhill skiing at *Fairfield Snowbowl,* 15 miles northwest of Flagstaff on U.S. 180, 774–1863, which features two triple chair lifts and a 14,300-square-foot lodge; at *Bill Williams Mountain,* 4 miles west of Williams, off I-40, 635–2041, which has a Poma lift and rope tow.

Cross-country skiing facilities include *Mormon Lake Ski Touring Center,* 28 miles southeast of Flagstaff on Mormon Lake Loop Road, 354–2240; and *Montezuma Nordic Center,* 25 miles southeast of Flagstaff at the base of Mormon Mountain, 354–2221.

Fishing. The forested mountains around Flagstaff abound with scenic lakes and streams regularly stocked with rainbow, brown, brook, and cutthroat trout; bass; crappie; northern pike; perch; and catfish. And the Colorado River lakes—Powell, Mead, and Mohave—are a fisher's paradise. Bring your own equipment or purchase it at several sporting goods stores in Flagstaff and Kingman. For fishing licenses and information on fishing in the area, contact *Arizona Game and Fish Department, Region II,* 310 S. Mary Rd., Flagstaff 85001; 774–5045.

Hunting. Deer, elk, wild turkey, antelope, buffalo, javelina, and mountain lion can be hunted in northern Arizona. For information on hunting and licenses, contact the *Arizona Game and Fish Department* at the address just given.

Horseback riding. Several scenic areas of northern Arizona just beg to be explored from the back of a trusty steed. *Canyon Country Outfitters,* Route 4, Box 739, Flagstaff 86001, 774–1676, can set up a trail ride for 2 or 20 people for an overnight or a two-week trip. The season runs from May through October, and they make all the arrangements. You just show up, climb on your horse, and enjoy. Prices range from $85 to $100 per person per day and include horse, meals, and guide. Trips are available to the San Francisco Peaks, Arizona's highest mountains; Supai Canyon, the hidden village at the bottom of the Grand Canyon; the Mogollon Rim, land of the Apache Indian wars; and Zane Grey Country. Other trips are available, and they can set up custom excursions anywhere in the West.

Hiking. Hundreds of miles of hiking trails wind throughout the Flagstaff area, over every type of terrain from high desert to pine-covered mountain to sheer-walled sandstone canyons. For information, contact the *Coconino National Forest,* 2323 E. Greenlaw Ln., Flagstaff 86004, 527–7400; and the *Kaibab National Forest,* 800 S. 6th St., Williams 86046, 635–2633.

Boating and waterskiing. *Lake Powell, Lake Mead,* and *Lake Mohave* feature four marinas renting houseboats, powerboats, and skis.

Golf. There are a number of golf courses open to the public across northern Arizona, including *Hidden Cove Golf Course* in Holbrook, 524–3097; *Winslow Municipal Golf Course,* 289–4915; *Fairfield Continental Country Club* in Flagstaff, 526–3211; *Williams Country Club* in Williams, 635–2122; *Glen Canyon Golf Course* in Page, 645–2715; *Kingman Golf Course,* 753–6593, and *Valle Vista Country Club,* 757–8744, both in Kingman.

Tennis. For public tennis courts in each town, contact the local chambers of commerce.

Navajo and Hopi Reservations

Hiking. The national and tribal parks feature miles of well-maintained hiking trails through some stunning scenery—wind- and sand-sculptured canyons, scenic overlooks with views of 100 miles.

Horseback riding. Several of the parks offer horse rentals, including *Navajo National Monument* and *Canyon de Chelly National Monument.* Reserve in advance.

Fishing. Fishing on the reservations is permitted with a reservation license. Contact the tribal governments for information on fees and where licenses can be purchased.

Boating. There are several lakes on the Navajo reservation, most notably *Lake Powell,* the huge (200 miles long) scenic lake along the northern border of the reservation. For boat rental and other information regarding Lake Powell, contact *Glen Canyon National Recreation Area,* Box 1507, Page 86040, 645–2471; or *Wahweap Lodge and Marina,* Box 1597, Page 86040, 645–2433.

Mogollon Rim and the White Mountains

The Rim Country and the White Mountains are a paradise for the outdoors type. For hundreds of miles, the Ponderosa pine forest stretches out, filled with wildlife, dotted with sapphire lakes and bubbling streams full of hungry fighting fish, and crisscrossed with hundreds of miles of hiking trails. In winter, both downhill and cross-country skiing draws thousands to the area each weekend.

Hiking. Late spring through early fall is the best time of year for hiking the Mogollon Rim and White Mountains. For information on trails, permits, wilderness areas, and camping, contact the *U.S. Forest Service* offices and the *Indian reservation* (see Mogollon Rim and White Mountains National Forests and Indian Reservations).

Fishing. The lakes, streams, and rivers teem with trout, northern pike, catfish, and more. The larger towns in the area have sporting goods stores, but you will probably want to bring your own equipment. For licenses and information on fishing, contact the *Arizona Game and Fish Department,* 2222 W. Greenway Rd., Phoenix 85023, 942-3000.

Hunting. Deer, elk, bear, turkey, and other game roam the rim and White Mountains. For information on hunting licenses, contact the *Arizona Game and Fish Department* at the address just listed.

Boating. A number of small lakes dot this area, and while use of powerboats is often restricted, canoes, rowboats, and sailboats are allowed. A few of the lakes feature rental boats. For information, contact the *U.S. Forest Service offices* listed above.

Downhill skiing. Arizona's largest ski area, *Sunrise Ski Resort,* is owned and operated by the White Mountain Apache Indians. Sunrise, near McNary, features restaurants, ski rentals, sales, instruction, and lodging. For information, call 735-7676. Also in the White Mountains is the *Greer Ski Area,* near the town of Greer. Greer Ski Area features a Poma lift and rope tow that take you to beginner and intermediate runs. Instruction, equipment rental, and sales are available.

Cross-country skiing. Hundreds of miles of cross-country ski trails crisscross this area. The touring centers are *Forest Lakes Touring Center,* 36 miles northeast of Payson on State Route 260; equipment rentals, instruction, and cabin rentals available, 535-4047; *White Mountain Ski Tours,* in Lakeside; lessons and ski tours by advance reservation, 368-5310; *Alpine Ski Tours,* in Alpine; tours, equipment rental, and instruction, lodging packages available, 339-4914.

Golf. Several challenging golf courses dot the Rim Country/White Mountains. Among them are *Alpine Country Club,* 339-4944; *Payson Country Club,* 474-2273; *Pinetop Lakes Golf and Country Club,* 369-4531; *Show Low Country Club,* 537-4564; *Silver Creek Golf Club,* Show Low, 537-7151; *Snowflake Municipal Golf Course,* 536-7233; *White Mountain Lake,* 537-2744.

SPECTATOR SPORTS. Northern Arizona seems to be more involved in get-out-and-do-it sports than in spectator sports. However, in June, there's the *Pine Country Rodeo.* The rest of the summer features *horse racing* at Fort Tuthill, southwest of Flagstaff on U.S. Route 179; December through February, Fairfield Snowbowl north of Flagstaff on U.S. Route

180 offers occasional *ski races.* Northern Arizona University has a full range of *intercollegiate sports* in the Big Sky Conference. For information, contact NAU Athletic Department at 523–5353.

Navajo and Hopi Reservations. Indian cowboys ride and rope in *All-Indian Cowboy Association Rodeos* nearly every weekend through the summer in different communities on the reservations. For hard-riding, colorful action, these events can't be beat. Check locally.

MUSEUMS. Rainbow Forest Musuem, Petrified Forest National Park, 86028 (602–524–6228). Open daily 6 A.M. to 7 P.M. June through September; 8 A.M. to 5 P.M. October through May. Closed Christmas and New Year's. Located at the south end of the park, the museum contains polished petrified wood, fossil leaves, fossil skulls, minerals, and exhibits on the history of the forest. Admission is $5 per car and includes entrance to the park.

FLAGSTAFF. Coconino Center for the Arts, Box 296, Flagstaff 86002. Open 9 to 5 daily. Donation requested. Take U.S. Route 80 north of Flagstaff to Fort Valley Road, turn right for one mile. The center is set back from the road on the same driveway as the Northern Arizona Pioneers' Historical Museum. Exhibits change every five to six weeks. The 200-seat theater features concerts, plays, dance performances, lectures, and films.

Lowell Observatory, Box 1269, Flagstaff 86002. On Mars Hill, one mile west of downtown Flagstaff on Santa Fe Ave. Generally open from 10 A.M. to 4:30 P.M., Tuesdays through Saturdays, summer; Fridays through Sundays, winter. Slide shows and lectures in the afternoons, with telescopic viewing the first evening of each month from 8 to 10 P.M. No advance tickets necessary for telescopic viewing nights. For information, phone 774–2096.

Museum of Northern Arizona, Route 4, Box 720, Flagstaff 86001. Off U.S. 180 nearly two miles north of downtown Flagstaff. Open 9 to 5 daily, closed major holidays. Admission: adults, $3; ages 5 to 21, $1.50. Since 1928, the museum has been interpreting through research and exhibits the cultural and natural history of the Colorado Plateau. It features displays of prehistoric cultures of the area as well as artwork and crafts of modern native peoples of the Southwest. Gift shop and bookstore on premises.

Northern Arizona Pioneers' Historical Museum, Box 1968, Flagstaff 86002. From downtown Flagstaff, take U.S. Route 180 north to Fort Valley Road, turn right for one mile. Museum is on the right. Open 9 to 5 Mondays through Saturdays, 1:30 to 5 Sundays, April through October; 9 to 4 and 1:30 to 4 in winter. Closed major holidays. Donation requested. Artifacts used by the early settlers of the area from the late 1800s to mid-twentieth century. Also a transportation exhibit featuring wagons, buggies, and a 1921 La France fire engine.

Riordan State Historic Park, Box 217, Flagstaff 86001. On Riordan Ranch Rd. off I-17 on the west end of Flagstaff. Open daily 8 to 5 mid-May through mid-September; 12:30 to 5 in winter. Closed Christmas. Admission: adults, $2; under 18, free. Guided tours are given hourly. This two-story mansion owned by the Riordan brothers, who made their fortunes in lumber, features everything a family of means should have owned in the West in the early twentieth century.

PAGE. John Wesley Powell Memorial Museum, Box 547, 6 North Lake Powell Blvd., Page 86040. Open daily 8 to 8 May through August;

9 to 5 weekdays, September through November, March through April. Closed December through February. Free admission. This museum highlights the life of Major Powell, the first man to run the Colorado River. Exhibits include Indian artifacts, geological displays, and videotapes of Colorado river runners.

PAYSON. Zane Grey's Cabin, Box 787, Payson 85541. Open 9 to 5 April through October; 10 to 4 March and November; closed December through February. Admission, $1. Northeast of Payson off State Route 260, five miles from Kohl's Ranch. The world's most popular Western novelist had this cabin built for him in 1918 through 1920 and used it for hunting, fishing, and writing for nine years. His saddlebags, jacket, vest, horsehair bridle, 1903 Winchester, and other memorabilia are displayed here, along with original and reprint editions of his books.

PINE. Pine-Strawberry Museum, Box 6307, Pine 85544. Open 1 to 4 Mondays through Saturdays; closed Sundays. Free. Located in the Pine Library on Randall Drive off State Route 87 near the center of Pine. On display are Indian and Anglo artifacts from prehistory to early twentieth century, including Tonto Apache Indian dolls, cradleboard, necklace and belt, 1878 quilt, bullet molds, and more. Also in Strawberry is Arizona's oldest schoolhouse, restored and open on weekends.

NAVAJO AND HOPI RESERVATIONS. There is a wide variety of fine museums and trading posts across both the Navajo and Hopi reservations that interpret and explain the rich history and life ways of these fascinating cultures. Inquire locally.

Canyon de Chelly National Monument, Box 588, Chinle 86503. Located three miles east of Chinle on Navajo Route 7. Open 8 to 5 October through April; 8 to 6, May through September. Closed Thanksgiving and Christmas days. Free admission. Exhibits explain the inhabitants of this canyon from the Anasazi people to the modern Navajo. Displays include murals, ancient brush shelters, baskets, pottery, hafted axes, cooking jars, sandals, bone tools, models of Navajo hogans, rugs, and concho belts.

Hubbell Trading Post National Historic Site, Box 150, Ganado 86505. On State Route 264, west of Ganado. Open 8 to 5 October to May; 8 to 6 May through September. Closed Thanksgiving, Christmas, and New Year's days. Free admission. This oldest trading post on the reservation hasn't changed much in 100 years and is a living museum. Featured are over 3,000 photographs of early reservation life and a huge assortment of baskets, rugs, jewelry, and pottery, all for sale. The Hubbell home is nearby, furnished in late nineteenth-century decor, and can be seen on guided tours. At the visitor center nearby, silversmiths and rug weavers demonstrate their crafts. Park rangers offer interpretive talks.

St. Michaels Historical Museum, St. Michaels Mission, Drawer D, St. Michaels 86511. On State Route 264, west of Window Rock. Open 9 to 5 Sundays through Fridays, Memorial Day through Labor Day; open by request only at other times of the year. Free admission. Restored Franciscan mission. Features display Navajo life before the coming of the Franciscans. Gift shop.

Hopi Cultural Center Museum, Second Mesa 86043. On State Route 264, five miles west of the junction with State Route 87. Open 9 to 5 daily except national and tribal holidays. Admission charge. Exquisite pottery and silvercraft of the Hopi people.

Navajo National Monument, HC 71, Box 3, Tonalea 86044. On State Route 564, nine miles north of U.S. 160. Open 8 to 5 in winter; 8 to 6 in summer. Free admission. Anasazi artifacts including pottery, arrows, shells, etc., from the thirteenth century, plus Navajo weaving and jewelry.

Ned A. Hatathli Center Museum, Navajo Community College, Tsaile 86556. North of Window Rock on State Route 12. Open 8:30 A.M. to noon and 1 to 5 P.M. Mondays through Fridays. Free admission. Culture and history of the Navajos and other tribes. Artifacts of various Indian cultures. Photo gallery of Navajo leaders. Sales gallery of silver and turquoise Navajo jewelry.

Navajo Nation Zoological and Botanical Park, Box 308, Window Rock 86515. Located in Tse Bonito Tribal Park on State Route 264. Open 8 to 5 daily except Christmas and New Year's days. Free admission. Thirty animal species at this eight-acre zoo. Only Native American-operated zoo in the U.S.

Navajo Tribal Museum, Box 308, Window Rock 86515. In the Navajo Arts and Crafts Enterprise building on State Route 264. Open 8 to 5 Mondays through Fridays; closed holidays. Donation requested. Prehistory and history of the area includes a dinosaur skeleton, Clovis and Folsom spear points, Anasazi artifacts, trading post replica, craft sales.

SHOPPING. Flagstaff has a variety of shopping opportunities, including **University Plaza Shopping Center** at I-17 and Milton Road, featuring a number of stores including Newberry's and Super X. South of University Plaza is **Green Tree Shopping Center,** with mostly locally owned stores. **Flagstaff Mall,** 4650 N. U.S. Route 89 has Dillard's, Sears, J. C. Penney, Baker's Shoes, and Casual Corner, among others.

Downtown Flagstaff is currently experiencing a renaissance, with more new stores and restaurants opening each month. The place to shop for quality Indian jewelry and crafts as well as a wide range of consumer goods.

Navajo and Hopi Reservations. Beautiful Navajo and Hopi crafts such as weaving, jewelry, and pottery are available at the museums and trading posts just listed. In addition, you'll see roadside stands along the highways featuring these crafts. Cameron, an hour north of Flagstaff, is home to the historic **Cameron Trading Post,** one of the original outposts which dealt with the Navajo. A good selection of baskets, pottery, and rugs is available.

DINING OUT. Northern Arizona has a number of good restaurants scattered along I-40 and its environs. The nicer ones are in the Flagstaff area, but a good meal can be found in the smaller, more remote areas too. Some of the better restaurants are listed here.

The price classifications of the following restaurants, are based on the cost of an average three-course dinner for one person for food alone; beverages, tax, and gratuity not included. *Expensive,* $16 to $20; *Moderate,* $10 to $16; and *Inexpensive,* under $10. Sales tax is 5 percent.

FLAGSTAFF

American

Western Gold. *Expensive.* 2515 E. Butler, in the Little America, 779–2741. Fine dining and gracious service in a comfortably elegant atmosphere. Good variety of items on the menu and a better than adequate wine list. Lunch Mondays through Fridays; dinner daily.

Horsemen Lodge Restaurant. *Moderate.* U.S. Route 89, three miles north of Flagstaff Mall, 526–2655. Western mountain lodge-style dining, including oak-broiled steaks, barbecue, mountain trout, chicken, lobster tail, cocktails. Dinner Mondays through Saturdays.

Kelly's Christmas Tree. *Moderate.* 1903 N. Second St., 779–5888. Chicken and dumplings is the specialty of the house, and the soups and cinnamon rolls are homemade. Cocktails. Reservations advised. Lunch Tuesdays through Fridays; dinner Tuesdays through Sundays.

Cookie's. *Inexpensive.* 100 N. San Francisco, 779–6971. In the historic Monte Vista Hotel. Steak and seafood. Cocktail lounge. Dinner daily.

Mexican

El Chilito. *Inexpensive.* 1551 S. Milton Rd., 774–4666. A great variety of Mexican dishes that taste the way authentic Mexican food should. The charming "south of the border" atmosphere puts you right in the spirit, and the margaritas are cold and tangy. Lunch and dinner daily.

Italian

Mama Luisa. *Moderate.* 2710 N. Steve's Blvd., 526–6809. Cozy yet elegant atmosphere. Good pasta and salad bar. Excellent daily specials. Decent wine list. Lunch Mondays through Fridays; dinner Mondays through Saturdays.

Chinese

Mandarin Garden. *Inexpensive.* 3518 E. Santa Fe Ave., 526–5033. Complete menu. Delightful Chinese atmosphere. Senior citizen discounts. Lunch and dinner daily.

WINSLOW

Best Western Town House Restaurant. *Moderate.* On West Highway 66 and 3rd St., 289–4611. American food served in the dining room, plus a coffee shop and cocktail lounge. Lunch and dinner daily.

Gabrielle's Restaurant. *Inexpensive.* 918 E. 2nd St., 289–2508. Homestyle chicken, steaks, chops, and homemade pies. Open for breakfast, lunch, and dinner seven days a week.

KINGMAN

Dambar and Steakhouse. *Moderate.* 1960 E. Andy Devine, 753–3523. Mesquite charcoal-broiled steaks and seafood in a Western atmosphere.

Cocktails; lunch, Mondays through Fridays; dinner, Mondays through Saturdays.

House of Chan. *Moderate.* 960 W. Beale St., 753–3232. A variety of good Cantonese food, plus prime rib and charcoal-broiled seafood and steaks. Lunch and dinner, Mondays through Saturdays.

La Poblanita. *Inexpensive.* 1921 Club Ave., 753–5087. Good Mexican food in a delightful south-of-the-border atmosphere. Lunch and dinner, Tuesdays through Sundays.

WILLIAMS

Rod's Steakhouse. *Moderate.* 301 E. Bill Williams Ave., 635–2671. A northern Arizona institution for over 30 years, serving thick steaks, prime rib, and seafood. Cocktails. Lunch and dinner daily.

Quality Inn Mountain Ranch Resort. *Inexpensive.* Deer Farm Rd., 635–2693. The dining room serves a wide range of good American cooking. Cocktails. Breakfast and dinner daily.

NAVAJO AND HOPI RESERVATIONS

Except for fast-food stands, restaurants on the reservations are scarce. Your best bets are restaurants associated with hotels and motels, where most meals are under $10 each. At the fast-food stands, small restaurants, and fairs, don't hesitate to try the Indian food: Navajo tacos, mutton stew, fry and piki breads are unusual treats.

PAYSON AND THE MOGOLLON RIM

Swiss Village Restaurant and Lounge. *Moderate.* One-half mile north of State Route 260 on State Route 87, 474–5800. Varied menu, cozy chalet atmosphere. Lounge with entertainment on weekends. Lunch and dinner daily.

Kohl's Ranch Resort. *Moderate.* On State Route 260, 17 miles east of Payson, 478–4211. Wide selection from steaks to prime rib to seafood to pasta. Lunch and dinner daily.

La Casa Pequena. *Inexpensive.* 911 S. Beeline Highway, Payson, 474–6329. Good selection of traditional Mexican food. Lunch and dinner daily.

WHITE MOUNTAINS

Charlie Clark's. *Moderate.* On State Route 260 in Pinetop, 367–4973. A White Mountains tradition, and still one of the best steakhouse/bars around. Lunch Mondays through Saturdays; dinner daily.

Greer Lodge. *Moderate.* In downtown Greer, 735–7515. Great food in this charming restaurant overlooking the Little Colorado River.

NIGHTLIFE. Flagstaff is a college town, and the clubs tend to cater to the younger crowd. Some more general night spots are:

The lounge at *Little America*, 2515 E. Butler, 779–2741. Mainstream entertainment nightly.

The lounge at *Monte Vista,* 100 N. San Francisco St., 779–6971. Mainstream entertainment every Thursday, Friday, and Saturday night except major holidays.

The Museum Club, 3404 E. Santa Fe, 526–9434. Country-western music in a huge, barnlike atmosphere.

Dillons, 1768 E. Santa Fe, 779–3602. Country-western music in a large turn-of-the-century lounge.

THE GRAND CANYON

When most people look down into the Grand Canyon for the first time, they tend to speak in hushed tones of wonderment. Of course, this awesome spectacle, which attracts some 4 million visitors from all over the world each year, does not produce the same reaction in everyone.

The area that includes the Grand Canyon originally was under a vast prehistoric sea, but a gradual upthrust of the earth created what is now the Kaibab Plateau. As the plateau was pushed upward, it developed faults or cracks, one of which became the course of the Colorado River. Over millions of years, the river has gradually eroded its rocky bed, grinding its way downward as the earth came upward. This "erosion upon a grand scale" reveals many of the rock formations that marked the beginnings of the Planet Earth back in the mists of time.

The first Europeans to discover the Canyon were a contingent of Spanish Conquistadores who had gone out to look for a "great river." They reported that they had found the river, but it ran between "high red walls" and it was impossible to cross. The Spaniards were awe-struck by the strange beauty of the area, but wrote it off as a great natural barrier.

This feeling was shared by early American explorers some three centuries later. Because the river couldn't be crossed for the 270 miles or so that it turns and twists through the great gorge, they felt it was "valueless."

But today, of course, it is officially designated as one of the Seven Natural Wonders of the World, and the Canyon is on the itinerary of almost everyone who wants to see Arizona.

THE GRAND CANYON THROUGH THE AGES

The name Grand Canyon comes from the Spanish *Gran Barranca,* which was what the conquistadores called it. They called the river the *Río Colorado,* Spanish for "red river," to describe the high red walls the soldiers found blocking their way to crossing the stream.

Early Indian Dwellers

Archeologists have found the canyon first was used by humans as a dwelling place at least 4,000 years ago. The first signs of their occupancy are small figures made of split twigs representing bighorn sheep and pronghorn antelope, which still may be seen there today. The figurines, which date back between 3,000 and 4,000 years, probably were made by nomadic hunters.

About 2,000 years ago, a group that historians call Basketmakers began living in caves and rock shelters at the bottom of the canyon, where the climate is mild because of its low elevation.

By about A.D. 700, the Basketmakers became what is known as Pueblo Indians, probably by association with other peoples. They built houses of masonry and mud on the surface of the ground. They also constructed *kivas,* places of worship, partly underground.

The Puebloans developed several styles of pottery—banded, decorated, and painted in various color patterns. They grew cotton, began to spin and weave into pleasing patterns, and domesticated dogs and turkeys.

Pueblo villages were independent, like the Greek city-states, and their rules and customs became highly formalized, reflecting their agrarian way of life. They held elaborate ceremonies to implore their gods for rain in a dry land and fertility for life-sustaining crops, and decorated the walls of their kivas as well as the caves and cliffs of the canyon.

Around A.D. 800, a western branch of Pueblo Indians, the Kayentas, built small houses on the North Rim of the canyon and, a century later, on the South Rim.

The Kayentas farmed fertile areas and built terraces and irrigation ditches. These Pueblo tribes dwelled in many parts of the canyon from rim to river until a short time after A.D. 1050.

This was the classic or high period of Pueblo civilization, during which they built multistory houses, some of them with hundreds of rooms. More than 500 Pueblo ruins have been found in the immediate vicinity of the canyon.

The biggest of these were located at Betatakin, Keet Seel, and Inscription House settlements. Other large dwellings were built at Mesa Verde and Chaco Canyon.

The Puebloans abandoned their locations in the Grand Canyon and appear to have withdrawn from the North Rim somewhere around A.D. 1150. Archeologists believe it may have been a withdrawal in stages, possibly as a result of hostility from nomadic tribes.

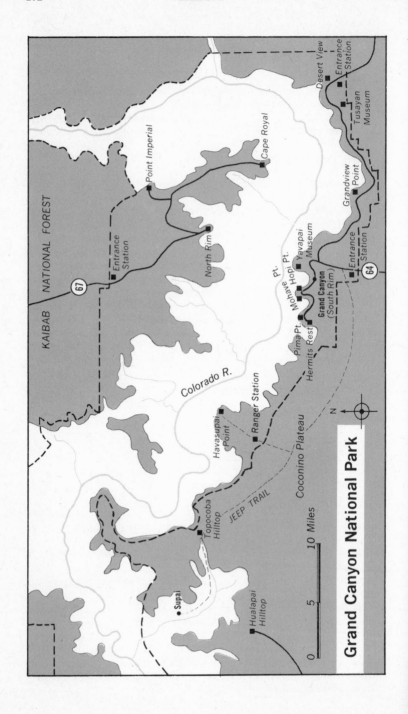

Grand Canyon National Park

Still other possibilities are a depleted game supply, scarcity of firewood, or exhaustion of their farmlands. It is known that a great drought took place from A.D. 1276 to 1299 and probably forced the Puebloans to move out of their population centers to locate near permanent springs. The Puebloans are the ancestors of the modern Hopi Indians, whose villages and farms are situated about 100 miles east of the Grand Canyon, where springs seep from under mesas.

Old Oraibi, established in about A.D. 1150, is the oldest continuously inhabited town in the United States. To get to Oraibi, take 160 from the junction with U.S. Route 89 (north from Flagstaff) to Tuba City, then turn right on State Route 264. The trip is about 65 miles and includes the other Hopi villages of Hotevila, Bacobi, Kykotsmovi, and Shongopavi.

In the Hopi religion, the Grand Canyon is the place where man emerged from the underworld. It also is believed that the dead return there. Sipapu, the entrance to the underworld, is located in the canyon of the Little Colorado River 4.5 miles above the junction with the Colorado. For centuries, it has been the route of pilgrimages by the Hopis.

The Hopis made trips to a ceremonial salt deposit near the Colorado below the mouth of the Little Colorado, and also had a trade route to the Havasupais. Hunting trips were another factor that brought them into the Grand Canyon. Evidence of their frequent visits to the canyon are shards of Hopi pottery and clan symbols on the rocks.

From around A.D. 600, the Coconino Plateau (the area south of the South Rim) was occupied by agricultural and hunting people called the Cohonina, meaning "people of the west" in the Hopi tongue. The Cohoninas (which later became Coconino) lived apart from their neighbors, the Basketmakers and the Puebloans, and pursued a simpler life. They used little ornamentation, and their stone objects were of poor quality.

Around A.D. 900, when the Puebloans occupied the South Rim, the Cohoninas moved west of Hermit's Rest. They also may have been driven down into Havasu Canyon by the arrival of other hostile tribes and thus became the ancestors of the modern-day Havasupais. Another theory is that the Cohoninas were driven out or exterminated by enemy tribes, and that invaders from the west were the ancestors of both the Hualapai and Havasupai Indians.

The Havasupais now are the only Indians living in the Grand Canyon, and are relatives of the Hualapais, who live farther west. *Havasupai* means "people of blue-green water" and refers to the pools in Havasu Creek, their source of water. The Havasupais were farmers in the summer, hunters and gatherers in the winter, who carried on trade with their neighbors.

The Havasupai tribe has stayed at a population of around 200 for several centuries. Their homes are surface shelters of willow, mud and thatch, or logs. Their religion is simple, with little ceremony and oriented toward the cycle of crops. However, with the continued exposure to the white man, their way of life is changing.

To the north of the Grand Canyon, the Paiutes claimed the territory south of the high plateaus of Utah. They were hunters and gatherers and trekked wherever they could find the necessities of life, traveling in an annual cycle.

In the fall, they went up on the Kaibab Plateau to hunt deer and collect pine nuts. Their annual deer hunt caused the later-arriving whites to call the plateau Buckskin Mountain.

The Paiutes, who speak a language distantly related to the Hopi tongue, lived in scattered family groups. Their clothing consisted of loincloths or skirts made of cliff rose bark and, occasionally, deerskin. The Paiute's houses were caves or crude brush shelters that they occupied for short periods.

During the 19th century, white settlers began taking the Paiutes' lands. The whites also shot Paiute men and stole their children. Diseases brought in by the white man also decimated the Paiute population, so that only about 160 of them are left. They live on a small reservation near Fredonia.

The Navajos, whose huge reservation includes part of the Grand Canyon, were late arrivals in the Southwest. Their oldest hogan (dwelling) dates to about A.D. 1540 in New Mexico. The Navajos wandered down the Rocky Mountains from western Canada.

They and the Apaches were the same people when they migrated south between A.D. 1000 and 1400. At times, they raided the Puebloans and took food, slaves, and wives. They adopted many Puebloan pursuits, such as growing corn and weaving, and even embraced some of their religious practices and myths.

Pueblo Indians called the Navajos Apaches de Nabahu, or "enemies with cultivated fields." As a result of exposure to the Spanish settlers in New Mexico, the Navajos increased their mobility and striking power by obtaining horses. In acquiring sheep, they also increased the economic quality of their lives.

Discovery and Exploration

The first white men to see the Grand Canyon were a detachment of Spaniards under the command of García López de Cardenas, an officer in the expedition of Francisco Vásquez de Coronado. Cardenas had been sent out to find a great river that had been reported to be not far to the west.

They found the river, but from the perspective of either Moran Point or Desert View, it appeared to be only about six feet wide. They climbed down about one-third of the way and saw that it was indeed a big river and that rocks that appeared to be only about man-size from the rim were actually bigger than some Spanish castles. The Spaniards could not explore farther, however, because they lacked water. No other Europeans saw the Grand Canyon for 225 years.

In 1776, the explorer-priest Francisco Tomás Garces was on an expedition with Juán Batista de Anza to found a mission and colony in Alta, California. Garces left the expedition to explore up the Colorado with Indian guides.

He came to Havasu Creek in June, 1776, by following a steep and hazardous trail. After spending five days with the Havasupai Indians, the priest emerged from the canyon by another dangerous trail onto a plateau of piñons, juniper, and grass.

A day later, he reached the rim, where he could see an endless series of canyons in which the Colorado River flowed. Garces then went on to Hopi country.

Some 50 years later, James Ohio Pattie, whose accounts of his travels in the Southwest became a bestseller in the mid-19th century, explored up the Colorado River looking for beaver. At the end of March, 1826, he arrived at a place "where the mountains shut in so close upon the shores" that he and his party "were compelled to climb a mountain and travel along the acclivity at a considerable height so that the river was far below." Pattie estimated that the canyon was only about a mile wide, but perhaps 300 miles long. He had to travel along the rim and eat bark and shrubs to survive. Perhaps this contributed to his dislike of the canyon when he wrote about it.

The United States acquired most of the Southwest, including the canyon, in 1848 after the war with Mexico, but much of the new territory was unknown. The government's main concern was setting up forts to control the Indians.

Some early military explorers, such as Lt. Amiel Weeks Whipple, skirted the canyon. Whipple surveyed a railroad route for today's Santa Fe along the 35th parallel. Another explorer was Lt. Edward Fitzgerald Beale, who used camels to open a major trail across northern Arizona between the Zuni villages and southern California, predecessor of Old Route 66 and today's Interstate 40.

Still another was Lt. Joseph Christmas Ives, who set out in 1857 to explore the navigability of the Colorado River for steamboats. Ives got as far as Black Canyon, near the present site of Hoover Dam, when his boat struck a rock. He explored on to what he called the Big Canyon and descended to the bottom along Diamond Creek.

Like Pattie, Ives was unimpressed with the canyon's possibilities. He wrote, "The region is, of course, altogether valueless. It can be approached only from the south, and after entering it there is nothing to do but leave. Ours has been the first, and will doubtless be the last, party of whites to visit this profitless locality."

Ives's report, accompanied by sketches done by artist F. W. von Egloffstein, was published in 1861 by the War Department.

On September 7, 1867, some residents of Callville, Nevada, fished a sunburned, half-starved, and somewhat incoherent man out of the Colorado River. His name was James White, and he told what was considered a wild tale of rafting through the canyon.

White's story was that he and two companions, Captain Charles Baker and George Stohle, had started out looking for gold in the San Juan River, a tributary of the Colorado. Baker was killed by Indians, White said. To escape, he and Stohle built a raft of cottonwood logs and floated along on smooth water for four days until they struck rapids which finally broke up their raft. They built a larger one and renewed their journey, but Stohle was washed overboard and drowned. White said he strapped himself to the raft and continued downriver. He lost almost all his food from being slammed around in the rapids, and finally became so hungry he ate the leather scabbard for his hunting knife.

After passing through the canyon, White continued, he was first robbed, then fed by some Indians. He traveled after that for some 14 days before he was pulled out of the river at Callville.

Although he was not believed at the time, White now is credited with being the first white man to go through the canyon. His garbled report of his adventures interested Major John Wesley Powell, a one-armed Union Army veteran of the Civil War, who was a professor of geology at Illinois Wesleyan University. Powell organized an expedition with the support of educational institutions, free passes from railroads, and scientific instruments from the Smithsonian Institution.

The Powell expedition started in four boats from the Union Pacific bridge over the Green River in Wyoming on May 24, 1869. They floated swiftly downstream through several rapids, made observations, and named canyons along the way. But on June 8, they hit Disaster Falls and lost one boat with 2,000 pounds of provisions. The crew barely escaped drowning. Powell and his group salvaged what they could of their wrecked boat's load, including barometers and a jug of whiskey.

After getting more provisions at the Uinta Indian Agency they started out again and went through the confluence of the Colorado and Green rivers on July 16. By this time, they were supplementing their food shortage with fish, deer, and mountain sheep. On August 10 they reached the mouth of the Little Colorado in the Grand Canyon.

Powell reported: "We are three-quarters of a mile in the depths of the earth, and the great river shrinks into insignificance as it dashes its angry waves against the walls and cliffs that rise to the world above; they are but puny ripples, and we but pygmies, running up and down the sands, or lost among the boulders. We have an unknown distance yet to run; an unknown river yet to explore. What falls there are, we know not; what rocks beset the channel, we know not; what walls rise over the river, we know not."

As the walls of Granite Gorge and the Inner Gorge of the Grand Canyon began to close them in, their provisions began to run out. They could no longer shoot sheep or deer to supplement their food supply.

The "mad waters" took a heavy toll of notes and maps that were washed overboard or thrown out. Oars were splintered and the boats were finally so damaged that the expedition stopped on August 15 at the mouth of a clear, cold stream for repairs.

Powell named his stopping place Bright Angel, from Milton's *Paradise Lost*. While the men repaired the boats, made new oars, and caught fish, Powell took notes and measurements and climbed formations to their summits, despite the fact that he had only one arm.

Three men who were fearful of an especially bad rapids ahead asked Powell to abandon the expedition and hike out to some Mormon settlements. When the trio arrived on the plateau to the north, they met a party of Paiute Indians who mistook them for prospectors who had mistreated and killed one of their squaws. The Indians killed the three men.

Powell and the five men remaining with him abandoned a damaged boat and, with the two remaining craft, went through the wild rapids and out into quiet water in one day's time. When they reached a Mormon settlement at the mouth of the Virgin River, they found three men seining for wreckage of the "lost" Powell expedition.

After his return to civilization, Powell found that while he had much new geological information, he had lost many valuable notes and another exploration was necessary. Powell planned a new voyage in sections, with supplies available at certain points along the way. His new expedition would include a full survey of the river and the bordering territory, for which he received support from the United States government.

Powell's second expedition started from Green River, Wyoming, on May 22, 1871, and his personnel included a geographer, an artist and writer, a mathematician and surveyor, a geologist, a surveyor and teacher, a cook, and a photographer. The boats this time were of a sturdier design, and Powell even had an armchair mounted on his craft.

Because of delays and many rapids, the group did not reach Lees Ferry until October 23. They went into winter camp at Kanab, Utah. The next year Powell explored the area north of the Grand Canyon and started down the river again on August 17.

The expedition reached the Grand Canyon in a week. Rough rapids and high river water threw the men into the water repeatedly. Because notes and maps of the Lower Grand Canyon from the 1869 expedition had survived, and because of the dangers ahead, Powell's second expedition left the river at Kanab Creek on September 8.

It was Powell who established *Grand Canyon* as the official name of the world-famous gorge. Before that, the Indians called it the Rough Rim; the Spaniards called it a *barranca* or canyon; and early American explorers referred to it as the canyon, Great Canyon, and Big Canyon.

Another important Grand Canyon explorer was Jacob Hamblin, a big, soft-spoken Mormon missionary who crossed the Colorado River several times trying to establish a mission among the Hopi. In 1862, he made the first recorded circle trip around the Grand Canyon. The following year he again made the journey and went down into the canyon to visit the Havasupais.

Hamblin, whose honesty and courage were respected by the Indians, was a successful peacemaker between the Paiutes and Mormons, who had many clashes in the period from 1865 to 1870. Jacob Lake on the North Rim is named for Hamblin.

By 1872 the general public's curiosity about the Grand Canyon began to grow. Since transportation in those days was limited to horse-drawn vehicles or horse- and muleback, sightseers had to be of a pioneer persuasion. It was not until 1901 that the railroad was completed to the South Rim.

The Grand Canyon, meanwhile, was considered fair game by prospectors who found some gold, silver, and copper. But the deposits were located in such inaccessible places that they were unprofitable. Many who failed as miners went into business as guides, and others built tourist hotels and camps.

The beauty of the Grand Canyon exploded on the world in the works of such artists as Thomas Moran. In the early 1870s, Moran accompanied Powell on his later explorations of the Grand Canyon area. His work so impressed Powell that he hired Moran to do engraved illustrations for his report, *The Exploration of the Colorado River of the West,* published in 1875.

Moran's almost photographic skill with the extravagant colors of the canyon led Congress to buy his classic *The Grand Chasm of the Colorado* for $10,000. The painting was hung in the Capitol. Moran also did illustrations for Clarence E. Dutton, a protégé of Powell's, who wrote the definitive *Tertiary History of the Grand Canyon District.* Moran Point at the canyon is named for the painter.

Dutton, besides being a geologist, was interested in oriental religions. It was he who named many of the canyon's buttes and other formations after temples in India and China. Some of these names are Brahma Temple, Vishnu Temple, and the Tower of Babel.

Another important scientific work on the canyon was a biological study by C. Hart Merriam in 1889. Merriam, studying plants and animals, established seven different life zones, according to elevation. They are desert (Sonoran); Piñon (Upper Sonoran); Pine (Neutral); Fir (Canadian); Spruce (Boreal and Hudsonian); Timber Line (Subalpine); and Alpine. The list of climatic zones ranges from Mexican desert to Canadian Arctic in the 10,000 feet of elevation.

As northern Arizona settlements increased with the influx of farmers, miners, ranchers, and lumbermen, the area around the Grand Canyon was thoroughly exploited. Concerned scientists and explorers began to press Congress to pass laws to protect this natural wonder.

When Yellowstone was declared a national park in 1872, a movement began to get similar status for the canyon. Benjamin Harrison, then a senator from Indiana, introduced the first bill in 1882, but it was never voted upon. He made two more attempts in 1883 and 1886, but failed.

In 1893, Harrison, by then President of the United States, exerted his influence to have the area proclaimed a forest reserve to exempt it from homestead laws and other public land regulations allowing mining and other commercial uses. As a forest reserve, the canyon came under the jurisdiction of the Department of the Interior in 1897.

During this time, other national parks were created, such as Sequoia and Yosemite, but sheep and cattle ranchers, miners, and others successfully postponed the Grand Canyon's case. In 1906, President Theodore Roosevelt proclaimed the the area a game reserve, thus protecting deer and other game animals. Two years later, Roosevelt proclaimed it a national monument under the terms of a new law.

It was not until 1919 that a bill passed both houses of Congress to make Grand Canyon a national park. The bill was signed into law on February 26, 1919. Additional territory on the North Rim and to the west was added between 1927 and 1932, in the late 1960s, and in 1975.

EXPLORING THE SOUTH RIM

Note: To make the most of your visit to the canyon, plan your activities so that you can make necessary reservations as far in advance as possible. During peak periods, activities such as raft trips and mule rides get booked months in advance.

To get to Grand Canyon Village, which is headquarters for sightseeing and accommodations, take State Route 180 north out of Flagstaff, which is situated on Interstate 40. If you are starting from Williams, take State Route 64, which joins 180 about 28 miles out of town.

The Grand Canyon varies from 4 to 18 miles wide along its 280-mile-long course, a continuation of nearly unbroken cliffs, naturally terraced down to the river.

These cliffs are crumbly for the most part, so it is well to stay inside guardrails and on defined paths. It is doubtful anyone with acrophobia will even come close to approaching the guardrails. The drop down to the river in most places along the South Rim is more than one mile. On the North Rim, the distance is more like a mile and a half.

The North Rim, by the way, is only about 11 miles away as the crow flies, but it takes a round-about 200-mile trip to reach it from the South Rim.

As you look out over the Grand Canyon, especially on a cloudy day, it is understandable how many visitors (especially writers) can go into rhapsodies of description or simply are dumbfounded.

Clarence E. Dutton, the geologist who wrote the first definitive scientific report on the canyon more than 100 years ago, must have had a strong esthetic sense as well as a cool scientific mind. He warned himself, "We must be frugal of adjectives, lest in the chapters to be written we find their force and meaning exhausted . . . "

To get the greatest perspective, hike or ride a mule down into the canyon. Or you can take an air tour. Still another way is a white-water trip in a rubber raft.

White-water trips vary in length up to 14 days. Twenty concessionaires have been authorized to take passengers. Private parties may obtain permits from the U.S. Park Service if the applicants can satisfy authorities that they are knowledgeable and experienced in white-water rafting.

Because the South Rim is more accessible and is open year-round, most of the action is there. However, some travelers prefer the North Rim—in season—because of the relative quiet and smaller crowds of sightseers. Winters on the North Rim can be severe because of its high altitude, so it is usually closed from November to May.

Grand Canyon Village

On your way into Grand Canyon Village on State Route 64/180, your first view of the gorge is at Mather Point. You'll see more of it at the village, where there is an overlook near Hopi House, a curio shop built along the lines of a Hopi pueblo. There also is Lookout Studio, where you can view the Canyon deeply—or darkly—through the glass of a powerful telescope.

There are great views too from the windows of El Tovar, a picturesque log-and-stone hotel dating back to 1906. El Tovar, named for Pedro de Tovar, one of the Spanish conquistadores, was built by Fred Harvey, a famous entrepreneur who founded the Harvey House restaurant chain along the Santa Fe Railroad.

The Harvey House at El Tovar was built to serve the public, who came in mainly by train when Grand Canyon was served by the Santa Fe line. The Harvey Girls, a special breed of waitresses who staffed the restaurant, were made famous in prose, poetry, and even a movie.

So many of them married as the result of their contacts in the restaurant that their boss, Fred Harvey, was often accused of operating a matrimonial bureau. A great number of Arizona's oldest families can trace their ancestry back to a Harvey Girl who married a rancher or miner, an engineer, or some other professional man.

West Rim Drive

Originally called the Hermit Rim Road, the drive was constructed by the Santa Fe Company in 1912 as a scenic tour drive. Cars were banned on the road because of the tendency to frighten horses pulling the open-topped touring stages.

Rebuilt in 1919, it was christened the West Rim Road. Since 1974, the West Rim Road has been closed to automobile traffic during the summer months when the number of visitors is at its peak. During the summer, visitors can ride a free shuttle bus or walk along the West Rim Road.

The first viewpoint is Trailview I and II (elevation 7,050 feet). This point is appropriately named. It offers a spectacular view of the Bright Angel and Plateau Point trails as they switchback down the canyon. In the deep canyon to the north flows Bright Angel Creek, one of the few permanent tributary streams of the Colorado River in the region. As you leave Trailview, look to the southern horizon and see Kendrick Peak, Red Butte, Sitgreaves Mountain, and Bill Williams Mountain.

Maricopa Point (elevation 7,050 feet) offers an advantageous view of Bright Angel Canyon, which won its name from John Wesley Powell during his 1869 expedition. From here, you can identify many of the buttes with their unusual names. There, to the west, is Osiris; to the right of it is Dragonhead, Shiva Temple, and Isis Temple. To the north are Cheops and Buddha temples.

The large red-rock formation in front of you is called The Battleship. As you drive to Powell Memorial, the Hopi Fire Tower can be seen on the left. This tower was built as a Civilian Conservation Corps project in 1941. Now it is used primarily for air quality monitoring.

Powell Memorial was built in remembrance of the man who twice ran the then-raging Colorado River into the uncharted Grand Canyon to measure, chart, and name the canyons and creeks of the Colorado, as well as record the geology of the canyon environment. It was here that the dedication ceremony for Grand Canyon National Park took place on April 30, 1920.

From Hopi Point (elevation 7,071 feet), you can see a large section of the Colorado River and to the west a portion of Granite Rapids at Monument Creek. Across the canyon to the north is Shiva Temple, which, until 1937, remained an isolated, unexplored section of the Kaibab Plateau.

In that same year, Harold Anthony of the American Museum of Natural History led an expedition to the rock formation in the belief that the formation supported life that had been cut off from the rest of the canyon. The expedition's real surprise was finding an empty Eastman Kodak film box atop the temple.

On a windless day on Mohave Point, it is still possible to hear the roaring din of water crashing over Hermits Rapids on the floor of the canyon. Two other rapids can be seen from this point: Granite and Salt Creek rapids.

The Abyss is the name given to the head of Monument Creek. As nowhere else in the canyon, the Abyss demonstrates the sheer steepness of the canyon walls. The Great Mohave Wall on the east side of the abyss drops 3,000 feet before it levels out on the Tonto Plateau.

The next stop, Pima Point, which takes its name from the Pima Indians of Central Arizona, is at an elevation 6,798 feet. If you look into the canyon from the west side of the point, you can still see very faint outlines of the building foundations of Hermit Camp and Hermit Trail on the Tonto Plateau.

In 1911, the Santa Fe Railroad built Hermit Trail and the camp to provide access to the inner canyon. The camp consisted of a group of tourist cabins, a corral, outbuildings, and a dining hall. The camp had many luxuries that were brought down on an aerial tramway that stretched from Pima Point to the camp.

If you look to the west, two dark, cone-shaped mountains—Mount Trumbull and Mount Logan—are visible on clear days. Their heights are a strong contrast to the surrounding flat-topped mesas and buttes.

Hermit's Rest is the westernmost viewpoint (elevation 6,050 feet). From it, you can see Pima Point and the Tower of Set and Horus Temple. Farther to the northwest are Mencius Temple and Confucious Temple, and farther in the distance is Point Sublime. Just east of Point Sublime is Hindu Amphitheater, a deep gorge cut through very old granite rock by Crystal Creek. Although this is the end of the drive, the canyon continues on for another 180 miles.

East Rim Drive

A similar, just as breathtaking, drive can be taken along the East Rim Drive.

Back in 1910, the stagecoach started at Yaki Point, inside the Grand Canyon Village, and two and one-half hours later ended at Grandview Point. To reach the final destination of Desert View required additional long hours on horseback. Today that same 25-mile stretch from Yaki Point to Desert View takes 40 minutes. Before beginning the trek, stop and see the exhibits and free mini-lectures offered by Park Naturalists at Yavapai Geology Museum, three quarters of a mile east of the Visitor's Center. After the verbal introduction to the canyon Yaki Point is your first visual introduction to this natural wonder.

From this perch you can see O'Neill Butte. To the east of O'Neill, there's Newton Butte with its flat top of red sandstone, and Lyell Butte, also red in color, can be seen a little farther up the canyon. Looking north across the canyon, the most conspicuous feature is Buddha Temple, capped by limestone. Behind it and to the right is Manu Temple and in front of it to the left is Isis Temple. Both have lost their resistant layer of limestone, and the sandstone is eroding the temples into rounded shapes. To the northeast a large flat-topped butte called Wotans Throne is visible. It was named by Francois Matthes, a U.S. Geological Survey scientist who developed the first topographical map of the Grand Canyon.

Also visible from this point to the west are sections of the South Kaibab Trail.

The view from Grandview Point (elevation 7,496 feet) is regarded by many to be one of the finest in the canyon. To the northwest, across Ottoman Amphitheater and Clear Creek Canyon, are Zoroaster, Brahma, and Deva temples. They are pinnacles on a ridge that extends south from Obi Point, the southwestern end of Walhalla Plateau. Beyond that flows Bright Angel Creek. Points of interest include Isis and Buddha temple formations, Bright Angel Point, and Angel's Gate.

Farther to the east is Vishnu Temple, which is at a higher elevation than where you are standing. Still farther east is Palisades of the Desert, and beyond that in the murky distance is the Painted Desert.

Next is Moran Point (elevation 7,157 feet), named after the nineteenth-century landscape artist Thomas Moran, whose paintings of the Grand Canyon did much to convince Congress to establish the Grand Canyon as a national park. He first visited the canyon with Major Powell in 1873.

Many of the steep slopes you see below Moran Point are the result of great movement in the earth's surface that took place before much of the overlying rock was formed.

Just west of Navajo Point is a trail that bears many names. First used by the Hopi and Havasupai Indians as a way to get to salt deposits near the Little Colorado River, the trail was later navigated by prospectors like Seth Tanner, a miner who trekked it to reach his claims near the river. The trail continues to bear the Tanner name.

Lipan Point is one mile west from Navajo Point and is the widest spot in the canyon. Here the river forms a winding S. From this point, you can follow the course of the river far to the east. The lookout was originally called Lincoln Point. The name was changed in 1902 to Lipan to commemorate an Apache Indian group in Texas. From here you can also see Escalante Butte and a group of bright red, black, and white rocks called the Grand Canyon Supergroup, which dates back to Precambrian time— about a billion years ago.

And off on the southern horizon are the San Francisco Peaks. These mountains are the highest in Arizona. The tallest, Humphreys Peak, stands higher than 12,600 feet above sea level.

Three miles before the final viewpoint is Tusayan Ruin and Museum, where visitors get a first-hand look at how the early Indians lived.

Last is Desert View (elevation 7,488 feet). You can see both ways from here because it's above the apex of a right-angle bend in the canyon. Desert View got its name from the view of *El Desierto Pintado,* "the Painted Desert."

This is the location of the 70-foot Desert View Watchtower, designed by architect Mary Jane Colter and built by the Santa Fe Railroad in 1932. Its design is based on similar stonework that prehistoric Indians used in their dwellings in the Four Corners region. It is built of native stone, steel, and concrete. The logs making up the ceiling were salvaged from the old Grandview Hotel. The Watchtower has a glass-enclosed observatory with powerful telescopes. Because Desert View is the highest point on the South Rim, the Watchtower offers marvelous canyon views as well as a panoramic sweep of the Painted Desert. From this viewpoint can be seen Siegfried Pyre and Gunther Castle. To the west is the pagodalike mass of Vishnu Temple. To the northwest is Escalante Butte. To the east is a small flat-topped mesa called Cedar Mountain, of special interest to geologists because it is formed of the same material that once covered the entire canyon area. The upper part of the tower contains ancient Indian pictographs; the lower part is a curio shop where paintings by contemporary Indians are sold.

Colter, both an architect and a designer—and a knowledgeable student of history, archeology, and Indian arts—worked for the Harvey Company for over 40 years until her retirement at the age of 79. During her career, she designed Hopi House on the South Rim, which opened in 1905, a re-creation of Southwestern Indian dwellings she personally researched at Colorado's Mesa Verde National Park. Her other works in the Grand Canyon include the Lookout, 1914; Hermits Rest, 1914; Phantom Ranch, 1922; the Watchtower, 1932; and Bright Angel Lodge, 1936. Mary Colter died on January 8, 1958.

THE GRAND CANYON

183
The Trail to Phantom Ranch

Back on the South Rim, you can either hike or take a mule ride (if you are over 12 years of age and weigh less than 200 pounds) from Grand Canyon Village down to Phantom Ranch at the very bottom of the Grand Canyon. There are fundamental accommodations as well as camping sites. Advance reservations are necessary for mule rides, lodging, and campground use.

By mule, it's a two-day trip, and you stay over at the ranch, a rustic resort where you are served dinner and breakfast. You also are provided a box lunch on the trail. As many as four riders may share a cabin at the ranch and get a bargain rate.

If you hike down from the South Rim, you also can stay at Phantom Ranch or camp free at one of the campgrounds near the main trails. This is where the admonition about being in shape comes in: Park Rangers consider the 16-mile round-trip hike to the river exhausting and strongly suggest you plan to make it a two-day outing. Outdoorsmen call the hike climbing a mountain in reverse. They also advise bringing one gallon of water per day per hiker.

The change in altitude from the rim down to the bottom of the canyon is more than a mile. The result is a series of six different botanical life zones ranging from ponderosa pine forest down to the subtropical.

Phantom Ranch has been a haven for weary adventurers since 1903, when David Rust established a camp for travelers and hunting parties. Then called Rust's Camp, it was a paradise of cottonwoods and fruit trees in an otherwise harsh environment. The lodge was so popular that in 1907 Rust put in a tramway that furnished a safe way to cross the Colorado River.

The name changed in 1913 when President Theodore Roosevelt visited the camp. It became known as Roosevelt Camp for a short time, until it was remodeled in 1922 by Mary Jane Colter. Miss Colter chose the name Phantom Ranch after a nearby tributary of Bright Angel Creek. Today the ranch covers 14 acres and includes a dining hall, cabins, dormitories, and a ranger station.

Havasu Canyon

For those who want something different and away from the crowds, there are two trips outside the park that offer some spectacular scenic adventures. These are Havasu Canyon, located south of the middle part of the national park, and the road to Diamond Creek. You arrive at Havasu Canyon via a 70-mile road from U.S. Route 66 about 7 miles east of Peach Springs. The entrance to the canyon is at Hualapai Hilltop, where you begin an 8-mile journey either by foot or horseback down to the canyon floor by a twisting trail along the edge of rock walls that go straight down for hundreds of feet. But for those who do brave the trip, the reward is incredible natural beauty in a place where people live much as they have for centuries.

Here in a subtropical life zone, Havasupai Indians dwell in lush surroundings little touched by the white man's culture. There are gurgling streams, waterfalls, green fields, and the red walls the Spanish soldiers reported to their leader, Francisco Vásquez de Coronado, in 1540.

Some people have called this canyon America's Shangri-la; certainly there's no better place to completely get away—if you don't mind plain accommodations or camping out. It is essential that you make reservations ahead if you want to visit this Eden. For camping, contact the Havasupai Tourist Enterprise, Supai 86435, 448–2121; there is a fee for hiking and one for horse rental, if you wish to ride. For reservations at the Havasupai Lodge, call 448–2111, or write Havasupai Lodge, General Delivery, Supai 86435.

Diamond Creek

Diamond Creek Road is the only road into the canyon. It begins in Peach Springs (on old Route 66) and makes a dusty run north to the Colorado River.

Before attempting to travel the rough, winding dirt road, you must stop at the Wildlife and Recreation Office, Hualapai Indian Reservation in Peach Springs, and obtain a permit and information on road conditions. This is important. A rainstorm can make the road unsafe for travel. Guides also are available.

The road is paved for approximately two miles, up to a cattle crossing where a sign tells visitors they are entering the reservation and need a permit before going any farther.

Several miles in, under the shadow of Diamond Peak, is a small picnic area. This is the site of the old Diamond Creek Hotel, which was a popular tourist attraction in the early 1900s. A stage, driven by the owner of the hotel, would pick guests up in Williams for a stay at the hotel.

The hotel was demolished by fire in 1914, and the only evidence that there was once a habitation in the area is an occasional rusty can found half buried in the desert soil.

Two miles farther the road enters the bed of Diamond Creek. During rainy seasons, the creek will flow and wash out the road. It is soon repaired, though, by a road crew.

After you've reached this point and if the river is high (a factor controlled by the spillways of Glen Canyon Dam), you can hear the rapids echoing against the canyon walls. Make another turn and you see sand dunes and—finally—water.

EXPLORING THE NORTH RIM

You have seen some beautiful country on the way from Flagstaff or Williams to the canyon, and you have also experienced some unforgettable facets of nature's works in the canyon from the South Rim. Now prepare for some classic viewing as you head toward the North Rim.

You can take State Route 64 east from Desert View to Cameron, a well-stocked old-time trading post on the Navajo reservation with an open invitation to travelers. Then turn left on U.S. Route 89.

Off to the right are those long views so typical of the American West, but this time with a bonus—the Painted Desert and the Echo Cliffs. The cliffs keep getting bigger until you reach a bend in the road beyond The

Gap, a trading post and small restaurant (a gas station is directly across the highway), and suddenly you have a new spectacle to consider—the Vermilion Cliffs, a scenic wonder of the Arizona Strip Country.

At Bitter Springs, the road junctions and Route 89 continues on to Page and Lake Powell, described in other chapters. Take U.S. 89A at this juncture and proceed to even better views of the Vermilion Cliffs. Here you cross the Colorado River—some 467 feet below—on the sturdy but narrow Navajo Bridge. At the northern end, a picnic area and viewpoint affords a relaxing spot from which to gaze at Marble Canyon, part of the park area, with its sheer 800-foot-high cliffs. The highway continues along the foot of the aptly named Vermilion Cliffs, through House Rock Valley, home of the state's buffalo herd.

You are now officially in the Arizona Strip—a virtually unpopulated area that stretches approximately from Route 89 on the east to Nevada on the west, and from the Colorado River on the south to Utah on the north. It is wide open, empty, and beautiful.

While the Indians told the old Spaniards it was forbidding country without much water, the later-arriving Mormons did well on the strip, establishing farms and lumbering in what is now the Kaibab National Forest.

By now U.S. Route 89A is taking you up a twisting mountain road to Jacob Lake, elevation 7,921 feet. Just before the lake, watch for the road running to the south that leads to House Rock Buffalo Ranch, open to visitors. It's about 23 miles to the headquarters. Back on 89A, as you turn left (south) at Jacob Lake onto State Route 67, you are in the heart of the Kaibab, which means "mountain lying down" in Paiute. (Route 67 will take you to the North Rim.)

The reclining mountain actually is a dome with the Grand Canyon cutting into its south slope. The canyon serves as a dividing line between the north and south rims. As you proceed southward, the elevation continues climbing to around 9,000 feet and, suddenly, you are launched onto a 44-mile drive described by several outdoor writers as one of the most scenic in America.

Here you travel between walls of 100-foot-tall red-barked ponderosa pine, with frequent companion stands of quaking aspen. Be on the lookout for the Kaibab squirrel, a species unique to this area. Its identifying characteristics are tufted ears and a parasol tail.

After you reach Murray Lake, usually wreathed in wildflowers in the summer, there is a chain of lovely meadows surrounded by aspen, Douglas fir, and Englemann and blue spruce. Be ready to see some mule deer as you come to Kaibab Lodge, a rustic log structure on the North Rim of the Grand Canyon.

You'll also see huge mule deer bucks, Merriam's turkeys, and blue grouse. The deer, accustomed to people, probably won't do more than glance at you, flip an ear, and go on with their grazing.

Bright Angel Campground is the only camping facility close in on the North Rim. There are 82 sites in a wooded spot only a short distance from the store and cafeteria. Water and firewood are available here. There is a small fee, and the camping limit is seven days. No trailer utility hookups are available.

For noncampers, Grand Canyon Lodge provides rustic cabins from mid-May to October. Reservations should be made in advance.

Because you are at a higher elevation here (8,200 feet) than on the South Rim, you get a different perspective of the Grand Canyon. Here you can see more freestanding rock formations and narrow promontories that jut out into the gorge.

There are four good observation points on the North Rim. The first, Bright Angel Point, is only about three city blocks from the road into the campground.

Cape Royal is the southernmost point on the North Rim. From here you can look across the canyon to the Painted Desert. You get to Cape Royal by a paved road from Bright Angel Point. The distance is 26 miles.

You get to Point Sublime after 17 miles over a primitive road that starts near the park entrance. This is the westernmost point of view of the canyon. This road is not always open so inquire at the Ranger Station or the information desk at the lodge.

Point Imperial has the highest (elevation 8,800 feet) and is the northern-most viewpoint. Here you can see the beginning of the Grand Canyon, where the Colorado River flows out of Marble Gorge. You can get to Point Imperial by going three miles off the Cape Royal road by an eastward turn-off about 5.5 miles from Grand Canyon Lodge.

You also can visit most of the major attractions, except Point Sublime, by hiking, horseback, or the single daily bus tour.

For hikers, there is the 1.5-mile-long Transept Canyon Trail along the rim between the lodge and Bright Angel Campground, and the Uncle Jim Trail starting at the Kaibab Trail parking lot that takes you 3 miles to an overlook above the main canyon.

There also is the Widforss Trail, a 10-mile jaunt to a canyon overlook from the next point west of Bright Angel Promontory, and the Ken Patrick Trail, which goes for 12 miles through the forest and along the rim from Point Imperial to the North Kaibab trailhead.

There is also the North Kaibab Trail, 14 miles one way. Because it's so rugged, the Park Service recommends staying overnight at one of the two inner-canyon campgrounds. Coming back up, you climb 5,800 feet in 14 miles.

One other point of interest on the North Rim is Toroweap Overlook, which requires a bit of backtracking through Jacob Lake and on north and west to Fredonia on U.S. Route 89A. At Fredonia, turn left on State Route 389 to a graded road about 9 miles southwest. You travel about 65 miles on this road to the Tuweep Ranger Station, then another 5 miles on to Toroweap Overlook.

From this viewpoint, you can see upstream to sedimentary ledges, cliffs, and talus slopes. Looking downstream, you can see miles of lava flow that forms steep deltas, some of which look like black waterfalls frozen on the cliffs.

The drop here is about 3,000 feet to the Colorado River, so you can see far below how the river has cut, exposed, and even polished the black basalt.

As always when you're traveling backcountry, it is well to fill your gas tank and water jugs before leaving the pavement behind. The last gas stop here is Fredonia.

On your way back to Flagstaff, stop and visit another scenic spot with some interesting history, Lees Ferry. You get there by taking a left turn just before you come back to the Navajo Bridge.

Lees Ferry was established during the 1860s by John Doyle Lee, a Mormon frontiersman involved in the massacre of 120 people in a Missouri wagon train. The wagons were crossing southern Utah in the summer of 1857, and the attack occurred at a place called Mountain Meadow.

Lee fled to Colorado for a time, then came to the mouth of the Paria River, where it flows into the Colorado, and started a ferry service. For a time, the settlement was called Lonely Dell, a name suggested by one of Lee's wives.

The crossing became especially popular with young Mormon couples who took the "Honeymoon Trail" to St. George, Utah, to have their marriages blessed in the temple there. Lee, who dodged federal authorities for nearly 14 years, finally was apprehended by federal officials and jailed. In 1877, 20 years after the massacre, Lee was executed by a firing squad. He was the only person to pay for the crime.

The ferry, as a river crossing, continued to operate until Navajo Bridge was built in 1929. Buildings there have been carefully preserved in their quaint, beautiful setting.

PRACTICAL INFORMATION FOR
THE GRAND CANYON

GETTING TO THE CANYON. By air. Grand Canyon Airport is located about 8 miles south of Grand Canyon Village. Direct flights to the airport are available from Los Angeles and Burbank (*Air LA* and *National Executives Airlines*), Phoenix (*America West*), Flagstaff (*America West*), and Las Vegas (*America West, Scenic Airlines, Air Nevada,* and *National Executive Airlines*). Rental cars, taxis, shuttles, and the *Harveycar* (Fred Harvey shuttle) are available to transport you from the airport to Grand Canyon Village.

By car. The South Rim is less than one and one-half hours from Flagstaff, four and one-half to five hours from Phoenix, five-and-a-half hours from Las Vegas, around seven hours from Tucson, less than an hour's drive from Cameron, and about one hour from Williams. The North Rim is less than an hour's drive from Jacob Lake on U.S. Route 89A and only two and one-half hours from Page–Lake Powell.

By bus. Bus transportation to Bright Angel Lodge at the Grand Canyon is available through Nava-Hopi Bus Lines from Flagstaff, 774–5003.

If you are a train-travel connoisseur, Amtrak travels to Flagstaff, where bus, plane, or rental car can take you on to the Grand Canyon.

WHEN TO GO. Summer is the height of the tourist season. Days are pleasant and nights cool, but there are large crowds at just about every attraction on the South Rim.

Those planning overnight hiking or camping activities within the park during summer season are required to make advance reservations. See the

"Permits and Reservations" section of *Grand Canyon National Park,* below.

During the winter, the Grand Canyon puts on a fabulous coat of many colors. Its rims draped in snow much of the time, the canyon presents glorious views. Much of the crowd is gone, and lodging is more readily available. The temperatures average 45 degrees during the day and 20 degrees at night on the South Rim.

Because of its relative inaccessibility and only one lodge, the North Rim offers visitors the opportunity to view the landscape in relative peace and quiet. One thousand feet higher than the South Rim, the North Rim is consistently cooler, with nights almost chilly during the summer. Visitor facilities are closed November through April.

CLIMATE. Due partially to changes in elevation and partially to the unique effect the canyon itself has on weather, climate can vary considerably, almost like traveling from northern Mexico to southern Canada.

In winter, a hiker can begin in snow on the South Rim and walk into springlike conditions on the canyon's floor in a few hours. In summer, the variation is even more noticeable. Starting a hike on a frosty summer morning on the North Rim can turn into a 110-degree crawl on the canyon floor eight or nine hours later. So be prepared for the variety of weather conditions that exist. Because the canyon is in Arizona doesn't mean that temperatures will remain warm, with blue skies and little rain. Only the Inner Canyon meets those criteria.

During the months of June through August, the average high temperature at Phantom Ranch on the canyon's floor exceeds 100 degrees with less than seven inches of rain per year. Even in January, the coldest month of the year, many of the days are in the low 60s in the Inner Gorge, even though the high canyon walls only allow a few hours of direct sunshine during the winter months.

The North Rim is much cooler than the canyon floor and cooler than the South Rim. The elevation ranges from 8,000 to 9,000 feet, resulting in Canadian life zone conditions. During the winter, October through April, the snows are 6 to 10 feet deep. The nights are cool even in the summer, and roads are open only from late spring to fall.

Even though the South Rim is only 1,000 feet lower than the North Rim, it receives half as much snow and rain. This rim's climate is moderated by the lower elevation and the warm air that rises out of the canyon. The South Rim's winter climate can include snow accumulations of up to two feet in depth and temperatures below zero.

During the summer, afternoon thunderstorms are frequent at the canyon. Lightning usually accompanies these storms. The canyon rim is a natural target for lightning bolts. If the hair on your head starts to stand on end and you detect the smell of ozone, an electrical charge is building up around you. Immediately move back from the rim into the trees. Lightning usually strikes the tallest object in the area of a charge, and if you stand away from the rim under the shorter trees, you may be better protected.

At best the weather at the canyon is unpredictable. At any time of the year, have rain gear available. Even if you plan a hike into the Inner Gorge, be prepared for some wet weather.

WHAT TO TAKE. Remember this is Arizona—where casual and comfort are king. If you are not planning to hike into the canyon, slacks, jeans, or shorts with blouses or sport shirts are the most practical. During the summer, don't forget a hat. Sandals can be worn, but the lookouts and some other areas are not paved, so sneakers are handy. If you are planning any type of walking, bring comfortable, good-quality walking shoes or hiking boots.

During the winter, sweaters and jackets are a must. Jeans or slacks will keep you warm and comfortable. You may want to pack some long johns for extended activities outside. Mittens or gloves are a nice luxury too.

For more formal dining at one of the lodges, a sports coat, button-down or open-necked shirt, and slacks are ideal for men. Women can take a basic outfit with enough accessories to change the look. No shorts are allowed at dinner in the El Tovar Hotel.

If you are planning a hike, jeans or corduroy slacks are a must; T-shirts, more than one pair of socks, hiking boots, and a hat are good staples to begin with. Check with the Backcountry Reservation Office or the National Park Service office for a more complete list of items necessary for hiking the canyon (see "Tourist Information and Useful Numbers," below).

HOTELS AND LODGES. You can stay in a turn-of-the-century hotel, in a cabin at the bottom of the canyon, or, if you don't have a flair for the unusual, a solid bed in a motel. The listings for both the North and South rims are in order of price categories. A lodging tax, which varies, is added to all accommodation bills.

The price categories in this section will average as follows: *Deluxe,* $85 and up; *Expensive,* $65–$85; *Moderate,* $35–$65; and *Inexpensive,* under $35. For a more complete description of those categories, see Facts at Your Fingertips.

The reservation office on the South Rim is open weekdays from 6 A.M. to 9 P.M. March through September and from 7 A.M. to 8 P.M. October through February; on weekends and holidays from 8 A.M. to 5 P.M. This office handles reservations for all lodgings on the South Rim. Write to Grand Canyon National Park Lodges, Box 699, Grand Canyon, 86023, or call 638–2401. In other cases a telephone number is included in the listing. One night's deposit per room must be received no later than 14 days after confirmation to hold your booking firm. There is no charge for children 12 years old and under. There are no cooking facilities in any of the lodges.

Pets are not allowed in the lodges. A kennel is available for a fee on the South Rim; phone 638–2631.

Check-in times are after 3:30 P.M. Check-out time for all lodges and hotels is 11 A.M.

South Rim

El Tovar Hotel. *Deluxe.* This historic landmark hotel is elegantly appointed and sits on the canyon rim. Built of native boulders and pine.

Best Western Grand Canyon Squire Inn. *Expensive.* Located in Tusayan, 7 miles south of Grand Canyon on State Route 64 (638–2681).

Kachina Lodge. *Expensive.* Interior is contemporary. Located near El Tovar.

Quality Inn Red Feather Lodge. *Expensive.* Part of Quality Inn chain. Located in Tusayan, 7 miles south of the Canyon. (638–2673).

Thunderbird Lodge. *Expensive.* A contemporary setting. Comfortable. Located on the rim, near Kachina Lodge.

Bright Angel Lodge and Cabins. *Moderate.* The main lodge, guest lodges, and individual cabins are of log and stone construction.

Maswik Lodge. *Moderate.* Located a short distance from the rim. Rustic cabins as well as modern accommodations.

Moqui Lodge. *Moderate.* Just outside the boundary of the South Rim (638–2424). Tennis courts. Horseback riding available in season. Open from March 1 to December 31.

Seven Mile Lodge. *Moderate.* Located in Tusayan, 7 miles south of Grand Canyon (638–2291).

Yavapai Lodges. *Moderate.* Located in the woodlands between Yavapai Point and the El Tovar. Closed Nov.–Feb. except for holiday periods.

Grand Canyon International Hostel. *Inexpensive.* Located in Grand Canyon Village. Dormitory accommodations available first come, first served (638–9018.) Open 5 P.M. to 9 A.M. nightly.

North Rim

Grand Canyon Lodge. *Moderate.* Near Bright Angel Point at the end of State Route 67 (801–586–7686). The lodge is constructed of native sandstone and rough-hewn ponderosa pine timbers from the Kaibab Forest. Cabins radiate out from the main lodge. The lodge offers beautiful views of the canyon. Lounge. Curio shop. Open from just before Memorial Day through early October.

Jacob Lake Inn. *Moderate.* Located in Jacob Lake, 45 miles from the North Rim (643–7232). Restaurant. Gas station. Groceries.

Kaibab Lodge. *Moderate.* Eighteen miles from the North Rim (638–2389). Closed in winter. Restaurant.

GETTING AROUND THE CANYON. By car. Once inside the park on the South Rim, you can leave the driving to someone else. Transportation is available by taxi, which runs daily from 6 A.M. to 8 P.M. Phone 638–2822.

Or, car rentals are available at Dollar Rent-A-Car, 638–2391, or Budget, 638–9360, both in the Grand Canyon Airport. The maximum speed limit inside the park is 45 mph; 15–25 mph in developed areas, and 15 mph in campgrounds.

By shuttle. A courtesy shuttle bus runs every 10–20 minutes from 5:45 A.M. to 10 P.M., mid-April to mid-September. It stops at the Visitor Center, Yavapai Museum, hotels, restaurants, campgrounds, and other facilities in the village area.

By air. Air transportation is available at Grand Canyon Airport, eight miles south of Grand Canyon National Park on State Route 64. The airport is open year-round. Grand Canyon Airlines has scheduled flights to the North Rim. However, flights to this dirt landing strip are dependent on field conditions. Contact Grand Canyon Airlines, Box 3038, Grand Canyon 86023 for more information. Phone 638–2407; (800) 528–2413 outside Arizona.

SERVICES. On the South Rim, services available in the Grand Canyon Village include a general store, service station, ambulance, medical clinic, pharmacy, trail equipment sales and rental, beauty and barber shops, dry cleaning, bank, souvenir shops, and post office. At Desert View, also on the South Rim, there are a general store, service station, and souvenir shops.

The North Rim, besides having food and lodging, has a service station, post office, laundry, showers, and general store. These are usually open from Memorial Day to mid-October.

TOURIST INFORMATION AND USEFUL TELEPHONE NUMBERS. The following list will provide a Grand Canyon visitor with vital numbers as well as phone numbers for tours, visitor activities, ranger station, and general park information. The area code in Arizona is (602).

South Rim. *National Park Service Visitor Activities and Programs* (recorded message), 638–9304.

Park Services switchboard, 638–7888, to connect you with any number you need.

Weather and Park Information (recorded message), 638–2245.

Emergency (doctor, ambulance, rangers), 911 (or 9–911 from your hotel room).

Clinic, 638–2551 or 638–2469.

Lodging, 638–2631 (same-day reservations) or 638–2401 for advance reservations.

Transportation Desk, Bright Angel Lodge Front Lobby, 638–2631.

Williams Chamber of Commerce, 635–2041.

Backcountry Reservations Office, 638–2474, for information only.

North Rim. *Grand Canyon Lodge,* (801) 586–7686.

Grand Canyon Scenic Rides, 638–2292.

RECOMMENDED READING. The following collection is not only informative but makes for interesting reading.

Arizona Trails: 100 Hikes in Canyon and Sierra. David Mazell. Wilderness Press, 2440 Bancroft Way, Berkeley, CA 94704. 1981. 312 pp. $12.95. Ideal for hikers and backpackers, this guide provides information on five major Arizona mountain areas: the Grand Canyon, Superstition Wilderness, the southeastern ranges, eastern (east-central) highlands, and the Mazatzal Wilderness northeast of Phoenix.

Grand Canyon Treks. Harvey Butchart. Grand Canyon Natural History Assn., Box 399, Grand Canyon 86023. The guide provides much useful data necessary for exploring the canyon's numerous trails.

The Man Who Walked Through Time. Colin Fletcher. Random House, Inc., N.Y. 1967. 239 pp. This veteran hiker spent one year preparing himself for a hike from one end of the canyon to the other. Overcoming incredible obstacles as he did, this account is that of one man alternately at odds and in tune with the elements.

Grand Canyon Wildflowers. Arthur M. Phillips III. Grand Canyon Natural History Assn., Box 399, Grand Canyon 86023. 145 pp. $6.50. A handy field guide of common and rare wildflowers found in Grand Canyon National Park.

Recollections of Phantom Ranch. Elizabeth Simpson. Grand Canyon Natural History Assn., Box 399, Grand Canyon 86023. 28 pp. $1.50. A history of Phantom Ranch, the guest quarters at the bottom of the Grand Canyon. Also provides suggestions for day hikes.

Canyon Maker. Ivo Lucchitta, Plateau Magazine of the Museum of Northern Arizona, Volume 59, Number 2, 1988. A geological history of the Colorado River. Explains the generally accepted theory of how the Grand Canyon was formed.

Grand Canyon; The Story Behind the Scenery. Merill D. Beal. K. C. Publications, Box 14883, Las Vegas, NV 89114. 1978 revised edition. 64 pp. $4.50. Over one million copies have been sold since its first issue in 1967. Written by a retired chief park naturalist at the Grand Canyon, the book is simple and readable. It presents a general history of the canyon, theories on its formation, fossils, and a history of its inhabitants. Numerous color photographs of excellent quality beautifully complement the text.

The Grand Canyon Natural History Association, Box 399, Grand Canyon 86023, publishes *The Grand Canyon Guide,* a free newspaper about accommodations, services, and seasonal activities at the Canyon. The Grand Canyon Natural History Association is a nonprofit corporation whose goal is to assist the National Park Service at the Grand Canyon in interpretive programs, education, and research. You can support these efforts by joining the association for a $10 annual fee or $150 life membership. As a member you receive the association newsletter and a 20 percent discount on all items purchased from the association.

Other pamphlets and brochures available from the Grand Canyon Natural History Association include: *A Guide to Hiking the Inner Canyon,* Scott Thybony, 43 pp., $1.75; *Guide to Grand Canyon Village Historic District,* Timothy Manns, 24 pp., $1.75; *John Wesley Powell and the Anthropology of the Canyon Country,* John Wesley Powell, 30 pp., $2.25; reprint of Powell's U.S. Geological Survey paper from the late 1800s.

Brochures: Available in English, French, German or Japanese. Specify language. Cost is 25¢ each. *A Slice of Time: Geological Eras of Grand Canyon; A Human Look: An Overview of Human History of Grand Canyon; A Place for Everything: Life Zones and Ecosystems in Grand Canyon.*

Arizona Highways Magazine, 2039 West Lewis Avenue, Phoenix 85009, has been publishing articles and photos about the Grand Canyon—and the rest of Arizona and the Southwest—for the past 60 years. Subscription rates: $15 a year, $25 for two years, in the U.S. and possessions. $18 a year elsewhere.

GRAND CANYON NATIONAL PARK. Welcome to the park that has acquired World Heritage status, signifying its universal importance as a natural wonder that must be protected as a common legacy for everyone.

Each year the park is visited by more than 4 million people. Of these, 20 to 40 percent are from foreign countries.

The area was first established as a national park by President Woodrow Wilson on February 26, 1919. The park's total acreage today is 1,218,375. Its length in air miles is 190, and its width in air miles is about 25.

The Grand Canyon owes all its praise to the browbeating received for more than 6 million years from the mighty Colorado River. Originally known as the *Rio Colorado* (Red River) by the Spaniards, it is more than 1,400 miles long and averages 300 feet in width. In certain areas, the river reaches a depth of 100 feet and flows at an average speed of 4 miles per hour (as measured at the river gauging station near the Kaibab Suspension Bridge within the canyon).

Before the gates of Glen Canyon Dam were closed in 1963, the river carried an average of half a million tons of suspended sand and silt through the Grand Canyon every 24 hours. Today that flow has been reduced to 80,000 tons a day. Most of the sand and rock are now settling to the bottom of Lake Powell behind Glen Canyon Dam. Pioneers said of it that it was too thick to drink and too thin to plow.

The Colorado flows west through the canyon, later turning to the south, and eventually emptying into the Gulf of California in Mexico.

That single river, running over and eventually through the Kaibab Plateau through the millenia, has created a canyon that is approximately 190 miles long (277 miles long measured by river course), reaching from Lees Ferry in the east to the Grand Wash Cliffs in the west, and up to 18 miles wide.

The canyon bottom below Yavapai Point is 2,400 feet above sea level, 4,500 feet below the South Rim, and 5,400 feet below the North Rim—an average depth of one mile. It is because of this diversity in height that the canyon can boast of six earth life zones. Hiking from the floor of the canyon (2,400 feet) to the very uppermost point of the South Rim (7000 feet) is much like passing from the Mexican border to Canada. Within each life zone exists a large variety of plant and animal life not usually found in the other zones.

The canyon acts as a Mason-Dixon line, physically separating north from south, creating different biotic communities. Certain plants and animals found on one side are absent on the other or have evolved into a subspecies. A case in point is the tassel-eared squirrel, found only in the zone between 7,000 and 8,000 feet. It was once a single undifferentiated species but has become two subspecies because of the cutting and separating of the two canyon rims. The tassel-eared squirrel has become known as the Kaibab squirrel, which lives only on the North Rim and is a different color than the Abert squirrel, which lives only on the South Rim.

Together the two rims are home to 70 species of mammals, including mule deer, bobcats, mountain lions, and coyotes; 250 species of birds; 30 species of reptiles and amphibians; 26 species of fish; and 1,500 species of plants.

The North Rim is only ten short miles away from the South Rim—if you have wings. Otherwise, it is 215 driving miles around the eastern end of the gorge, across the only bridge at Marble Canyon, and over pine-studded Kaibab National Forest. Less popular because of the added mileage and heavy winter snowfall, the North Rim is open only from mid-May through mid-October.

During the winter season, the access road into the North Rim from Jacob Lake is closed to vehicular traffic due to snow and ice. Water, facilities, and overnight accommodations are not available.

It is during this time—and longer if trail conditions warrant—that you can explore the North Rim from the park boundary to Roaring Springs plus the North Kaibab Trail, only with a Backcountry Use Permit. Application can be made at the Backcountry Reservation Office (see Permits and Reservations). If you want to ski into the North Rim from Jacob Lake (43 miles), you can snow camp at the parking lot north of the North Kaibab Trailhead.

Park Rangers

Within the National Park, uniformed park rangers are responsible for enforcement of rules and regulations, fire detection and suppression, operation of entrance stations, and general supervision of activities in several districts into which the park is divided. Rangers also patrol those campgrounds that are under National Park Service jurisdiction. Because the rangers act as police officers in the park, they are authorized to issue summonses for the violation of a park regulation and to appear before the U.S. Magistrate at Park Headquarters.

If you encounter any difficulties or need information, go to the Ranger Station near the El Tovar Hotel on the South Rim. Other stations are located at Indian Gardens on the Bright Angel Trail, Phantom Ranch, Desert View, the lodge at the North Rim, and at Cottonwood on the North Kaibab Trail.

Park rangers also have a wealth of knowledge about the canyon and provide a variety of talks at the National Park Service Evening Program in the Grand Canyon Village year-round and at Desert View during the summer. Specific times are available at the Visitor Center.

Permits and Reservations

Because of the number of visitors to the park, it was necessary for the National Park Service to establish a permit system to limit and distribute use in the Inner Canyon.

Before 1971, the park had few regulations on backcountry camping. But with an increase in use, resources were being damaged and popular areas were being overcrowded. Use limits were adopted to protect the fragile desert ecosystem and to allow each visitor to experience a true wilderness adventure.

A revised plan was set in motion in 1983. Its long-range goals include maintaining and perpetuating the natural ecosystem processes at work in the park; preserving and protecting prehistoric and historic cultural resources; and providing a number of recreation opportunities to the ever-growing number of visitors.

Today advance reservations are necessary to ensure that you will be able to hike when and where you wish. Reservation requests for overnight backcountry camping are accepted by mail or in person only. Beginning October 1st, reservation requests are accepted for the remainder of the current year and for all of the following calendar year. Your requests should be directed to: *Backcountry Reservations Office,* Grand Canyon National Park, Box 129, Grand Canyon 86023. The heaviest demand for permits is from March through May, far exceeding the use limits established to protect the backcountry resources and the quality of your experience.

With your request, include the proposed dates you expect to be in specific campgrounds and on specific trails, as well as the number of people in your group. Groups are limited to 16 people. There is a two-night limit at each campsite. A maximum of seven nights can be spent at each use area, but the overall trip length is not limited.

Permits for hikes beginning on the North Rim or in remote areas of the park will be issued by mail only when the North Rim is closed or when it is otherwise unreasonable for a hiker to go to the Backcountry Reservations Office. The mail-out permits require four to five weeks to process.

If you have an advance reservation, the use permits must still be picked up in person the day before your hike begins or before 9 A.M. Mountain Standard Time (MST) on the day of the hike. If the permit is not picked up by 9 A.M. on the day of the trip, reservations will automatically be canceled.

Hikers without reservations also should contact the Backcountry Office on the South Rim or at the North Rim Ranger Station (summer only). You may be able to obtain a use permit by putting your name on a waiting list for cancellations. You may list your name up to 24 hours in advance of your proposed hike and in person only, then return at 9 A.M. the morning you plan to hike into the canyon to determine the availability of permits.

The Backcountry Use Permit is valid only at the locations and on the dates specified. The permit itself should be attached to your pack or clothing in plain view so that it can be easily checked by Backcountry Patrol Rangers.

The Backcountry Office does not make reservations for campground space on the rims, or for river trips or mule trips, Phantom Ranch lodging, or excursions into the Havasupai Indian Reservation. These must be made with each individual service.

TIPS FOR PHOTOGRAPHERS. The Grand Canyon is probably one of the most photographed places in the world. Because of its dramatic, ever-changing lighting, it is a challenge to professional and amateur photographers alike.

During the summer on the South Rim, the only time that is not ideal for taking pictures is between 10 A.M. and 2 P.M., when the light is flat and the usual brilliant colors of the landscape are dulled.

From midafternoon to sunset is the best time for color photography, as the canyon is at its handsomest. Early morning is good after the sun is high enough to hit points within the canyon. At this hour, dust in the air is limited. The air is especially clear after thunderstorms during the summer. Not only does the air smell fresh and clean, but the canyon takes on sparkling clarity. If the air is hazy, try using filters for both your color and black-and-white film.

For panoramic shots, stop down your lens, dig out your tripod, and shoot more slowly—nothing is moving out there.

The South Rim provides numerous panoramas that can be seen from the 20 viewpoints along the East and West Rim drives. Other picture-taking spots include the head of Kaibab Trail, Yavapai Museum, Pima Point, and along the Bright Angel and Kaibab trails.

The same hours for photography stand true for the North Rim during the summer. The best times are before 10 A.M. and after 2 P.M. For panoramic shots, try any of the three major lookout points—Royal, Imperial, or Sublime. For sunsets, try Vista Encantada. The setting sun plays tricks on the desert that will make unique backgrounds for your photos.

If you are on the rim during the winter, the light is not as strong, so be careful when reading your light meter.

SEEING THE GRAND CANYON. With so much to see and do, you will need careful planning to get the most out of your Grand Canyon visit.

If you have only two or three hours to spend at the canyon, begin your tour at the Visitor Center on the South Rim, and explore the exhibits that trace the various natural and human histories of the canyon. Or consider visiting the Yavapai Museum, located about one mile from the center.

If you have six or seven hours to explore, in addition to those activities already mentioned, take in the breathtaking views from the West Rim Drive. (There is a two-hour narrated shuttle-bus tour of the eight-mile West Rim Drive during the summer.)

Another half-day schedule of activities could find you taking a stroll along any portion of the self-guided Rim Trail. This nearly level trail is 10 miles long and begins at Mather Point.

If you have a full day to discover the canyon, take a ride along the East Rim Drive. This scenic drive is 25 miles long and takes about 45 minutes to complete. It begins at Desert View at the east entrance of the park.

There are quite a number of day hikes on both rims, too, that you can take. No hiking permit is necessary. For more information see *Hiking,* below.

There also are quite a few bus tours available to various points in and around the canyon. Or consider a special tour of the lands of the Navajo and Hopi Indians.

A special way to appreciate the canyon is with a bird's-eye view, either from a helicopter or an airplane. The length of flight and cost depends on what tour you choose.

If you plan an extended visit of two days or more, plan a float trip down the Colorado River or a backpacking trip within the canyon. Permits are required. Hiking equipment can be rented in the village spring through fall. Or take a ride on a mule to the bottom of the canyon.

Helicopter tours. While it used to take more than two hours and a trip of 150 miles just to arrive at Hualapai Hilltop, then begin the 8-mile hike down to the floor of the Grand Canyon to the Havasupai Indian village of Supai, it now takes just 55 to 60 minutes for the entire trip by helicopter. The Havasupai flight lets you land at the bottom of the canyon, play in the Havasu falls, and explore the Havasupai Indian village.

Grand Canyon Helicopters. Located 3 miles south of the Grand Canyon's South Rim entrance station on State Route 64, the service has been flying canyon tours since 1965. It currently offers 30-, 50-, and 60-minute sightseeing flights over the Grand Canyon as well as 6-hour and overnight flights into Supai Canyon. Contact Grand Canyon Helicopters, Box 455, Grand Canyon, AZ 86023; 638–2419; (800) 528–2418 outside Arizona.

Kenai Helicopters is also located 3 miles south of Grand Canyon National Park on Route 64 in Tusayan, and offers 30- and 60-minute scenic flights. 638–2764 or 638–2412. Closed during the winter.

Airplane flights. Or see the canyon from the vantage point of a soaring eagle. Several airlines fly in and around the canyon. *Grand Canyon Airlines,* Box 3038, Grand Canyon 86023; 638–2407 or (800) 528–2413 outside Arizona, has been offering scenic flights into the area since 1927. *Air Grand Canyon,* Box 3028, Grand Canyon, AZ 86023; 638–2686; (800) 247–4726 outside Arizona. *Explorer Air Tours,* Box 3412, Grand Canyon, AZ 86023; 638–2422.

Scenic Airlines, 241 E. Reno Ave., Las Vegas, NV 89119, (702) 739–1900, and *National Executive Airlines,* 6005 Las Vegas Blvd. South, Las Vegas, NV 89119; (702) 798–6666, (800) 634–6616 outside Nevada, offers a variety of multilingual Grand Canyon tours. All flights are round-trip from Las Vegas or Los Angeles (NEA tours only).

Bus tours. Another way to see the Grand Canyon in cool comfort is a scenic bus tour with the Fred Harvey Transportation Company. Operating year-round, the tours visit scenic and historic viewpoints along the South Rim. So you don't miss any sights along the way, the driver/guide explains the Canyon's geology, flora and fauna, history, and contemporary events. The *Hermit's Rest Tour* covers 16 miles in two hours. *The Desert View Tour* covers the East Rim Drive (52 miles round trip) and lasts 4 hours. A sunset tour is available during the summer.

The *Ancient Ones Tour* is an all-day, 225-mile excursion that explores the lives of the earliest inhabitants of the Grand Canyon. You visit the Sinaguan ruins of Wupatki National Monument; Sunset Crater, the remains of a volcano active 750 years ago; and Walnut Canyon National Monument, once a thriving community of cliff dwellers. Your trip completely circles the San Francisco Peaks, Arizona's highest mountains, and includes a stop at the Museum of Northern Arizona. A picnic lunch is provided. The tour operates year-round and has four person minimum.

An enjoyable side trip while staying at the Grand Canyon is the *Monument Valley Tour* offered by Fred Harvey Transportation year-round. During the ride from the Canyon to Kayenta, you will tour the East Rim Drive, the Little Colorado River Gorge, and Black Mesa. At Kayenta, passengers will take a four-hour 4-wheel-drive tour of Monument Valley provided by Crawley's Navajo Nation Tours. Lunch is provided during the tour of the Valley.

The tour runs seven days a week and has a four-person minimum. Check in at the Bright Angel Transportation Desk before 5 P.M. the day before the tour.

To reserve a space on any of the above-mentioned tours or to obtain specific departure and price information, write or call Grand Canyon National Park Lodges, Reservations Department, Box 699, Grand Canyon 86023, 638–2401.

RAFTING. Want to test your ability to stay seated while shooting a white-water rapids in a rubber raft? Then team up with one of 20 qualified Colorado River concessionaires that run river trips.

Because of the popularity of riding the rapids, it is suggested that you make your reservations at least six months before your planned trip. To make your reservations, it is best to contact directly the particular operator you have chosen. At that time, ask any questions you have pertaining to the trip, such as what to wear, what to bring, etc. Be sure to ask how you will get out of the canyon at the conclusion of your river trip. They'll supply you with plenty of pamphlet information to make your trip a success. Grand Canyon National Park Lodges, Box 699, Grand Canyon 86023, 638–2631, can furnish you with a complete list of all river operators. Here are a few of the more popular ones:

Georgie's Royal River Rats. Georgie Clark. Box 12057, Las Vegas, NV 89112; (702) 451–5588. Georgie is a very popular river runner and has been for more than 20 years. She has both motorized and oar-powered trips and offers half or partial excursions. Her trips run from 4 to 14 days.

Canyoneers, Inc. Gaylord Stavely. Box 2997, Flagstaff 86003; 526–0924; (800) 525–0924 outside Arizona. This operator offers 3- to 14-day motorized and oar-powered trips, and kayak-support trips.

Arizona Raft Adventures, Inc. Robert Elliott. 4050-X E. Huntington Dr., Flagstaff 86001, 526–8200. Raft Adventures provides both motorized and oar-powered trips, paddle trips, kayak-support trips, and half or partial trips. Adventures last from 6 to 15 days.

Grand Canyon Expeditions. Ron Smith. Box 0, Kanab, UT 84741, (801) 644–2691. This operator offers both motorized and oar-powered trips for either 9 or 14 days.

Outdoors Unlimited. John Vail. Box 854, Lotus, CA 95651; (916) 626–7668. Offers oar-powered, paddle trips, and kayak-support trips. In addition to trips of 5 to 13 days, he also offers half or partial trips.

Expeditions, Inc. Dick McCallum. R.R. 4, Box 755, Flagstaff, 86001; 774–8176 or 779–3769. McCallum has oar-powered, paddle, and kayak-support trips. In addition to 5- through 18-day trips, he offers half or partial trips, too.

Oars, Inc. George Wendt. Box 67, Angels Camp, CA 95222; (209) 736–2924 or (209) 736–4677. Oar-powered trips, kayak-support trips, and half-day or partial trips. Tours are 4 to 18 days in length.

Tour West, Inc. Howard Lewis. Box 333, Orem, UT 84057; (801) 225–0755 or (800) 453–9107. Tour West sells both motorized and oar-powered raft trips from 4 to 12 days in length, plus half or partial trips.

Colorado River and Trail Expeditions, Inc. David Mackay. Box 7575, Salt Lake City, UT 84107; (801) 261–1789. This river runner has motorized and oar-powered rafts, paddle trips, and kayak-support trips running from 3 to 12 days. Also offered are half-day or partial trips.

Moki Mac River Expeditions, Inc. Richard Quist. Box 21242, Salt Lake City, UT 84121; (801) 943–6707. This river expeditions outfit has both motorized and oar-powered trips, kayak-support tours, and trips from 4 to 18 days in length.

Wilderness River Adventures. Dean Crane. Del Webb Recreational Properties, Inc. Box 717, Page, 86040; 645–3296. Both motorized and oar-powered trips from 3 to 10 days in length.

One-day smooth-water trips are available daily April through October from either **Fred Harvey Transportation Co.**, Box 699, Grand Canyon 86023, 638–2401; or **Del Webb Wilderness** River Adventures, Inc., 645–3279. A one-day white-water trip is available every Friday, May through September, from **Canyoneers, Inc.**, Box 2997, Flagstaff 86003; 526–0924.

Most raft trips depart from Lees Ferry, Arizona, but some companies offer partial trips from Phantom Ranch or from other points along the river. The majority of trips occur between April and October, although there are several companies that offer trips year-round.

Excursions run from one to 15 days. Pick the one you'll most enjoy. Even though you are on a boat and in water, it does get hot during the summer, so remember to wear a hat. Bring swimwear and clothing that is comfortable and shoes that you don't mind getting wet and that will work well for hiking.

Because of limited space, most of the concessionaires will allow only two bags per person. One bag is for sleeping gear, the other for clothing

and necessities. Your river-running company will provide yo
of what to bring.

You don't need bulging muscles, but you must be able to (
own gear. During much of the actual float trip, you will be ha
to the ropes while the boat is going over rapids, so the trip doe.
some physical stamina.

The Park Service wants the park to remain pristine for all visitors. This
means anything you take along—magazines, tin cans, cigarette butts—will
also have to be taken out of the canyon.

Sample rates for motor-powered raft trips depending on number of days,
can range from $400 to $1,200. Rates for oar-powered rafts and dories,
depending again on number of days, can range from $450 to $1,800. One-
day trips start at about $50. These rates include all food costs, some or
all necessary camp items, guide services, and, in many cases, transportation to and/or from the river.

Reduced family and/or children's and/or group rates are available from
some operators. Most raft concessionaires offer private charter trips in addition to the regularly scheduled trips. A number of operators, in addition
to those mentioned, also offer kayak-support trips.

Rafting trips let you experience the canyon and the forces that created
it while spending quiet nights on the banks of the river, under stars that
never seemed so luminous.

HIKING. "Go hike the canyon." Most times, easier said than done. But
thousands do it yearly and say it is the only way to enjoy all the canyon
has to offer. Two types of trails are open to hikers. Maintained trails are
ideal for short hikes, especially for children and adults who do not want
to test their stamina or surefootedness by attempting to make the entire
trek to the river and back.

You can follow the maintained trails for full-day or overnight trips.
There is no charge for camping permits, but reservations are necessary
for any overnight hike. Guided day and overnight hikes are available April
through November from **Grand Canyon Trail Guides,** Box 735, Grand
Canyon 86023, 638–2391.

The Grand Canyon is a beautiful environment, but it can be hostile if
you're not prepared or in good shape. While backpacking anywhere requires an amount of preparation, it is especially true of hiking in the desert
environment in the Inner Canyon. Unlike hiking elsewhere, the Inner Canyon does not afford shade, and you must carry your own water, a gallon
per person per day, minimum. A hiker's greatest threats are exposure, extreme variations in temperature, and unreliable water sources. Inner-
canyon temperatures can exceed 105 degrees in summer and drop below
freezing in winter. So plan ahead.

During winter hiking, be prepared for snow, rain, or sunshine. Be sure
to wear adequate footgear for snow or mud. And appropriate clothing
should be packed in for rain and foul weather. One big danger, besides
becoming disoriented, is hypothermia, caused by exhaustion and exposure
to cold, wet, windy weather. The symptoms are uncontrollable shivering,
poor muscle control—and a careless attitude. Treatment includes a change
into dry clothes, staying dry, getting out of the wind, and getting warm.

Hiking in the summer can mean walking with a 40-pound backpack
down into the canyon in temperatures over 105 degrees. Always wear a

hat. To avoid the extreme heat, hike early in the morning or late in the afternoon. Wear clothing that will cover your body, arms, and legs to prevent excessive water loss and sunburn. And adequate broken-in footwear can prevent blisters. Another good way to prevent blisters is to wear two pair of socks.

One of the biggest and most serious mistakes made by inexperienced canyon hikers is not taking enough water. Always carry at least one gallon per person per day. More may be required, depending on temperatures and where you are hiking. Your body must replace the water lost through perspiration. Do not wait until you feel thirsty to drink, as thirst doesn't always accompany the body's need for water.

Salt depletion can be another serious problem. The first symptoms are often leg cramps. If the salt is not replaced, you may become ill. Do not take salt tablets, as they generally cause more harm than good when there is not sufficient water. Instead use an electrolytic replacement powder in your drinking water or drink fruit juices to replace needed salt.

Two ailments that can strike summer canyon hikers are heatstroke and heat exhaustion. Dry skin, weak and rapid pulse, high body temperature, and even unconsciousness are signs of heat stroke, indicating that a person is in danger. Put the victim in shade, cool him or her with water, and then go for help.

Strenuous exercise in hot weather will cause heat exhaustion. The symptoms are nausea, cool and moist skin, headache, and cramps. Again, find some shade, drink water, cool down the body temperature, and allow the victim to rest.

All canyon trails are deceiving—they do not seem very strenuous or very long from the rims. At any time of the year, allow plenty of time for your hike. Hiking alone is never recommended.

When packing your backpack, travel light. The heaviest item in your pack during the summer should be water. For sleeping, take only a foam pad and a light sleeping bag or blanket. In the winter, be prepared for cold, rain, or snow. Pack a flashlight, well-equipped first aid kit, signal mirror or reflector. The Backcountry Permit Office or Ranger Station can provide you with a full list of items that should and should not be taken. If you have overlooked any camping gear, equipment can be rented April through November from Grand Canyon Trail Guides (638–2391), next to the Backcountry Permit Office.

Emergencies. Your Backcountry Permit lists your hiking itinerary. Stay with it. If an accident occurs, search efforts will be much more difficult, time consuming, and costly if you are not in the area you said you would be.

Causes for evacuation from the canyon range from heatstroke and hypothermia to disorientation and fractures with accompanying shock. If a hiker does get hurt or sick, don't leave him alone. If possible, at least two people should go for help, and be sure to carry a description of the injuries, the treatment given, and the precise location of the injured party. If you have a topographic map of the area, it is a good idea to mark the location of the injured person. This will aid evacuation, which will probably be made by helicopter.

If you should get lost, try to retrace your steps to where you left the trail. If all attempts to find a reference point fail, sit down, calm your thoughts, and then stay in one place; you will be found more quickly. Use your signal mirror on passing aircraft. They can spot you and radio for help. And/or make a large X on the ground with your spare clothes and gear.

Regulations. If commonsense precautions are taken, hiking the Inner Canyon can be an experience to last a lifetime. But responsibility and challenge are inherent in hiking the canyon. Backpackers make up a small percentage of the total park visitors, but it is with backpackers that the greatest potential lies for damaging the Inner Gorge environment. Littered trails and campsites, polluted water sources, denuded vegetation, fire scars, improperly buried fecal matter, and unnecessary multiple trails are testaments to this environment's vulnerability to humans. There are regulations that must be followed to ensure that the Grand Canyon experience can be passed on to the next generation. See "Regulations for Back Country Camping for Hiking" which follows.

Some other regulations for hikers:

• Select designated campsites or choose places that previously have been used as camps. Camping in the designated campsites is limited to two consecutive or nonconsecutive nights per campsite per hike. Throughout the rest of the backcountry, you can spend up to seven nights in each area. You will have the least impact if you choose sites with an absence of vegetation and organic soil. Sandy areas, dry washes, and slickrock benches make the best campsites. (See "Camping.")

• Any campsite must be located at least 100 feet from water sources to prevent pollution and to allow wildlife unobstructed access. Never wash clothes, dishes, or yourself directly in a water source. Instead, carry water 100 feet from the source in a clean container. Dirty water should be thrown on vegetated soil, away from the source. Do not swim in the Colorado River. Strong currents and constant 45-degree temperatures have claimed the lives of numerous hikers.

• Stay on designated trails. Straying off the trails causes severe erosion and is unsafe for you and hikers who might be below you. When exploring off-trail, walk single-file, and make your route over slickrock, in dry washes, or through sandy and unvegetated areas.

• No pets are allowed on the trails below the rim of the canyon. The Fred Harvey Lodge on the rim operates kennels.

• Mules have the right-of-way on the trails. If you do encounter a mule train, stand quietly on the side and obey the instructions of the mule guide.

• The greatest problem encountered in the Grand Canyon is human waste. It decomposes very slowly in desert soil. Use toilets. Where they are not available, bury feces at least 100 feet from trails, campsites, and water sources. Choose an area with rich, dark soil and dig a small hole. When finished, cover it with the soil you just removed. All toilet paper must be packed out in plastic bags with your other trash.

South Rim Maintained Trails

Now that you are ready for a hike, you may want to try the **Bright Angel Trail** for a hike halfway down the canyon or all the way to the Colorado River. If you do plan on an overnight trek to the river, remember, a permit is necessary.

Bright Angel Trail was originally a bighorn sheep path and later was used by the Havasupai Indians. In 1890–91, the Bright Angel Trail was widened. Following this, 10 years later, the trail was extended to the Colorado River. Today the Bright Angel begins just west of the Bright Angel Lodge and descends 4,460 feet in 7.8 miles to the river.

Because of the strenuous nature of the hike, there are rest houses available for hikers at the 1.5- and 3-mile points, and at Indian Gardens. Plateau Point, which is 1.5 miles below Indian Gardens or 6 miles into the canyon, is usually a good turnaround point for a day hike. From here, you can look down 1,300 feet to the Colorado River.

If the river continues to lure you after this, it is still four more miles to the bottom. This trip should be attempted only by persons in good physical condition. The climb out is a vertical 4,600 feet. It is not recommended for anyone during the summer. If you are planning to camp at either Indian Gardens or Bright Angel campgrounds, your food supply should not include too many extras because of weight. Instead, snack often along the way, particularly on the way back; it will keep your strength up. Small containers of fruit in syrup or granola bars are good to munch.

Another much used trail is the **Plateau Point Trail** that spurs off the Bright Angel Trail at Indian Gardens and leads out 1.5 miles to the edge of the Tonto Platform, with a spectacular view of the Inner Gorge and the river.

The **South Kaibab Trail** begins near Yaki Point on East Rim Drive east of Grand Canyon Village and descends 4,800 feet in just 7 miles. This is a steep trail with no campgrounds or water and very little shade. A day hike on this trail would take you either to Cedar Ridge, 1.5 miles into the Canyon or Tipoff, which is 5 miles into the canyon. From Tipoff, the trail begins its descent into the Inner Gorge to Phantom Ranch. This trail is recommended for descent only. Use the Bright Angel Trail for your ascent.

The South Kaibab Trail connects with the **North Kaibab Trail** after the Kaibab Bridge across the Colorado. The North Trail will take you directly to the North Rim through Bright Angel Canyon.

Hikers who plan to stay overnight in the canyon after walking the Bright Angel or Kaibab trails have two alternatives: camping at *Indian Gardens* or *Bright Angel Campgrounds* or staying at *Phantom Ranch*. Reservations must be made in advance at the Backcountry Office for camping at either Indian Gardens or Bright Angel campgrounds.

Reservations for dates from April 1 through October 31 or for holiday stays at Phantom Ranch should be made at least six months in advance. Reservations for lodging and for meals can be obtained by writing or calling Grand Canyon National Park Lodges, Reservations Dept., Box 699, Grand Canyon 86023, 638–2401.

Indoor accommodations at Phantom Ranch mean segregated dormitories, and limited cabin space. And after your seven-mile trek straight down into the canyon, you can look forward to a home-cooked meal served family-style. You must reserve your meal when you make lodging reservations.

After a night's rest, it's back on the trail. The best ascent is by the Bright Angel Trail.

If you really don't want to work that hard on your vacation, there is a pleasant, nearly level **10-mile walk along the South Rim** that will take you from Hermits Rest to Mather Point. The trail is paved from Maricopa Point to Yavapai Point. The rest is an undeveloped dirt path. A self-guided nature trail pamphlet is available at the Visitor Center for sections of this rim walk.

For a short walk, you might try the **Desert View Nature Trail.** This 15-minute rim stroll begins at the watchtower or the campground at Desert View.

Unmaintained and Abandoned Trails of the South Rim

It is impossible to grade these trails as the best or worst. It depends greatly on the stamina and fitness of the hiker.

There are approximately 30.7 miles of maintained trails and 400 total miles of primitive and undeveloped trails within the canyon. It is strongly recommended that hikers without previous Grand Canyon hiking experience use those maintained trails before attempting hikes in more remote areas of the backcountry. Also, none of these trails has water sources. For information, contact the Ranger Station at the South Rim.

If you're interested in old mines and mining in the canyon in the last hundred years, **Horseshoe Mesa Trail** will take you to Last Chance Mine, operated from 1883 to 1907 by Peter Berry. The ore collected from this mine was 70 percent pure, but hauling the ore out of the canyon made the venture a money-loser. After this, Berry quit the mine and built the Grandview Hotel, a two-story log structure. It was popular for several years until Grand Canyon Village was developed. The Grandview's doors closed in 1908. Today several buildings still stand and several mine shafts can be seen on the east side. The three-mile trail to this site is rough.

Hermit Creek Trail is semi-maintained. The trail begins west of the Hermit's Rest parking area. The difficulty of this trail should not be underrated. A particularly tricky area is a 1/3-mile section of rock slides. It is 6.2 miles from the head of the trail to now-abandoned Hermit Camp, operated as a tourist resort by the Santa Fe Railroad after 1912. After the camp, the trail follows Hermit Creek to the river.

The **Tanner Trail** is primitive. The trail head lies several hundred feet east of the Lipan Point parking area. This is the South Rim's longest rim-to-river route (12 miles). It has no water and little shade. The Tanner is almost twice the length of the South Kaibab Trail and contains steeper ascents than anything found on the Kaibab or Bright Angel trails. The trail is vague, but the route appears on a topographic map.

North Rim Maintained Trails

If you are planning a stay on the North Rim, the **North Kaibab Trail** is the only maintained trail into the canyon. The trail, built by the National Park Service in 1925, begins at Roaring Springs, which is below the rim, and descends 14.2 miles to the river. From Roaring Springs, the trail follows Bright Angel Creek to the Colorado.

Other forest and rim trails on the North Rim include the **Transept Trail.** The Transept is 1.5 miles long. It follows the rim from the Grand Canyon Lodge to the campground. You can return along the same trail or take the Bridle Path, which follows the main road.

Ken Patrick Trail is 12 miles long and takes six hours to walk one way. It winds through the forest and along the rim from Point Imperial to the North Kaibab Trail parking area.

Uncle Jim Trail is five miles long and takes approximately three hours to complete. It begins at the North Kaibab Trail Parking Lot and winds through the forest to a point that overlooks the canyon and the North Kaibab Trail switchbacks.

The **Cape Royal Trail** is an easy walk of less than one mile. The trail is flat and paved. Beginning at the southeast side of the Cape Royal parking lot, the path is dotted with photo markers that interpret the area's natural history. From this trail you can view the canyon from Angel's Window Overlook and see a portion of the Colorado River.

Cliff Springs Trail is approximately one mile in length and travels down a forested ravine past a small Indian ruin to the spring. The trail begins directly across the road from the Angel's Window Overlook.

Widforss Trail. This 10-mile, five-hour hike blends forest and canyon scenery. Take the road directly opposite the North Kaibab trailhead one mile to the Widforss Trail parking area.

Unmaintained Trails of the North Rim

Clear Creek is not very difficult to follow. The trailhead can be found one-half mile north of Phantom Ranch. The trail climbs up to the Tonto Plateau, and much of the route follows the southern edge of the plateau. The distance from Phantom Ranch to the campsite at Clear Creek is 8.1 miles.

The **North Bass Trail** is primitive. It is 12.6 miles from rim-to-river. The trail begins at Swamp Point, approximately 20 miles west of the North Rim Entrance Station.

CANYON MULE TRIPS. If just reading about all this hiking has worn you out, but you would still like to venture into the depths of the canyon, consider a mule ride.

The canyon mule rides on the **South Rim** are available year-round. There is a one-day trip to *Plateau Point,* which is 1,400 feet above the Colorado River.

A two-day trip includes an overnight stay and dinner and breakfast at the Phantom Ranch. From December 1 through March 31st there is also a three-day trip with two nights at Phantom Ranch. Overnight mule trips should be reserved at least 9 months in advance to assure availability. Write or call the Reservations Dept., Grand Canyon National Park Lodges, Box 699, Grand Canyon 86023; 638–2401.

From the **North Rim,** mule trips go only as far as *Roaring Springs,* a one-day trip. For North Rim reservations, write to Grand Canyon Trail Rides, Box 1638, Cedar City, UT 84720.

Although the mule is doing the walking, the trip still is rigorous for the rider. Because the grades are steep, you must have sufficient strength to maintain your balance in the saddle. And you can be in the saddle for up to seven hours at a time.

To make the trip as safe as possible, precautions are taken for both the mule and the rider. Also the mule trips are limited to persons weighing less than 200 pounds fully dressed. Persons near this weight will be weighed at the Transportation Desk before being allowed in the corral. The ride is prohibited for pregnant women.

Also, riders must be at least 4 feet, 7 inches tall and in good physical condition. If you are afraid of heights, this trip is not recommended. Previ-

ous riding experience is not mandatory, but it does help. Before the
begins, you may be asked to demonstrate your riding competency. Yo
must be fluent in English, because instructions will be given to you frequently by the guide during the trip.

Because you have to concentrate on riding the mule (a crossbreed between a female horse and a male donkey), riders are not allowed to have
a lot of encumbering items hanging on their person, such as purses, camera
bags, spare camera lenses, or backpacks. You can, however, carry one
camera or one pair of binoculars, which has to hang around your neck.
A limited amount of water is provided, as well as a box lunch; however,
a one-quart canteen that straps over the shoulder is permitted at the discre-
tion of livery personnel.

On overnight trips a plastic bag is provided for overnight necessities
such as pajamas, underclothing, toothbrush, and the like. It is a good idea
to take some cash on this trip, as there are snacks and first-aid items available at Phantom Ranch.

Because this trip can be a little uncomfortable after a while in the saddle,
it is best to wear clothing that will add to your comfort. However, long
pants and solid shoes are required; no open-toed shoes or sandals are allowed.

During the summer months, a long-sleeve shirt and a broad-brimmed
hat will prevent sunburn and water loss. Hats can be rented at the Transportation Desk. Any hat you wear must have a chin strap.

If you are hesitant about the ride, you can order through the mail a
150-foot color movie (Super8 or VHS/Beta video formats) for $16 post-
paid that prepares visitors for the mule rides by showing the mules de-
scending the switchbacks on the trail. To order the movie, write to Fred
Harvey Movies, Box 709, Grand Canyon 86023.

HORSEBACK RIDING. There are several guided rides available on the
South Rim at *Moqui Lodge,* Box 369, Grand Canyon 86023, 638-2424.
From one to four hours in length, the rides either follow the rim or wind
through the beautiful Kaibab National Forest. The lodge also provides
wagon rides and a cowboy breakfast ride.

CAMPING. Do you want to take it easy but still enjoy the canyon the
natural way? There are several campgrounds located on the rims. **Mather
Campground** at Grand Canyon Village is under the jurisdiction of the National Park Service (638-7851). Reservations through Ticketron are required from May 15 to September 30. Mather sites are available either
through Ticketron or on a first come, first served basis the rest of the year.
Mather Campground has a store, shower and laundry facilities, and a sani-
tary dump station. Pets are allowed.

To reserve a site through Ticketron, write to Ticketron, Dept. R, 401
Hackensack Ave., Hackensack, NJ 07601. Include a check payable to Ticketron for $8 per site per night and provide the following information:
name; address; phone; number of persons in the party; pets; name of campground; your first, second, and third choice of arrival; length of stay; type
and size of camping equipment you plan to bring (motor home, tent, trailer, etc.); and the serial number of your Golden Access or Golden Age
Passport (when applicable).

ı be made up to eight weeks in advance, and you should
quest to Ticketron at least two weeks before you start
ll mail you a reservation ticket, which must be presented
into the campground. If you are late, contact the park
arrangements. Otherwise your site will be reserved until
after your expected arrival. If you fail to arrive by then
and have .... , notified the ranger, your reservation will be canceled and
given to another camper.

For groups of more than 6 people, write to the Park directly for a group campsite: Mather Campground Group Reservations, Grand Canyon National Park, Box 129, Grand Canyon 86023.

Desert View Campground, also under National Park Service jurisdiction, is located 25 miles east of the Grand Canyon Village area. It also operates on a first-come, first-served basis and is open from mid-May through mid-October. The fee is $6 per site, per night.

Trailer Village, located in Grand Canyon Village, is a concession-operated trailer campground open year-round. Hookups are available. The sites are $13.50 per night for the first two people. For additional persons over the age of 12, add 50¢ each. Reservations can be made by writing or calling the Grand Canyon National Park Lodges, Inc., Box 699, Grand Canyon 86023, 638–2401.

Tusayan, located seven miles south of Grand Canyon Village, has several commercial campgrounds. For specific information, contact the Chamber of Commerce, Box 3007, Grand Canyon 86023.

Camping at the **North Rim** is available at three campgrounds and one trailer campground. They are:

The North Rim Campground, open during the season and operated on a first-come, first-served basis at a cost of $6 per site, per night. Group reservations are available. Write to North Rim, Grand Canyon National Park, Box 129, Grand Canyon 86023.

DeMotte Campground is operated by the National Park Service and is located 18 miles north of the North Rim. The sites are available on a first-come, first-served basis at a charge of $5 per site, per night.

Jacob Lake Campground is at Jacob Lake, at the junction of State Route 67 and U.S. Route 89A near the North Rim. This campground also is operated by the Park Service on a first-come, first-served basis. The fee is $5 per site, per night.

Jacob Lake Recreational Vehicle Trailer Camp is about 200 yards away from the campground. Full hookups, electricity, water, and sewage facilities are provided. The fee is $7 per site, per night.

Regulations for Back Country Camping for Hiking. Campsites and campgrounds are limited to specific numbers of individual parties (1–8 people) and groups (9–16 people) per night. *Groups* means hiking parties of 9 to 16 people traveling together, and the maximum size is 16. If a group includes more than 16, it must divide membership between different campgrounds or use areas.

Only one group from the same organization may be in the same noncorridor use area on the same night. No more than three groups from the same organization may camp within the backcountry on the same night.

Camping is limited to two nights (either consecutive or nonconsecutive) per campground at Hermit, Monument, Horseshoe Mesa, and Tapeats areas and the campgrounds on the Bright Angel and Kaibab trails. In other parts of the backcountry, campers may spend up to seven nights per area.

Other regulations for campers and hikes are:

• You must have a use permit, which must be in your possession while you are in the backcountry.

• No wood or charcoal fires. Use canned heat or a backpack stove, or carry cold foods. Fires and fire rings leave scars on the landscape that cannot be healed easily by nature in this arid climate.

• Carry out your own trash. Do not bury or burn it or stuff it in or under anything other than a plastic bag in your backpack. The Park Service takes the position that if you packed it in, you should be courteous enough to pack it out. This includes cigarette butts, eggshells, and orange peels.

• No firearms are allowed. This also means bows and arrows. Firearms cannot be used anywhere in the park, and wildlife is unlikely to bother you as long as you respect their rights and remember you are a visitor in their home.

• No dogs or other pets are allowed below the rim because they disturb wildlife, other hikers, and mule parties.

• Do not throw or roll rocks into the canyon. This is dangerous to hikers on the trails below you. Serious injuries and a fatality have resulted from such activity.

• Do not feed wild animals. It is detrimental to their health and encourages them to beg. It also might encourage them to chew into your pack to obtain food, and they might bite you, too.

• Do not dig up, collect, or otherwise remove plants, rocks, animals, or other natural or cultural features. Such collecting is allowed only with a special permit for research or educational purposes.

• No motorized or wheeled vehicles are allowed on trails. The trails are not designed for motorcycles, baby buggies, bicycles, or similar vehicles. They create a hazard to you and other hikers on the trail.

• Fishing by persons 14 years or older requires a valid Arizona fishing license or nonresident permit, which can be obtained at Babbitt's General Store inside the park.

• No writing, scratching, or other defacing of natural features, signs, buildings, or other objects is allowed.

MUSEUMS. When you arrive at the Grand Canyon, your first inclination will be to leave the luggage in the trunk, rush to the first overlook, and gaze awestruck into the blue and purple depths of the Inner Canyon.

This first glance serves only to make you thirst for more. The National Park Service realizes that to drink in all the beauty the canyon presents can take a lifetime. But, because most visitors have only several days to enjoy the canyon, the Park Service maintains several museums and a Visitor Center that can add to your understanding of the chasm and the people who have called it home—making your gazing twice as enjoyable.

The Visitor Center is three miles north of the South Rim Entrance Station. Using dioramas and exhibits, the center details the discovery of the canyon in 1540, and first Colorado River voyage made by John Wesley Powell and associates.

Also on display are various Indian artifacts found within the canyon, including split-twig figurines, animal images found on the canyon walls, and bone awls. The center has a slide show each hour that depicts the various moods of the canyon.

Yavapai Geology Museum. South Rim. Located three-quarters of a mile east of the Visitor Center, the museum has a glass-enclosed viewing area that affords a view of the canyon. This museum also offers early-morning rim and geology walks, as well as canyon and geology talks during the summer.

Museum displays include fossils found in the area, a geologic time line of the canyon and pictorial exhibits on the formation of the canyon.

Tusayan Museum. South Rim. Located on the East Rim Drive, 21 miles east of the Visitor Center, this one-room stone museum is next to the Tusayan Ruins. This ruin, originally built and occupied by the Anasazi Indians around A.D. 1185, was excavated in 1930 by Emile W. Haury, of the University of Arizona.

The museum contains reproductions of various kinds of Indian dwellings found in and around the canyon, including basketmaker, slabhouse, and pueblo. Also on display are Hopi, Coconino, Navajo, and Kayenta Anasazi arts and crafts.

ARCHEOLOGICAL AND HISTORIC SITES. "Found some Moquis ruins and cactus-apples; the latter were good but the former we cared little about." So wrote Major John Wesley Powell during his exploration of the Grand Canyon. Considering the hardships he and his team endured, his lack of enthusiasm over the discovery of some ruins is understandable.

But 113 years later, the scene is quite different, as is evident at the Tusayan Museum. Today Park officials take every precaution to preserve and study the artifacts left by prehistoric cultures.

The Grand Canyon is a storehouse of information on how Southwestern Indians lived before A.D. 1540 in the canyon. There are approximately 2,000 known prehistoric ruins here. It is from these and other similar sites around Arizona that archeologists have been able to piece together how these Indians lived, what they ate and wore, and how they spent their time. Besides Indian habitations, there also are 312 historic structures.

With a little planning and effort, visitors can tour some of the ruins and historic structures. Thanks to television, most people have a preconceived idea of what a "ruin" is supposed to look like (i.e., either dilapidated dwellings or empty teepees). That is not the case. Taking into consideration each site's age and that they are unlike "buildings" as we know them, most ruins are not evident to the untrained eye. What to look for:
•Surface evidence such as straight alignments of rock, especially in the absence of natural linear rock outcrops, or structures with corners aligning at right angles. These may once have been houses, storerooms, or agricultural terraces.
•Stone-lined or circular depressions. Were these perhaps pit houses, kivas, or fire pits?
•Broken pottery or lithics (stone tools and flint-knapping debris). These are remains of trash deposits.
•Pictographs (paintings) and petroglyphs (engravings) are also indications of habitation.

Historic sites generally have wooden or stone structures still standing, or rectangular mine shaft openings, or metal, china, or wooden objects strewn about.

If you do take the time to scout out these sites, be careful, and respect their age. Do not walk or lean on walls or terraces or remove any fragments of mortar or other objects you happen to see lying around.

If you discover an archeological site that you suspect has not been previously identified, provide the National Park Service with information about the type of architecture and artifacts, and the location on a topographic map. We stress that you must not remove anything from these sites. The placement of objects relays important information to archaeologists.

All ruins and historic sites are under the protection of the National Park Service. If you are found tampering in any way with a site, you can be fined heavily and prosecuted.

THEATERS. Over The Edge Theatre, Community Building, South Rim. A 20-minute multimedia presentation of a guided tour around the Canyon rim. Shows begin at half past the hour, Monday through Saturday, 9:30 A.M. to 8:30 P.M.; $3.50 for adults, $2 for children, under 8 are free (638–2224).

IMAX Theatre, *Grand Canyon—The Hidden Secrets,* Tusayan, 7 miles south of the Grand Canyon. *The Hidden Secrets,* a 34-minute documentary about early Grand Canyon explorations, is shown on a 70-foot-high screen. Shows begin at half past the hour daily, from 8:30 A.M. to 8:30 P.M. Admission is $6 for adults, $3 for children 3–11 (638–2468).

DINING OUT. The Grand Canyon's motels and lodges cater not only to your every sleeping comfort but also to your taste buds. The price categories are as follows: *Deluxe,* $15 and up; *Expensive,* $10 to $15; *Moderate,* $5 to $10.

Generally speaking, the dining rooms carry a full array of food, prepared to your specifications by competent chefs. All the dining rooms are tastefully appointed. There are several lodges that offer cafeterias or restaurants for a quick but tasty meal. The only lodges that do not have a restaurant are *Kachina* and *Thunderbird.*

El Tovar. *Deluxe.* An excellent continental/American menu.

Arizona Steakhouse. *Expensive.* South Rim, next to Thunderbird Lodge. Closed January-February.

Bright Angel. *Expensive.* A coffee shop offering a variety of satisfying temptations.

Grand Canyon Lodge. North Rim. *Expensive.* Beautiful vistas. Food is well prepared.

Moqui Lodge. *Expensive.* Located outside the park boundary, the dining room offers a selection of both Mexican and American cuisine.

Babbitt's General Store. *Moderate.* Delicatessen located in the store.

Maswik Lodge. *Moderate.* Cafeteria-style.

Yavapai Lodge. *Moderate.* Large cafeteria.

Index

Airplane flights, Grand Canyon, 196–197
Airport, 36
Aleh-Zhon, 8
Ambos Nogales, 101
Anasazi Indians, 6
Apaches, 9–10
Arcadia Park, 46
Archaeological sites, 208–209
Arcosanti, 126
Arizona Heritage Center, 89–90
Arizona Historical Society Museum, 50
Arizona History Room, 51
Arizona Military Museum, 51–52
Arizona Mineral Museum, 50
Arizona Museum, 49–50
Arizona Museum of Science and Technology, 50–51
Arizona Sonora Desert Museum, 15, 86–87
Arizona State Museum, 90
Arizona State University (Tempe), 62
Arizona Strip, 185–187
Arizona Veterans Memorial Coliseum, 34
Art galleries, 53, 93
Ash Fork, 152
Automobiles, 18–19
Auto racing, 34

Ballooning, 27, 46, 69
Baseball, 34, 70, 123
Basketball, 46
Basketmakers, 171
Bed & Breakfasts, 17–18, 21
Betakin, 139
Bicycling, 70
Bird-watching, 27
Bisbee, 5, 12, 103–104, 107, 112
Black Canyon City, 126
Bloody Basin, 126
Boating and waterskiing, 27, 69, 123, 162
Bradshaw Mountains & Canyons, 126

Bright Angel Trail, 201–202
British visitors, 15–16
Budget tips, 18
Bullhead City, 150
Business hours, 23
Bus tours of Grand Canyon, 197

Cactuses, 26
Camelback Mountain, 32, 45
Cameron, 184
Camping, 25, 66–67, 108, 116–117, 134, 154–157, 205–207
Camp Verde, 131
Canyon De Chelly National Monument, 139, 160, 165
Canyon Diablo, 144
Cape Royal, 186
Carefree, 62, 66
Carson, Kit, 9, 10
Casa Grande, 105, 113–114, 116
    Ruins National Monument, 117
Cathedral Cave, 148
Cave Creek, 62
Celito Park, 46
Children's activities, 87
Chiricahua National Monument, 104, 109
Civic Plaza (Phoenix), 35
Civil War, 10–11
Climate, 2–3, 16–17, 145, 188
Clothing, 17, 189
Cochise, 10, 104
Coconino National Forest, 159
Cohoninas (Coconinos), 173
Colorado River, 4–5, 170, 192–193. *See also* Grand Canyon
Colter, Mary Jane, 182, 183
Cordes Junction, 126
Coronado, Francisco Vásquez de, 7, 103, 174, 183
Coronado National Forest, 100

Coronado National Memorial, 103, 109
Coronado Trail, 7
Costs, 17–18

Desert, 2–4, 26
Desert Botanical Garden Living Museum, 3,
    34, 51
Desert Dangers, 3–4
Desert View Watchtower, 182
Diamond Creek, 184
Dining. *See* Restaurants
Disabled, hints for, 28–29
Douglas, 104, 107, 112
Dragoon, 110–111
Drinking laws, 23
Duppa, Lord Darrell Philip, 11, 31
Dutton, Clarence E., 177

East Rim Drive, 181–182
Elderhostel program, 24
El Tovar, 179
Emergencies, in Grand Canyon, 200–201
Encanto Park, 34, 45
Estrella Mountain County Regional Park, 44

Fishing, 28, 69, 110, 123, 135, 162, 163
Flagstaff, 144–146, 152, 164–165, 167–168
Flandreau Planetarium, 90
Football, 47
Fort Bowie National Historic Site, 109
Fort Huachuca, 103
Fort Verde, 131, 135–136
Four-wheeling, 28

Gadsden Purchase, 10
Ganado, 8, 139
Garces, Francisco Tomas, 8, 174
Gardens, 87
Geronimo, 10
Ghost towns, 114
Gila Bend, 113–114, 116
Gila River Indian Crafts Center and Heritage
    Park, 118
Gila Trail, 113
Glen Canyon National Recreation Area,
    159–160
Gold rush, 9–10
Golf, 27, 35, 46, 66, 87–88, 110, 117, 123,
    135, 162
Goldwater, Barry, 12
Grand Canyon, 4, 170–209
    hiking in, 199–205
    history of, 171, 173–178
    horseback riding in, 205
    museums and archaeological and historic
        sites in, 207–209
    National Park, 192–195
    North Rim of, 184–187
    rafting Colorado River in, 197–199
    services in, 190–191
    South Rim of, 178–184, 189–190, 201–203

Grand Canyon Caverns, 160
Grand Canyon Village, 179
Grand Falls of the Little Colorado River, 159
Grandview Point, 181
Green Valley, 100
Guadalupe, 63
Guest ranches, 21, 133

Hall of Flame Museum, 51
Hamblin, Jacob, 177
Handball, 88
Handicapped travelers, 28–29
Hart Prairie, 146
Harvey, Fred, 179
Hashknife cowboys, 141
Havasu Canyon, 183–184
Havasupais, 173
Hayden, Charles, 12
Health and safety hints, 29–30
    for hiking, 197–199
Heard Museum of Anthropology and
    Primitive Art, 50
Heat exhaustion, 200
Heatstroke, 30, 200
Helicopter tours of Grand Canyon, 196
Heritage Square, 48–49
Hermit Creek Trail, 203
Highways and roads, 18, 33
Hiking, 27, 69, 110, 117, 162, 199–205
Historic sites and houses
    in Grand Canyon, 208–209
    in North-Central Arizona, 135–136
    in Phoenix, 47–49
    in Southern and Southeastern Arizona,
        109–110
    in Tucson, 89
    in Yuma, 122–123
History of Arizona, 5–13
    of Grand Canyon, 171, 173–178
Hohokams, 5
Holbrook, 141, 151
Hoover Dam, 149
Hopi Cultural Center, 147, 165
Hopi Mesas, 146–147
Hopi Point, 180
Hopi Reservation, 14, 153, 155–156,
    160–161, 164, 165, 168
Hopis, 146–147, 173
Horseback riding, 27, 47, 69, 88, 162, 205
Horseracing, 34–35
Horseshoe Mesa Trail, 203
Horsethief Basin, 126
Hostels, 21–22
Hot air ballooning, 46–47
Hotels and motels, 19–21
    costs of, 20–21
    in Grand Canyon, 189–190
    in North-Central Arizona, 132–133
    in Northern Arizona, 151–154
    in Phoenix, 38–40
    in Phoenix suburbs, 64–67

Hotels and motels (*continued*)
  in Southern and Southeastern Arizona,
    107–108
  in Tuscon, 79–81
  Valley Reservation System for, 14
  in Western Arizona, 116
  in Yuma, 121–122
Hours of business, 23
Houses. *See* Historic sites and houses
Hualapai Mountain Park, 149, 160
Hubbell Trading Post National Historic Site,
  139, 165
Humboldt, 128
Humphrey's Peak, 4
Hunt, George W.P., 12
Hunting, 28, 69, 110, 117, 123, 135, 162,
  163

Indian reservations, 25
  camping in, 155–156
  hotels and motels in, 153
  museums in, 165–166
  national and tribal parks in, 160–161
  Navajo, 139, 153
  participant sports in, 162–163
  restaurants in, 168
  shopping in, 166
Indians (Native Americans), 5–6, 9–10, 171,
  173–174
  archaeological and historic sites of,
    138–139
Inner tubing, 35, 69–70
Introduction to Arizona, 1–13

Jerome, 129–130, 135

Kabotie, Fred, 147
Kaibab, 170
Kayaking, 27, 197–199
Kayentas, 171
Keet Seel, 139, 171
Kingman, 149, 152, 167–168
Kino, Eusebio Francisco, 7–8, 74, 100, 119
Kofa Mountains, 114

Lake Havasu City, 150
Lake Mead, 149
  National Recreation Area, 160
Lake Pleasant, 125
Lake Powell, 146, 148
Lees Ferry, 187
Litchfield, Paul,
Litchfield, 105
Litchfield Park, 66, 105
London Bridge, 150
López de Cardenas, García, 174
Los Olivos Park, 46
Lowell Observatory, 164
Lynx Lake, 128

McDowell Mountain Regional Park, 45

McFarland Historic State Park, 118
Madison Park, 46
Mayer, 128
Medical Museum, 51
Merriam, C. Hart, 178
Mesa, 63, 66, 73
Meteor Crater, 4, 144, 159
Mexican War, 119
Mining Camps, 128
Mishongnovi, 147
Misson San Xavier del Bac, 8, 109
Mogollon Indians, 6
Mogollon Rim, 4, 144, 151, 153–154,
  156–157, 161, 163, 168
Montezuma Castle, 131, 135
Monuments. *See* National parks and
  monuments
Monument Valley, 147–148
Moran, Thomas, 177
Moran Point, 181
Motels. *See* Hotels and motels
Motorist hints, 18
Mountain climbing, 27
Mule trips, 204–205
Museum of the Horse, 101, 103
Museums
  in Grand Canyon, 207–208
  in North-Central Arizona, 135–136
  in Northern Arizona, 164–166
  in Phoenix, 49–52
  in Prescott, 129
  in Phoenix suburbs, 68
  in Southern and Southeastern Arizona,
    110–111
  in Tucson, 89–92
  in Yuma, 122–123
Music, 3, 52, 92

National forests, 14–15
  Coconino, 159
  Coronado, 100
National parks and monuments
  Canyon de Chelly National Monument,
    139, 160, 165
  Chiricahua National Monument, 104, 109
  Coronado National Memorial, 103, 109
  Grand Canyon National Park, 192–195
  handicapped accessibility to, 29
  Navajo National Monument, 161, 166
  in North-Central Arizona, 134–135
  in Northern Arizona, 159–161
  Organ Pipe Cactus National Monument,
    113
  Petrified Forest National Park, 140–141,
    159
  Saguaro National Monument, 86
  in Southern and Southeastern Arizona,
    109–110
  Tuzigoot National Monument, 130–131,
    135
  in Western Arizona, 117–118

Native Americans. *See* Indians
Navajo National Monument, 161, 166
Navajo Reservation, 139, 153, 160–161, 166, 168
Navajos, 174
Nightlife, 59–60, 73, 97–98, 168–169
Nogales (Arizona), 107
Nogales, Sonora (Mexico), 101
North-Central Arizona, 125–137
Northern Arizona, 138–169
  camping in, 154–157
  forests, parks, monuments, and scenic attractions in, 159–160
  hotels and motels in, 151–154
  Indian lands and tribal parks, 160–161
  museums in, 164–166
  restaurants in, 166–168
  seasonal events in, 157–159
  sports in, 161–164
Northern Arizona University (Flagstaff), 145
North Kaibab Trail, 202, 203
North Mountain Park (Phoenix), 45
North Rim (Grand Canyon), 184–187, 190, 193

Oak Creek Canyon, 130, 135
Old Fort Bowie, 104
Old Oraibi, 14, 146–147, 173
Organ Pipe Cactus National Monument, 113, 117

Page, 148, 152, 164–165
Painted Desert, 4, 140
  State Park, 114, 118
Paiutes, 174
Papago Indian Reservation, 114
Papago Park (Phoenix), 34, 45
Park rangers, 194
Parks. *See also* National parks and monuments
  in Phoenix, 34, 44–46
  in Southern and Southeastern Arizona, 109–110
  in Tucson, 85–86
  in Western Arizona, 117–118
Patagonia, 101, 103
Pattie, James Ohio, 119, 174–175
Payson, 144, 153, 165, 168
Peeples Valley, 131
Permits, for Grand Canyon National Park, 194–195
Petrified Forest National Park, 4, 140–151, 159
Phantom Ranch, 183
Phoenix, 31–32
  historic sites and houses in, 47–49
  history of, 34–35
  hotels and motels in, 38–40
  museums in, 49–52
  parks in, 34, 44–46
  recommended reading, 42

restaurants in, 54–59
seasonal events in, 42–43
senior citizens' programs in, 24–25
shopping in, 53–54
sports in, 34–35, 46–47
suburbs of, 60–73
telephone numbers, 37–38
theater in, 52–53
tourist information, 41–42
tours of, 43–44
transportation in, 40–41
transportation to, 36–37
weather in, 16–17
Phoenix Art Museum, 50
Phoenix Zoo, 34
Photography, 25, 195
Picacho, 105
Picacho Peak State Park, 117–118
Pima Air Museum, 90
Pima Point, 186
Pine, 165
Pioneer Arizona Museum, 125–126
Plant and animal life, 2–3, 26
Plateau Point Trail, 202
Poisonous animals and insects, 3, 30
Powell, John Wesley, 175–177
Powell Memorial, 180
Prehistoric Peoples, 5–6
Prescott, 126, 128–129, 133, 136, 137
Presidio, 74
Protected plants, 26
Puebloans, 171, 173–174
Pueblo Grande Museum, 48

Quartzite, 106

Rafting, 27, 197–199
Railroads, 12
Rainbow Forest Museum, 164
Rainbow Bridge National Monument, 148
Ramsey Canyon, 109–110
Ranches, 21, 133
Recreational vehicle parks, 122, 157
Red Rock Country, 130–132
Regulations, for camping in Grand Canyon, 201
Reid Park Zoo, 87
Rental cars, 18–19, 64, 81, 122, 132, 150, 190
Reservations, for Grand Canyon National Park, 189, 194–195
Restaurants, 22
  in Grand Canyon, 209
  in North-Central Arizona, 136–137
  in Northern Arizona, 166–168
  in Phoenix, 54–59
  in Phoenix suburbs, 70–73
  in Southern and Southeastern Arizona, 112
  in Tucson, 94–98
  in Western Arizona, 118
  in Yuma, 123–124

Rincon Mountains, 85–86
Rockhounding, 28
Rock Springs, 126
Rodeos, 163–164
Roosevelt Dam, 31
Running, 70

Saguaros, 26
Saguaro National Monument, 86
Salt River Project History Center, 52
San Francisco Peaks, 4, 144
Santa Anna, Gen. Antonio Lopez de, 9
Santa Catalinas, 85
Santa Rita Mountains' Madera Canyon, 86
San Xavier del Bac, 8, 100
Scottsdale, 60, 62, 70–73
Seasonal events
    in North-Central Arizona, 134
    in Northern Arizona, 157–159
    in Phoenix, 42–43
    in Phoenix suburbs, 67–68
    in Southern and Southeastern Arizona, 108
    in Tucson, 83–84
    in Western Arizona, 117
    in Yuma, 122
Sedona, 130, 132–133, 136, 137
Seligman, 149
Senior citizens' programs & discounts, 24–25
Shemer Arts Center, 50
Shongopovi, 147
Shooting, 69
Shopping
    in North-Central Arizona, 136
    in Northern Arizona, 166
    in Phoenix, 53–54
    in Phoenix suburbs, 70
    in Scottsdale, 70
    in Southern and Southeastern Arizona,
        111–112
    in Tucson, 93–94
    in Yuma, 123
Show Low, 141, 154
Sierra Vista, 112
Sinaguas, 6, 145
Skiing, 28, 88, 161, 163
Skydiving, 28
Snakes, 3
Snow Bowl, 146
Snowflake, 141
Soaring (sail planing), 28
Sonora Desert Museum, 2
Southern and Southeastern Arizona, 99–112
    hotels and motels in, 107–108
    museums in, 110–111
    parks, monuments, and historic sites in,
        109–110
    restaurants in, 112
South Kaibab Trail, 202
South Mountain Park (Phoenix), 34, 44
South Rim (Grand Canyon), 178–184,
        189–190, 201–203

Spaniards, 6, 170
Sports, 26–28
    in North-Central Arizona, 135
    in Northern Arizona, 161–164
    in Phoenix, 34–35, 46–47
    in Phoenix suburbs, 69–70
    in Southern and Southeastern Arizona, 110
    in Sun City, 63
    in Tucson, 87–89
    in Western Arizona, 117
    in Yuma, 123
Squaw Peak, 45
State Capitol (Phoenix), 35–36, 43
Sunburn hazards, 29–30
Sun Circle Trail (Phoenix), 44
Sun City, 63–64, 66
Sunset Crater, 145
    National Monument, 159
Sunset Point, 126
Superstition Mountain, 63
Swilling, Jack, 11, 31
Swimming, 27

Taliesin West, 48, 68
Tanner Trail, 203
Telephones, 23
Tempe, 11, 62, 65, 73
Tennis and racquetball, 26–27, 162
    in North-Central Arizona, 135
    in Phoenix, 35, 46
    in Phoenix suburbs, 69
    in Tucson, 88
    in Western Arizona, 117
    in Yuma, 123
Theater, 52–53, 92–93, 209
Time zone, 23
Tipping, 22–23
Tohono Chul Park, 86
Tombstone, 103, 108, 109, 112
Tonto Natural Bridge, 144
Tourist information, 14–15
    in Grand Canyon, 15, 191
    in North-Central Arizona, 134
    in Northern Arizona, 157
    in Phoenix, 41–42
    in Phoenix suburbs, 67
    in Southern and Southeastern Arizona, 108
    in Tucson, 82
    in Western Arizona, 117
    in Yuma, 122
Tours
    of Grand Canyon, 196–197
    of Phoenix, 43–44
    of Phoenix suburbs, 68
    of Tucson, 84–85
Trailers, 19
Trails. *See also* Hiking
    in Grand Canyon, 185, 201–204
    to Phantom Ranch, 183
Trailview I and II, 180
Trains, 12

Transept Trail, 203
Transportation
  in Grand Canyon, 187, 190, 195–197
  in North-Central Arizona, 132
  in Northern Arizona, 150–151
  in Phoenix, 40–41
  in Phoenix suburbs, 64
  in Southern and Southeastern Arizona,
    106–107
  in Tucson, 81–82
  in Western Arizona, 116
  in Yuma, 121
Trappers, 9
Tubac, 100–101
Tuba City, 146
Tubac Presidio State Historic Park, 110
Tucson, 74–98
  excursions out of, 99–106
  hotels and motels in, 79–81
  museums and historic sites in, 89–92
  music, theater, and art in, 92–93
  parks and zoos in, 85–87
  restaurants in, 94–97
  seasonal events, 83–84
  sports in, 87–89
  telephone numbers, 78–79
  tours, 84–85
  transportation in, 81–82
  transportation to, 78
  walking tour of, 75, 77–78
  weather in, 2
Tucson Botanical Gardens, 87
Tucson Museum of Art, 90
Tumacacori National Monument, 101, 110
Tusayan Museum, 208
Tuzigoot National Monument, 130–131

Vacation crooks, 30
Valley of the Sun, 60
Valley Reservation System, 14
Verde Valley, 132–133, 137
Visitor Center (Grand Canyon), 207–208

Wahweap Marina, 148
Walnut Canyon, 145
  National Monument, 159
Walpi, 147
Weaver, Paulino, 9
Waterskiing, 27, 69, 123, 162
Weather. *See* Climate
Western Arizona, 113–118
  Yuma, 119–124
West Rim Drive, 179–181
White, James, 175
White Mountains, 4, 151, 153–154,
    156–157, 161, 163, 168, 173
White Tank Mountains County Preserve, 44
White-water trips, 197–199
Wickenburg, 131, 132
Willcox, 107
Willcox Playa, 109
Williams, Bill, 9, 148
Williams, 148, 152
Winslow, 144, 152, 167
Wupatki National Monument, 159

Yavapai Geology Museum, 208
Young, Ewing, 9
Yuma, 118–124

Zoos, 34, 86–87

Fodor's Travel Guides

U.S. Guides

Alaska
Arizona
Atlantic City & the
  New Jersey Shore
Boston
California
Cape Cod
Carolinas & the
  Georgia Coast
The Chesapeake Region
Chicago
Colorado
Dallas & Fort
  Worth

Disney World & the
  Orlando Area
Florida
Hawaii
Houston &
  Galveston
Las Vegas
Los Angeles, Orange
  County, Palm Springs
Maui
Miami, Fort Lauderdale,
  Palm Beach
Michigan, Wisconsin,
  Minnesota

New England
New Mexico
New Orleans
New Orleans (Pocket
  Guide)
New York City
New York City (Pocket
  Guide)
New York State
Pacific North Coast
Philadelphia
The Rockies
San Diego
San Francisco

San Francisco (Pocket
  Guide)
The South
Texas
USA
Virgin Islands
Virginia
Waikiki
Washington, DC
Williamsburg

Foreign Guides

Acapulco
Amsterdam
Australia, New Zealand,
  The South Pacific
Austria
Bahamas
Bahamas (Pocket
  Guide)
Baja & the Pacific
  Coast Resorts
Barbados
Belgium & Luxembourg
Bermuda
Brazil
Britain (Great Travel
  Values)
Budget Europe
Canada
Canada (Great Travel
  Values)
Canada's Atlantic
  Provinces
Cancún, Cozumel,
  Mérida, the
  Yucatán
Caribbean

Caribbean (Great
  Travel Values)
Central America
China
China's Great Cities
Eastern Europe
Egypt
Europe
Europe's Great Cities
Florence & Venice
France
France (Great Travel
  Values)
Germany
Germany (Great Travel
  Values)
Great Britain
Greece
The Himalayan
  Countries
Holland
Hong Kong
Hungary
India, including Nepal
Ireland
Israel

Italy
Italy (Great Travel
  Values)
Jamaica
Japan
Japan (Great Travel
  Values)
Jordan & the Holy Land
Kenya, Tanzania,
  the Seychelles
Korea
Lisbon
Loire Valley
London
London (Great Travel
  Values)
London (Pocket Guide)
Madrid & Barcelona
Mexico
Mexico City
Montreal &
  Quebec City
Munich
New Zealand
North Africa
Paris

Paris (Pocket Guide)
Portugal
Rio de Janeiro
The Riviera (Fun on)
Rome
Saint Martin &
  Sint Maarten
Scandinavia
Scandinavian Cities
Scotland
Singapore
South America
South Pacific
Southeast Asia
Soviet Union
Spain
Spain (Great Travel
  Values)
Sweden
Switzerland
Sydney
Tokyo
Toronto
Turkey
Vienna
Yugoslavia

Special-Interest Guides

Bed & Breakfast
  Guide: North America
Health & Fitness
  Vacations

Royalty Watching
Selected Hotels of
  Europe

Selected Resorts
  and Hotels of the U.S.
Shopping in Europe

Skiing in North
  America
Sunday in New York